THE ETHNOGRAPHIC INTERVIEW

James P. Spradley

Macalester College

HOLT, RINEHART AND WINSTON
New York   Chicago   San Francisco   Dallas
Montreal   Toronto   London   Sydney

Library of Congress Cataloging in Publication Data

Spradley, James P.
  The ethnographic interview.

  Bibliography: p. 229.
  Includes index.
  1. Interviewing in ethnology.   I. Title.
GN346.3.S66   301.2′07′2   78-26426
ISBN 0-03-044496-9

A quiet revolution has spread through the social sciences and many applied disciplines. Ethnography, the study of culture, has come of age. A new appreciation for this unique approach to understanding humankind has emerged among educators, urban planners, sociologists, nurses, psychologists, public interest lawyers, political scientists, and many more. There has come a profound realization: the people we study or seek to help have a way of life, a culture of their own. Like a stream that rises slowly, then spills over its banks sending rivulets of water in many directions, the ethnographic revolution has overflowed the banks of anthropology. This stream had its beginning in field work expeditions to places like the Kalahari desert, remote Micronesian atolls, coastal villages of New Guinea, and communities of Arctic Eskimo. No longer relegated to exotic cultures in far-off places, ethnography has come home. It has become a fundamental tool for understanding ourselves and the multicultural societies of the modern world.

Not far from where I live, in St. Paul, Minnesota, stands a large brick building surrounded by black asphalt. During the school year it is crowded with young adolescents. One researcher set out to understand this ordinary junior high school using the tools of ethnography. She watched the students going to and from classes; she observed them smoking in the bathrooms, talking in the hallways, and eating in the lunchroom. She listened to lectures and interviewed teachers. Over a period of months she learned the special language and culture of this school, then described it from the participants' point of view (Gregory 1976). She was doing ethnography.

Across the Mississippi River, in the city of Minneapolis, lives a man whose arms and legs were paralyzed when he broke his neck in a trampoline accident. Physicians call him a quadriplegic. He spends much of his time in a wheelchair; although he works full time as a professional, he must depend on others for many of the things that most of us take for granted. A premed student in one of my classes became interested in the culture of "quads" and spent many hours interviewing this man. He also visited other quads who lived in nursing homes and slowly came to understand life from their point of view. He did field work in another culture that had direct applicability to his chosen field of medicine (Deveney 1974). He was doing ethnography.

Several years ago I became interested in alcoholism and the difficulties in treating the skid row alcoholic. Using the ethnographic approach, I set out to study men who had lived long years on skid row. I listened, watched, and allowed these men to become my teachers. I discovered a complex culture that gave shape and meaning to the lives of men whom most people wrote off as "derelicts" (Spradley 1970). Similar examples of contemporary ethnography could be drawn from all parts of the country.

With the new surge of interest in the ethnographic approach have come two pressing needs. First, there is an urgent need to clarify the nature of ethnography. As scholars and students from many disciplines begin using the tools of ethnography, they often bring their own disciplinary assumptions to this approach. In many cases, ethnography has become confused with qualitative and descriptive studies of another kind. Because interviewing and participant observation can be used for other forms of investigation, it has become necessary to make clear what is meant by *ethnographic interviewing* and participant observation that leads to an *ethnographic description*. In Part One, "Ethnographic Research," I define ethnography, identify some of its underlying assumptions, and distinguish it from other investigative approaches. I also discuss the ethics of doing ethnography and some criteria for selecting strategic ethnographic research projects.

The growing excitement about ethnography in many disciplines has given rise to a second need: specific guidelines for doing ethnography for professionals and students without long years of training in anthropology. Most ethnographers have learned the skills of their trade through the apprenticeship system or by themselves in a kind of on-the-job training while doing their first field research. This book is a response to the need for a systematic handbook for doing ethnography. With its companion volume, *Participant Observation* (Spradley 1980), I have tried to make explicit the basic concepts and skills needed for doing ethnography. I call the approach in both of these books the Developmental Research Sequence (D.R.S.) Method. My interest in this approach began from a rather simple observation: *some tasks are best accomplished before other tasks when doing ethnography*. Ethnographers cannot do everything at once, even though field work sometimes appears to demand it. Both ethnographic interviewing and participant observation, whether done separately or in combination, involve a series of tasks best carried out in some kind of *sequence*. The ethnographer, for example, must locate an informant before asking questions; some questions are best asked before others; interviews must precede analysis of interview data. As I began to work with this idea of *sequenced tasks,* I found it was not only valuable for my own research, but it had special importance to students and professionals trying to learn the skills for doing ethnography. What emerged over a period of the last twelve years was a procedure for *learning* as well as *doing* ethnography. In a real sense this book is thus designed both for beginners who want to learn to do ethnography and for professional ethnographers who will necessarily want to adapt the procedures to their own style of investigation.

Part Two, "The Developmental Research Sequence," sets forth a series of twelve major tasks designed to guide the investigator from the starting point of "Locating an Informant," to the goal of "Writing the Ethnography." Each of these larger tasks is broken down into many smaller ones that simplify the work of asking ethnographic questions and making ethnographic analyses. Those interested in a more extensive discussion of the D.R.S. Method as well as how the use of that method has placed certain limits on this book should consult Appendix C, "The Developmental Research Sequence Method."

Ethnography is an exciting enterprise, the one systematic approach in the social sciences that leads us into those separate realities that others have learned and use to make sense out of their worlds. In our complex society the need for understanding how other people see their experience has never been greater. Ethnography is a tool with great promise. It offers the educator a way of seeing schools through the eyes of students; it offers health professionals the opportunity of seeing health and disease through the eyes of patients from a myriad of different backgrounds; it offers those in the criminal justice system a chance to view the world through the eyes of those who are helped and victimized by that system. Ethnography offers all of us the chance to step outside our narrow cultural backgrounds, to set aside our socially inherited ethnocentrism, if only for a brief period, and to apprehend the world from the viewpoint of other human beings who live by different meaning systems. Ethnography, as I understand it, is more than a tool for anthropologists to study exotic cultures. It is a pathway into understanding the cultural differences that make us what we are as human beings. Perhaps the most important force behind the quiet ethnographic revolution is the widespread realization that cultural diversity is one of the great gifts bestowed on the human species. It is my hope that this book will enable those who use it to more fully apprehend the nature of that cultural diversity.

J. P. S.

ACKNOWLEDGMENTS

Many people have contributed to the ideas developed in this book. I am indebted to the hundreds of students, both graduate and undergraduate, who have taken my courses in ethnographic field work during the past dozen years. They have taught me much about doing ethnography, and their experiences have been the basis for much that appears in this book. In particular I am grateful to Macalester College and the Department of Anthropology for the freedom to experiment with different styles of teaching and learning.

Many of the ideas developed in this book have been enriched by my close collaboration with Professor David McCurdy of Macalester College, who participated in my ethnographic research course on more than one occasion, offering many valuable suggestions. In 1972 we co-authored *The Cultural Experience: Ethnography in Complex Society,* which offered guidance to undergraduate students doing ethnographic field work. This book includes brief ethnographic descriptions written by undergraduate students which have been useful models in our teaching. The present volume focuses more specifically on the ethnographic interview and is organized around the sequence of tasks as they occur in doing ethnography. It also goes beyond *The Cultural Experience* in discussing the nature and theory of ethnography. Professor McCurdy and I alternately teach a research course at Macalester College, which was selected in 1977 by *Change Magazine*'s project on notable improvements in American undergraduate teaching ("The New Ethnography: Language as the Key to Culture," by Evan Jenkins in *Report on Teaching, No. 5,* pp. 16-19). Professor McCurdy has been a partner in testing many of the ideas in this book with undergraduate students.

I am also grateful to Professor Thomas Correll of Bethel College, St. Paul, Minnesota, for many suggestions and long hours of discussing many of the ideas in this book. In 1978 he participated in a class I taught at Bethel College on ethnographic interviewing. His expertise in linguistics has been a valuable resource given freely on many occasions.

Professor Oswald Werner of Northwestern University has been of great assistance in many ways. He invited me to participate as a consultant to an ethnographic research project on Navaho schools, an experience that greatly enriched my understanding of ethnography. His comments on an earlier draft of this manuscript as well as his writings on ethnographic theory have been of enormous value.

Many others have made comments on this manuscript or have contributed by comments and suggestions, including George Spindler, Calvin Peters, Richard Furlow, David Boynton, and Don Larson. In 1976-77, through a Chautauqua-type short course sponsored by the American Association for the Advancement of Science, I presented many of these ideas to professionals from the fields of anthropology, sociology, history, psychology, education, and political science who were interested in ethnographic research. Many of them made use of this approach in their own research and teaching and their ideas have helped refine and clarify what is presented here.

The most important contribution was made by Barbara Spradley. As my wife and colleague she listened to the development of all these ideas, offered many suggestions, and provided constant encouragement. Without her assistance this book would not have been possible.

Contents

Part One

ETHNOGRAPHIC RESEARCH

Field work is the hallmark of cultural anthropology. Whether in a New Guinea village or on the streets of New York, the anthropologist goes to where people live and "does field work."[1] This means asking questions, eating strange foods, learning a new language, watching ceremonies, taking field notes, washing clothes, writing letters home, tracing out genealogies, observing play, interviewing informants, and hundreds of other things. This vast range of activities often obscures the most fundamental task of all field work—doing ethnography. This book concerns this central task of anthropological field work. In Part One, I want to explore the meaning of ethnography in some detail. Part Two examines, in step by step fashion, how to conduct ethnographic interviews.

Ethnography is the work of describing a culture.[2] The essential core of this activity aims to understand another way of life from the native point of view. The goal of ethnography, as Malinowski put it, is "to grasp the native's point of view, his relation to life, to realize *his* vision of *his* world" (1922:25). Field work, then, involves the disciplined study of what the world is like to people who have learned to see, hear, speak, think, and act in ways that are different. Rather than *studying people,* ethnography means *learning from people*. Consider the following illustration.

Elizabeth Marshall, a young American, had traveled for miles across the Kalahari Desert with her family and several research scientists. Finally the party came upon two shallow depressions "scooped in the sand and lined with grass, like the shallow, scooped nests of shore birds on a beach—the homes of the families, where the people could lie curled up just below the surface of the plain to let the cold night wind which blows across the veld pass over them" (Thomas 1958:41). And then a young woman who appeared to be in her early twenties came out of the house.

"Presently she smiled, pressed her hand to her chest, and said: 'Tsetchwe.' It was her name.

" 'Elizabeth,' I said, pointing to myself.

" 'Nisabe,' she answered, pronouncing after me and inclining her head graciously. She looked me over carefully without really staring, which to Bushmen is rude. Then, having surely suspected that I was a woman, she put her hand on my breast gravely, and, finding that I was, she gravely touched her own breast. Many Bushmen do this; to them all Europeans look alike.

" 'Tsau si' (women), she said.

"Then after a moment's pause, Tsetchwe began to teach me a few words, the names of a few objects around us, grass, rock, bean shell, so that we could have a conversation later. As she talked she took a handful of the beans out of her kaross, broke them open, and began to eat them" (Thomas 1958:43).

"Tsetchwe began to teach me. . ." This is the essence of ethnography. Instead of collecting "data" about people, the ethnographer seeks to learn from people, to be taught by them.

"Tsetchwe began to teach me. . ." In order to discover the hidden principles of another way of life, the researcher must become a *student*. Tsetchwe, and those like her in every society, become *teachers*. Instead of studying the "climate," the "flora," and the "fauna" which make up the Bushmen's environment, Elizabeth Marshall tried to discover how the Bushmen define and evaluate drought and rainstorm, *gemsbok* and giraffe, *torabe* root and *tsama* melon. She did not attempt to describe Bushmen social life in terms of what we know as "marriage" or "family"; instead she sought to discover how Bushmen identified relatives and the cultural meaning of their kinship relationships. Discovering the *insider's* view is a different species of knowledge from one that rests primarily on the *outsider's* view. Even when the outsider is a trained social scientist.

Imagine that Tsetchwe, curious to know our way of life, traveled to Cushing, Wisconsin, a small farm town with a population of about 100 people. What would this young woman, so well schooled in the rich heritage of Bushmen society, have to do in order to understand the culture of these Wisconsin townsfolk? How would Tsetchwe discover the patterns that made up their lives? How would she avoid imposing Bushmen ideas, categories, and values on everything she saw?

First, and perhaps most difficult, Tsetchwe would have to set aside her belief in *naive realism*. This almost universal belief holds that all people define the *real* world of objects, events, and living creatures in pretty much the same way. Human languages may differ from one society to the next, but behind the strange words and sentences, all people are talking about the same things. The naive realist assumes that *love, rain, marriage, worship, trees, death, food,* and hundreds of other things have essentially the same meaning to all human beings. Although there are few of us who would admit to such ethnocentrism, the assumption may unconsciously influence our research.

Ethnography starts with a conscious attitude of almost complete ignorance. "I don't know how the people of Cushing, Wisconsin, understand their world. That remains to be discovered."

Like Elizabeth Marshall, Tsetchwe would have to begin by learning the language spoken in Cushing. Obsrvations alone would not be sufficient. She could walk up and down the one or two streets in this farm community and record what she saw, but only when she asked questions and learned what the natives saw would she grasp their perspective. Observing the co-op creamery, where each morning local farmers bring their cans of fresh milk, the post office filled with letters and advertising circulars about farm implements, the two bars which attract a jovial crowd on Saturday nights, the row of white houses that line the main street, or the Lutheran church around the corner, would not, in themselves, reveal much. Tsetchwe would have to learn the *meanings* of these buildings and the *meanings* of all the social occasions that took place in them. She would have to listen to townsfolk and farmers, depending on them to explain these things to her.

The essential core of ethnography is this concern with the meaning of actions and events to the people we seek to understand. Some of these meanings are directly expressed in language; many are taken for granted and communicated only indirectly through word and action. But in every society people make constant use of these complex meaning systems to organize their behavior, to understand themselves and others, and to make sense out of the world in which they live. These systems of meaning constitute their culture; ethnography always implies a theory of culture.

CULTURE

Culture has been defined in hundreds of different ways.[3] Let's begin with a typical definition, one proposed by Marvin Harris: "the culture concept comes down to behavior patterns associated with particular groups of people, that is to 'customs,' or to a people's 'way of life' " (1968:16). Now, although this definition is helpful for some purposes, it obscures the crucial distinction between the outsider's and insider's points of view. Behavior patterns, customs, and a people's way of life can all be defined, interpreted, and described from more than one perspective. Because our goal in ethnography is "to grasp the native's point of view" (Malinowski 1922:25), we need to define the concept of culture in a way that reflects this objective.

Culture, as used in this book, refers to *the acquired knowledge that people use to interpret experience and generate social behavior*. The following example will help to clarify this definition. One afternoon in 1973 I came across the following news item in the *Minneapolis Tribune:*

CROWD MISTAKES RESCUE ATTEMPT, ATTACKS POLICE

Nov. 23, 1973. Hartford, Connecticut. Three policemen giving a heart massage and oxygen to a heart attack victim Friday were attacked by a crowd of 75 to 100 persons who apparently did not realize what the policemen were doing.

Other policemen fended off the crowd of mostly Spanish spreaking residents until

5

an ambulance arrived. Police said they tried to explain to the crowd what they were doing, but the crowd apparently thought they were beating the woman.

Despite the policemen's efforts the victim, Evangelica Echevacria, 59, died.

Here we see people using their culture. Members of two different groups observed the same event but their *interpretations* were drastically different. The crowd used their culture to (a) interpret the behavior of the policemen as cruel, and (b) to act on the woman's behalf to put a stop to what they saw as brutality. They had acquired the cultural principles for acting and interpreting things in this way through a particular, shared experience.

The policemen, on the other hand, used their culture (a) to interpret the woman's condition as heart failure and their own behavior as a life saving effort, and (b) to give cardiac massage and oxygen to the woman. Furthermore, they interpreted the actions of the crowd in a manner entirely different from how the crowd saw their own behavior. These two groups of people each had elaborate cultural rules for interpreting their experience and for acting in emergency situations. The conflict arose, at least in part, because these cultural rules were so different.

By restricting the definition of culture to shared knowledge, we do not eliminate an interest in behavior, customs, objects, or emotions. We have merely shifted the emphasis from these phenomena to their *meaning*. The ethnographer observes behavior, but goes beyond it to inquire about the meaning of that behavior. The ethnographer sees artifacts and natural objects but goes beyond them to discover what meanings people assign to these objects. The ethnographer observes and records emotional states, but goes beyond them to discover the meaning of fear, anxiety, anger, and other feelings.

This concept of culture (as a system of meaningful symbols) has much in common with symbolic interactionism, a theory which seeks to explain human behavior in terms of meanings. Symbolic interactionism has its roots in the work of sociologists like Cooley, Mead, and Thomas.[4] Blumer has identified three premises on which this theory rests (1969).

The first premise is that "human beings act toward things on the basis of the meanings that the things have for them" (1969:2). The policemen and the crowd interacted on the basis of the meanings things had for them. The geographic location, the types of people, the police car, the movements of the policemen, the behavior of the sick woman, and the activities of the onlookers were all *symbols* with special meanings. People did not act toward these things, but toward their meanings.

The second premise underlying symbolic interactionism is that the "meaning of such things is derived from, or arises out of, the social interaction that one has with one's fellows" (Blumer 1969:2). Culture, as a shared system of meanings, is learned, revised, maintained, and defined in the context of people interacting. The crowd came to share their definitions of police behavior through interacting with one another and through past associations with the police. The police officers acquired the cultural meanings they used through interacting with other officers and members of the community. The culture of each group was inextricably bound up with the social life of their particular communities.

The third premise of symbolic interactionism is that "meanings are handled in, and modified through, an interpretive process used by the person dealing with the things he encounters" (Blumer 1969:2). Neither the crowd nor the policemen were automatons, driven by their culture to act in the way they did. Rather, they used their culture to interpret the situation. At any moment, a member of the crowd might have interpreted the bahavior of the policemen in a slightly different way, leading to a different reaction.

We may see this interpretive aspect more clearly if we think of culture as a cognitive map. In the recurrent activities that make up everyday life, we refer to this map. It serves as a guide for acting and for interpreting our experience; it does not compel us to follow a particular course. Like this brief drama between the policemen, a dying woman, and the crowd, much of life is a series of unanticipated social occasions. Although our culture may not include a detailed map for such occasions, it does provide principles for interpreting and responding to them. Rather than a rigid map that people must follow, culture is best thought of as

a set of principles for creating dramas, for writing scripts, and, of course, for recruiting players and audiences. . . . Culture is not simply a cognitive map that people acquire, in whole or in part, more or less accurately, and then learn to read. People are not just map-readers; they are map-makers. People are cast out into imperfectly charted, continually shifting seas of everyday life. Mapping them out is a constant process resulting not in an individual cognitive map, but in a whole chart case of rough, improvised, continually revised sketch maps. Culture does not provide a cognitive map, but rather a set of principles for map making and navigation. Different cultures are like different schools of navigation designed to cope with different terrains and seas (Frake 1977:6-7).

If we take *meaning* seriously, as symbolic interactionists argue we must, it becomes necessary to study meaning carefully. We need a theory of meaning and a specific methodology designed for the investigation of meaning. This book presents such a theory and methodology. It is sometimes referred to as ethnographic semantics[5] because of its primary focus on understanding cultural meanings systems.

MAKING CULTURAL INFERENCES

Culture, the knowledge that people have learned as members of a group, cannot be observed directly. In his study of sky divers, for example, Richard

Reed (1973) observed sky divers at their clubhouse and on the airfield. He saw them jumping from airplanes, but only by "getting inside their heads" could he find out what jumping meant to these sky divers. If we want to find out what people know, we must get inside their heads. Although difficult, "this should not be an impossible feat: our subjects themselves accomplished it when they learned their culture and became 'native actors.' They had no mysterious avenues of perception not available to us as investigators" (Frake 1964 a:133).

People everywhere learn their culture by observing other people, listening to them, and then *making inferences*. The ethnographer employs this same process of going beyond what is seen and heard to *infer* what people know. It involves reasoning from evidence (what we perceive) or from premises (what we assume). Children acquire their culture by watching adults and making inferences about the cultural rules for behavior; with the acquisition of language, the learning accelerates. Elizabeth Marshall could infer that *"tsau si"* meant "woman" because Tsetchwe said it immediately after touching her own breast. Whenever we are in a new situation we have to make such inferences about what people know. One American student studying in a European country observed all the other students immediately rise to their feet when the professor entered the classroom. She made an inference—"standing recognizes the authority or position of the teacher." Later, the students explained further the importance of standing when a professor entered the class and gave reasons for doing it. Through what they said she made additional inferences about their cultural knowledge.

In doing field work, ethnographers make cultural inferences from three sources: (1) from what people say; (2) from the way people act; and (3) from the artifacts people use. At first, each cultural inference is only a hypothesis about what people know. These hypotheses must be tested over and over again until the ethnographer becomes relatively certain that people share a particular system of cultural meanings. None of the sources for making inferences—behavior, speech, artifacts—are foolproof, but together they can lead to an adequate cultural description. And we can evaluate the adequacy of the description "by the ability of a stranger to the culture (who may be the ethnographer) to use the ethnography's statements as instructions for appropriately anticipating the scenes of the society" (Frake 1964b: 112).

Sometimes cultural knowledge is communicated by language in such a direct manner that we can make inferences with great ease. Instructions to children such as "wash your hands before dinner" and "don't go swimming after you eat or you'll get cramps" represent expressions of such *explicit cultural knowledge*. In his study of sky divers, Reed learned from informants that the jumps he observed actually involved three different kinds: *fun jumps, single work* (to perfect three forms of falling), and *relative work* (jumping in groups in preparation for competition). Informants could easily talk about this cultural knowledge. It is important to point out that studying explicit culture through the way people talk does not eliminate the need for making inferences. It only makes the task less difficult.

However, a large part of any culture consists of *tacit knowledge*. We all know things that we cannot talk about or express in direct ways. The ethnographer must then make inferences about what people know by listening carefully to what they say, by observing their behavior, and by studying artifacts and their use. With reference to discovering this tacit cultural knowledge, Malinowski wrote:

. . . we cannot expect to obtain a definite, precise and abstract statement from a philosopher, belonging to the community itself. The native takes his fundamental assumptions for granted, and if he reasons or inquires into matters of belief, it would be always in regard to details and concrete applications. Any attempts on the part of the ethnographer to induce his informant to formulate such a general statement would have to be in the form of leading questions of the worst type because in these leading questions he would have to introduce words and concepts essentially foreign to the native. Once the informant grasped their meaning, his outlook would be warped by our own ideas having been poured into it. Thus, the ethnographer must draw the generalizations for himself, must formulate the abstract statement without the direct help of a native informant (1950:396).

Every ethnographer makes use of what people say in seeking to describe their culture. Both tacit and explicit culture are revealed through speech, both in casual comments and in lengthy interviews. Because language is the primary means for transmitting culture from one generation to the next, much of any culture is encoded in linguistic form. In this book I will focus exclusively on making inferences from what people say. This focus on language is not intended to rule out the use of behavior and artifacts as a basis for making cultural inferences. Indeed, those who do ethnographic research following the steps in this book may wish to use these other sources also. I focus exclusively on language because it is such an essential part of all ethnographic field work, and because such a narrow focus will facilitate the task of learning to do ethnography. The ethnographic interview is one strategy for getting people to talk about what they know, and this book deals primarily with this kind of interviewing. However, the techniques presented in this book can be used for making cultural inferences from language samples collected in other ways besides interviews.

ETHNOGRAPHY FOR WHAT?

Ethnography is a culture-studying culture. It consists of a body of knowledge that includes research techniques, ethnographic theory, and hundreds of cultural descriptions. It seeks to build a systematic understanding of all human cultures from the perspective of those who have learned them. Ethnography is based on the following assumption: knowledge of all cultures is valuable. This assumption warrants a careful examination. To what end does the ethnographer collect information? For what reasons do we try to find out what people have to know to traverse the polar cap on dog sled, live in remote Melanesian villages, or work in New York skyscrapers? Why should anyone do ethnography?

Understanding the Human Species

Let's begin with the goal of scientific anthropology: to describe and explain the regularities and variations in social behavior. Perhaps the most striking feature of human beings is their diversity. Why does a single species exhibit such variation, creating different marriage patterns, holding different values, eating different foods, rearing children in different ways, believing in different gods, and pursuing different goals? If we are to understand this diversity, we must begin by carefully describing it. Most of the diversity in the human species results from cultures each human group has created and passed on from one generation to the next. Cultural description, the central task of ethnography, is the first step in understanding the human species.

It is one thing to describe differences, another to account for them. Explanation of cultural differences depends, in part, on making cross-cultural comparisons. But this task, in turn, depends on adequate ethnographic studies. Much of the comparative work in anthropology has been hampered by shoddy ethnographies, by investigations that impose Western concepts onto non-Western cultures, thereby distorting the results. Comparison not only reveals differences but also similarities, what is common among all cultures of the world. In the most general sense, then, ethnography contributes directly to both description and explanation of regularities and variations in human social behavior.

Many of the social sciences have more limited objectives. In any study of human behavior ethnography has an important role to play. We can identify several specific contributions.

Informing culture-bound theories. Each culture provides people with a way of seeing the world. It categorizes, encodes, and otherwise defines the world in which people live. Culture includes assumptions about the nature of reality as well as specific information about that reality. It includes values that specify the good, true, and believable. Whenever people learn a culture, they are, to some extent, imprisoned without knowing it. Anthropologists speak of this as being "culture-bound," living inside a particular reality that is taken for granted as "the reality."

Social scientists and their theories are no less culture-bound than other human beings. Western educational systems infuse all of us with ways of interpreting experience. Tacit assumptions about the world find their way into the theories of every academic discipline—literary criticism, physical science, history, and all the social sciences. Ethnography alone seeks to document the existence of *alternative* realities and to describe these realities in their own terms. Thus, it can provide a corrective for theories that arise in Western social science.

Take, for example, the theory of cultural deprivation. This idea arose in concrete form during the 1960's to explain the educational failure of many children. In order to account for their lack of achievement, it was proposed that they were "culturally deprived." Studies of cultural deprivation were undertaken, focusing on Indians, Blacks, Chicanos, and other cultural groups. This theory can be confirmed by studying children from these cultures through the protective screen of this theory. However, ethnographic research on the cultures of "culturally deprived children" reveals a different story. They have elaborate, sophisticated, and adaptive cultures which are simply different from the ones espoused by the educational system. Although still supported in some quarters, this theory is culture-bound. Cultural deprivation is merely a way of saying that people are deprived of "my culture." Certainly no one would argue that such children do not speak adequate Spanish or Black English, that they do not do well the things that are considered rewarding in *their* cultures. But the culture-bound nature of psychological and sociological theories extends far beyond notions of cultural deprivation. All theories developed in Western behavioral science are based on tacit premises of Western culture, usually the middle-class version most typical of professionals.

Ethnography, in itself, does not escape being culture-bound. However, it provides descriptions that reveal the range of explanatory models created by human beings. It can serve as a beacon that shows the culture-bound nature of social science theories. It says to all investigators of human behavior, "Before you impose your theories on the people you study, find out how those people define the world." Ethnography can describe in detail the folk theories that have been tested in actual living situations over generations of time. And as we come to understand personality, society, individuals, and environments from the perspective of other than the professional scientific cultures, it will lead to a sense of epistemological humility; we become aware of the tentative nature of our theories and this enables us to revise them to be less ethnocentric.[6]

Discovering grounded theory. Much social science research has been directed toward the task of *testing* formal theories. One alternative to formal theories, and a strategy that reduces the ethnocentrism, is to develop theories grounded in empirical data of cultural description. Glaser and Strauss have called this *grounded theory*.[7] Ethnography offers an excellent strategy for discovering grounded theory. For example, an ethnography of successful school children from minority cultures in the United States could develop grounded theories about school performance. One such study revealed that, rather than culturally deprived, such children are *culturally overwhelmed,* that success in school performance required the capacity to become *bicultural.*[8] But grounded theory can be developed in any substantive area of human experience. Personality theories can be informed by discovering the folk theories of personality each culture has developed.[9] Medical theories of health and disease can be informed by careful ethnographies of folk medical theories. Decision-making theory could be informed by first discovering the cultural rules for decision-making in a particular organization. The list could go on and on for almost every area of social science theory has its counterpart in the taken for granted cultures of the world.

Understanding complex societies. Until recently, ethnography was largely relegated to small, non-Western cultures. The value of studying these societies was readily accepted—after all, we didn't know much about them, we couldn't conduct surveys or experiments, so ethnography seemed appropriate. However, the value of ethnography in understanding our own society was often overlooked.

Our culture has imposed on us a myth about our complex society—the myth of the melting pot. Social scientists have talked about "American culture" as if it included a set of values shared by everyone. It has become increasingly clear that we do not have a homogeneous culture; that people who live in modern, complex societies actually live by many different cultural codes. This is not only true of the most obvious ethnic groups but each occupation group exhibits cultural differences. Our schools have their own cultural systems and even within the same institution people see things differently. Consider the language, values, clothing styles, and activities of high school students in contrast to the high school teachers and staff. The difference in their cultures is striking, yet often ignored. Guards and prisoners in jails, patients and physicians in hospitals, the elderly, the various religious groups—all have cultural perspectives. The physically handicapped live in a different world even though they live in the same town with those not handicapped. As people move from one cultural scene to another in complex societies, they employ different cultural rules. Ethnography offers one of the best ways to understand these complex features of modern life. It can show the range of cultural differences and how people with diverse perspectives interact.

Understanding human behavior. Human behavior, in contrast to animal behavior, has various meanings to the actor. These meanings can be discovered. We can ask a person collecting seashells about her actions: what she is doing, why she is doing it. Even when people participate in carefully contrived scientific experiments, they define the experiment and their involvement. And these definitions are always influenced by specific cultural backgrounds. Any explanation of behavior which excludes what the actors themselves know, how they define their actions, remains a partial explanation that distorts the human situation. The tools of ethnography offer one means to deal with this fact of meaning.

One end of ethnography, then, is to understand the human species. Ethnography yields empirical data about the lives of people in specific situations. It allows us to see alternative realities and modify our culture-bound theories of human behavior. But is knowledge for understanding, even scientific understanding, enough? I believe it is not. However, ethnography offers other dividends to anyone involved in culture change, social planning, or trying to solve a wide range of human problems.

Ethnography in the Service of Humankind

There was a time when "knowledge for knowledge's sake" was sufficient reason for doing social science, at least for those who believed in the inevitability of progress and the inherent goodness of science. That time has long since passed. One reason lies in the changes in the human situation:

In the last few decades, mankind has been overcome by the most change in its entire history. Modern science and technology have created so close a network of communication, transport, economic interdependence—and potential nuclear destruction—that planet earth, on its journey through infinity, has acquired the intimacy, the fellowship, and the vulnerability of a spaceship (Ward, 1966:vii).

This vulnerability makes our responsibility clear, if not easy. To ignore this vulnerability is similar to (to change Auden's metaphor slightly) astronauts studying the effects of boredom and weightlessness on fellow astronauts while the spaceship runs out of oxygen, exhausts its fuel supply, and the crew verges on mutiny.

In addition, scientists can no longer ignore the uses to which research findings are put. This applies, not only to research in genetics and atomic energy, but also to ethnographic studies. Cultural descriptions can be used to oppress people or to set them free. I know of one case where the South African government made use of ethnographic descriptions to make its apartheid policy more effective. I knew that my own descriptions of the culture of skid row drunks could be used by police departments to arrest these men more easily. That knowledge placed a special responsibility on me regarding where and when to publish the ethnography.[10] In our world-become-spaceship, where knowledge is power, ethnographers must consider the potential uses of their research.

In spite of these facts, some people continue to maintain that scientists need not concern themselves with the practical relevance of their research.

This view has deep roots in the academic value system. More than forty years ago, in his classic book, *Knowledge for What?*, Robert Lynd described the dichotomy.

The time outlooks of the scholar-scientist and of the practical men of affairs who surround the world of science tend to be different. The former works in a long, leisurely world in which the hands of the clock crawl slowly over a vast dial; to him, the precise penetration of the unknown seems too grand an enterprise to be hurried, and one simply works ahead within study walls relatively sound-proofed against the clamorous urgencies of the world outside. In this time-universe of the scholar-scientist certain supporting assumptions have grown up such as "impersonal objectivity," "aloofness from the strife of rival values," and the self-justifying goodness of "new knowledge" about anything, big or little. . . . The practical man of affairs, on the other hand, works by a small time-dial over which the second-hand of immediacy hurries incessantly. "Never mind the long past and the infinite future," insists the clattering little monitor, "but do this, fix this—now, before tomorrow morning." It has been taken for granted, in general, that there is no need to synchronize the two time-worlds of the scholar-scientist and of the practical man. Immediate relevance has not been regarded as so important as ultimate relevance; and, in the burgeoning nineteenth century world which viewed all time as moving within the Master System of Progress, there was seemingly large justification for this optimistic tolerance (1939:1–2).

One force at work today that makes it imperative for the ethnographer to synchronize these two perspectives comes from the people we study. In many places we can no longer collect cultural information from people merely to fill the bank of scientific knowledge. Informants are asking, even demanding, "Ethnography for what? Do you want to study our culture to build your theories of poverty? Can't you see that our children go hungry? Do you want to study folk beliefs about water-witching? What about the new nuclear power plant that contaminates our drinking water with radioactive wastes? Do you want to study kinship terms to build ever more esoteric theories? What about our elderly kinsmen who live in poverty and loneliness? Do you want to study our schools to propose new theories of learning? Our most pressing need is for schools that serve our children's needs in the language they understand."

One way to synchronize the needs of people and the goals of ethnography is to consult with informants to determine urgent research topics. Instead of beginning with theoretical problems, the ethnographer can begin with informant-expressed needs, then develop a research agenda to relate these topics to the enduring concerns within social science. Surely the needs of informants should have equal weight with "scientific interest" in setting ethnographic priorities. More often than not, informants can identify urgent research more clearly than the ethnographer. In my own study of skid row men, for example, I began with an interest in the social structure of an alcoholism treatment center. My informants, long-time drunks who were spending life sentences on the installment plan in the Seattle city jail, suggested more urgent research possibilities. "Why don't you study what goes on in that jail?" they would ask. And so I shifted my goals to studying the culture of the jail, the social structure of inmates, and how drunks were oppressed by the jail system. My theoretical and scholarly interests could have been served by either project; the needs of tramps were best served by studying the oppression in the jail.

Another way to synchronize human needs with the accumulation of scientific knowledge is through what I call "strategic research." Instead of beginning ethnographic projects from an interest in some particular culture, area of the world, or theoretical concern, strategic research begins with an interest in human problems. These problems suggest needed changes and information needed to make such changes. For example, in a discussion on strategies for revitalizing American culture, I suggested the following priorities for strategic research (Spradley 1976:111):

1. A health care system that provides adequate care for all members of the society.
2. The provision of economic resources for all people sufficient to eliminate poverty and provided in a way that does not destroy the privacy and dignity of any recipient.
3. Equal rights and opportunities for all classes of citizens, including women, blacks, native Americans, Chicanos, the elderly, children, and others.
4. Public institutions, such as schools, courts, and governments that are designed for a multicultural constituency.
5. Socially responsible corporations that operate in the public interest as well as for a private interest.
6. Zero population growth.
7. An ecologically-balanced economy based on recycling and responsible for the protection of natural resources.
8. Education for all people, at every stage of life, that equips them to cope with the complexity of choice in our rapidly changing society.
9. Work roles and environments that contribute directly to the workers' sense of meaning and purpose in life.
10. Opportunity for alternative career patterns and more flexible life cycle sequencing with multiple occupational careers and meaningful involvement for youth, retired persons, and the elderly.

After identifying a general area such as an adequate health care system, strategic research translates that into a specific research project. This can lead to consultation with informants and a strategic project. For example, Oswald Werner, an anthropologist at Northwestern University, has been conducting ethnographic research among the Navaho for many years. In consultation with informants and out of a concern for adequate medical care, he selected a strategic research project: to develop an encyclopedia of Navaho medical knowledge. Three volumes in a ten-volume cultural description have been completed. It has many immediate uses in both preserving Navaho medical knowledge and also adapting Western medicine for the most effective use among the Navaho. As Navaho healers and Western health professionals increasingly work together, there is an urgent need for each to understand the medical knowledge of the other. Ethnographic research, in this case, is serving both the needs of the Navaho in solving pressing health problems and also the accumulation of theoretically important information for understanding human behavior.[11]

Consider the need identified above for "socially responsible corporations that operate in the public interest as well as for a private interest." This suggests hundreds of strategic ethnographic research projects. We need to know how decisions are made in corporate board rooms, something that could be discovered through ethnography. We need to know how lobbying efforts of corporations affect the legislature in every state; in short, an ethnography of corporate lobbying. We need to know how corporations bypass laws enacted to control them. As some corporations change to act more and more in the public interest, we need ethnographic descriptions of their efforts to serve as models for others. In short, we need extensive ethnographic research to understand this form of social organization in our own society and to know the extent to which corporations affect all our interests.

Ethnography for what? For understanding the human species, but also for serving the needs of humankind. One of the great challenges facing every ethnographer is to synchronize these two uses of research.

Language occupies such a large part of human experience that most of us take it for granted. We talk to others and ourselves. We listen to people talking. We make plans silently and review things in our minds by means of language. In doing ethnography, language structures our field notes and enters into every analysis and insight. Language permeates our encounters with informants, and the final ethnography takes shape in language. Whatever approach the ethnographer uses—participant observation, ethnographic interviews, collecting life histories, or a mixture of strategies—language enters into every phase of the research process. Ethnographers must deal with at least two languages—their own and the one spoken by informants. If we divide the work of ethnography into two major tasks, *discovery* and *description,* we can see more clearly the important role played by language.

LANGUAGE AND DISCOVERY

Language is more than a means of communication about reality: it is a tool for constructing reality. Different languages create and express different realities. They categorize experience in different ways. They provide alternative patterns for customary ways of thinking and perceiving. In setting out to discover the cultural reality of a particular group of people, the ethnographer faces a crucial question: *What language shall I use for asking questions and recording the meanings I discover?* The answer to this question has profound implications for the entire ethnographic enterprise.

Because ethnography was first undertaken in non-Western societies, learning the native language took the highest priority. The ethnographer who went to study the Bushmen, a remote village in the Andes, or an isolated New Guinea tribe, knew that understanding the language was a necessary prerequisite to thorough research. Early months in the field were spent with informants who taught the ethnographer to speak and understand the native language. But in the process, in addition to acquiring the ability to communicate, ethnographers learned something of great significance. They discovered how the natives categorized experience. They discovered how informants used these categories in customary thought. They discovered how to ask questions that made sense to informants. They discovered what questions lay behind everyday activities.

Language learning became the cornerstone of field work. It was the first and most important step to achieving the primary goal of ethnography—to describe a culture in its own terms. The anthropologist Franz Boas, one of the founders of ethnography, clearly stated this objective:

We know what we mean by family, state, government, etc. As we overstep the limits of one culture we do not know how far these may correspond to equivalent concepts. If we choose to apply our classification to alien cultures we may combine forms which do not belong together. . . . If it is our serious purpose to understand the thoughts of a people the whole analysis of experience must be based upon their concepts, not ours (1943:311).

But in recent years, as ethnographers have increasingly undertaken research in our society, the necessity of studying the native language is frequently ignored. In part, this neglect occurs because informants *appear* to use a language identical to that spoken by the ethnographer. But such is not the case; *semantic* differences exist and they have a profound influence on ethnographic research. Let me give one example.

When I began studying skid row men I set out to learn their language. Actually I was learning a dialect or special argot used by this population. Although not as difficult for me to learn as some non-Western language, the very similarity with my own dialect of English made it easy to overlook the necessity to learn it at all. My informants referred to themselves and others like them as *tramps*; one topic of conversation was *making a flop*.[1] I thought I understood these English words but I also recognized them as interesting words with slightly different usages. As the months passed, my tramp informants taught me more and more, helping me to understand the subtle meanings attached to these terms. It was as if they were leading me into a strange new world. I discovered, for example, that *making a flop* was such a rich phrase that I scarcely scratched the surface of its meaning. My informants identified more than a hundred different categories of *flops*. They had strategies for locating flops, for protecting themselves from the weather and intruders in these flops. Making a flop defined their friendship patterns and even their police record was affected by making a flop. I realized that, in some ways, a flop was like a home to a tramp, but I did not merely translate the one term into the other for my ethnography. Instead I worked to elucidate the full meaning of this concept, to describe their culture in its own terms.

In social science literature about skid row men I discovered that most scholars called them "homeless men." I found books on the homeless man and journal articles that described the characteristics of homeless men with suggestions for improving their lot. It became apparent that many scholars saw them as homeless men because *they had not taken the time to learn the native language.* They described the lives of skid row men, not in terms of *that* culture, but in terms appropriate to the middle-class lifestyle of professionals. One of the first questions asked by researchers of skid row men is "Where do you live?" or "What is your present address?" or "Where have you lived for the last year?"

Because tramps know the language and culture of researchers, social workers, and counselors, they know this question does not mean, "Where do you usually make a flop?" They translate it into something like, "Do I have a room, a house, or an apartment with an address like most people?" They almost always answer, "I don't have a home," and, on the basis of this answer, tramps are transformed into "homeless men." In all the months of interviewing tramps, I never heard one say "I'm a homeless man" or even "I have no home." I did hear them say, "I made a good flop last night" or "I used to jungle up down by the waterfront."

It might seem like a small matter to call them homeless men, but it represents only the tip of the iceberg. For one thing, it closes off a most important area of research: what kind of "homes" do tramps have? One of the most important identity features for tramps has to do with the kind of homebase they have—a car, a mission, a place of work, a bedroll, or none at all. But if they are *homeless,* we need not investigate this aspect of their lives, an assumption reflected in the dearth of literature on the flops tramps make.

The ethnographer working with people in our complex society must recognize the existence of subtle but important language differences. I began to test this idea in my own family and discovered my young children spoke a slightly different language with their friends at school than with me at home. At the university, students gave words different meanings than did their teachers. Occupational groups had their own argots. To do ethnography in our own society, it would be necessary to begin with a serious study of the way people talk. Ethnographers at home have to learn the language no less than ethnographers overseas.

As I worked with tramp informants I discovered they not only spoke their own language but they had acquired an ability I call *translation competence.* This is *the ability to translate the meanings of one culture into a form that is appropriate to another culture.* In our complex society, nearly everyone acquires this special kind of linguistic competence and it has a profound influence on ethnographic discovery. In addition to competence in speaking a native language, almost everyone learns to translate when communicating with outsiders who speak a dialectic variation of that same language. We learn to shift back and forth between the language of work and home, school and home, or men and women. We do not speak to the local minister in the same dialect of English spoken at the local bar. The secretaries change from one dialect to another between coffee break and the executive staff meeting.

When someone unfamiliar with our particular cultural scene[2] asks us a question about it, we make use of our *translation competence* to help them understand. Let us look more closely at how translation competence affects the work of ethnography in various kinds of settings.

In a society completely isolated from Western influence (a rare occurrence today), no one can speak the ethnographer's language. It becomes necessary to spend months learning to speak the native language. Both the ethnographer and informants are *naive* about the others' culture. The informant finds it extremely difficult to translate or interpret for the ethnographer. Only after months and months of language study can the ethnographer conduct wide-ranging interviews and begin to make sense out of many things. On the surface, this looks like a difficulty when, in truth, it is an unparalled opportunity for cultural discovery. Such isolated societies are the ethnographer's first choice for research, not because ethnographers want to romanticize such groups, but because they are groups in which all the assumptions we often share with those we study are absent.

This does not mean that translation competence does not exist in isolated societies. In his classic study of the Iatmul of New Guinea, Gregory Bateson showed how even the men and women in this small society spoke somewhat different dialects of the same language.[3] Undoubtedly, when communication takes place between subgroups in any society, people employ their translation competence to bridge the subtle differences in culture.

Most societies today have had some contact with Western culture and can be called *contact societies*. The natives have met missionaries, soldiers, or traders. Some natives have traveled widely; others have worked in factories or attended schools. Although informants may speak a strange language, one the ethnographer must learn, individuals do know something about the ethnographer's culture. This means that informants can begin to act as translators or interpreters. Some may even speak English or some pidgin language well enough to interpret during interviews. At first glance, the ethnographer may believe these interpreters would make the best informants. But their very ability to interpret, to use the ethnographer's language, presents a handicap to discovering their culture.

As I stated earlier, language not only functions as a means of communication, it also functions to create and express a cultural reality. When ethnographers do not learn the language, but instead depend on interpreters, they have great difficulty learning how natives think, how they perceive the world, and what assumptions they make about human experience. The barrier to learning their particular frame of reference, their cultural reality, has not been removed. The more an informant translates for your convenience, the more that informant's cultural reality becomes distorted.

In most urban areas and many other parts of the world, large aggregates of people live in close proximity and still maintain somewhat different cultures. In such *multi-cultural societies,* members of groups (usually called subcultures or ethnic groups) sometimes speak a different language. Some are bilingual, others merely use a different dialect of the national language. Cultural differences, while apparent, are not always striking. Compared to isolated societies, these groups do not appear exotic, strange, or completely alien. However, the necessity of learning the language is as important as ever if we want to avoid distorting what people know.

Finally, within the same cultural groups in complex societies, there are *cultural scenes* known to some people but not others. Our everyday lives are lived in different social situations, dealing with different problems, doing different things. The thousands of career specializations represent different cultural scenes. So do hobbies, clubs, service organizations, and even different neighborhoods. Any single individual will have knowledge of many cultural scenes and could serve as an informant for them. One woman, for example, may have detailed knowledge of the local P.T.A., the local synagogue, midwife culture, and the culture of skiers.

Take her work as a midwife in a nearby culture. She speaks English and shares with others this common language. Yet when she works as a midwife she uses words in slightly different ways. If an ethnographer decided to study midwives and hospital delivery rooms, such an informant would not only have the ability to translate her knowledge into the ethnographer's terms, she would have had much experience doing so. Many times she has been asked, "What kind of work do you do?" and in answering she has made use of her translation competence. As an ethnographer, if you begin asking questions, she will suspect your ignorance and actually find it difficult *not* to translate.

How does one overcome this tendency of informants to translate things? The major way is by asking ethnographic questions designed to reduce the influence of translation competence. Such questions will be described in detail as we go through the steps of the Developmental Research Sequence Method. In a sense, this book is a set of instructions for learning another language. It involves discovery procedures for the study of the meanings inherent in the way people use their language, whether in isolated societies, contact societies, multi-cultural societies, or within a particular cultural scene in complex societies.

LANGUAGE AND ETHNOGRAPHIC DESCRIPTION

The end product of doing ethnography is a verbal description of the cultural scenes studied. Even ethnographic films do not describe without verbal statements that tell the viewer what the people filmed would see and how they would interpret the scenes presented. Thus, ethnographic description inevitably involves language. The ethnographer usually writes in his native language or the language of a particular audience of students, professionals, or the general public. But how is it possible to describe a culture in its own terms when using an alien language? The answer lies in the fact that *every ethnographic description is a translation*. As such, it must use both *native* terms and their meanings as well as those of the ethnographer.

This does not mean that the mixture contained in such translations is always the same; ethnographic descriptions are not equally faithful to the concepts of informants. At one extreme we find descriptions that ignore the native point of view altogether and distort the culture. They are written almost entirely in the language of outsiders. At the other extreme we find monolingual ethnographies and ethnographic novels written by native authors. I have identified six types of descriptions in Figure 2.1 to illustrate differences in the degree to which descriptions reflect the native point of view.

Ethnocentric descriptions make almost no use of the native language; they certainly ignore what things mean. The people and their way of life are characterized in stereotypes such as lazy, dirty, ignorant, primitive, weird,

FIGURE 2.1. Types of Descriptions

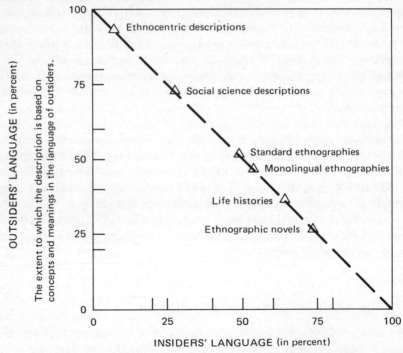

The extent to which the description is based on concepts and meanings in the language of informants.

This illustration provides a comparison of the different types of descriptions in terms of the languages used to describe the culture.

and uneducated. Ethnocentric descriptions appeared frequently in the writings of some early missionaries and other observers of non-Western peoples. Consider Alexander Henry's description of bodily decorations for women in a non-Western tribe:

Most of the women have their faces tattooed in a very savage manner, lines a quarter of an inch broad passing from the nose to the ear, and down each side of the mouth and chin to the throat. This disfigures them very much; otherwise, some would have tolerably good faces (1953).

Ethnocentric descriptions continue to appear today in the popular literature about other cultures or about cultural scenes within our society.

Social science descriptions take place in a variety of disciplines that study other people. They usually appear as part of theoretically-focused studies which test hypotheses. Based on observations, interviews, questionnaires, or psychological tests, they may appear to reflect the native point of view. However, social scientists are outsiders to these cultures and their analytic concepts are not the ones employed by informants. Tramps, for instance, become homeless men with characteristics that are merely stereotypes by outsiders. Consider the following statement by a social scientist: "The patient may then resemble a burned-out, back-ward schizophrenic who has forgotten what his troubles were and why he retreated from life. The alcoholic is now a 'bum,' inhabits skid row, and no longer knows or cares why he drinks, so long as he can just get his hands on another bottle" (Solomon 1966:165). Like many social science descriptions, this one does not reflect the cultural knowledge of skid row men.

Standard ethnographies show great variety in the extent to which they employ native languages. Some give lip service to informants' concepts and may even include a few native terms in parentheses throughout the description. Other ethnographies deal thoroughly with native concepts in some places, then fit the culture into analytic categories in other places. Still others are firmly rooted in the insider's language; the concepts and meanings of informants permeate the description and give one a profound sense of being on the inside of another way of life.

Monolingual ethnographies move a step closer to a description of a culture in its own terms.[4] In this type of study, a member of the society who is thoroughly enculturated writes the ethnography in the native language. Then the ethnographer, after carefully working out the semantic system for that language, translates the ethnography into English (or the investigator's language). This type of ethnography has not been developed extensively in its full form. One example of the monolingual ethnography is *The Navajo Ethno-Medical Encyclopedia* by Oswald Werner and his associates. In the past, many ethnographers have made extensive use of informant-written descriptions, including folk tales, historical events, and personal experiences. In some respects, the monolingual ethnography shares similarities with the next category of description, the life history.

Life histories are another kind of description that offers an understanding of alien cultures. They reveal the details of a single person's life and in the process show important parts of the culture. They may be recorded in the native language, then translated into English, or sometimes, if the informant is bilingual, recorded in the language of the investigator. Some life histories are heavily edited by the ethnographer, others are presented in the same form in which the recording occurred. Multiple life histories, such as Oscar Lewis's *Children of Sanchez,* employ the native language to a very great extent and broaden the description to include more than a single person.

Ethnographic novels written by native authors provide descriptions close to the insider's point of view. Chinua Achebe, the great Ibo novelist, has given us excellent examples of this kind of writing in such books as *Things Fall Apart* and *Arrow of God*. Ethnographic novels are rich in descriptions; they make use of the language spoken in the communities from which the characters come. It is important to recognize that novels about selected aspects of our own culture are often ethnographic in character. Such novels can capture the subtle meanings of a culture and portray them in a way that gives the reader a deep insight into another way of life.

Ethnographers cannot escape the use of language in carrying out their investigations. Asking questions, listening to casual conversations, interviewing, taking field notes, analyzing data, writing rough drafts, and finally writing the final ethnography *all* involve words, phrases, sentences, and most of all *meanings*. I would argue that the meanings expressed in both the ethnographer's language and the informant's language deserve the most serious considerations. With Franz Boas, I would reiterate that "if it is our serious purpose to understand the thoughts of a people the whole analysis of experience must be based upon their concepts, not ours" (1943:11). In ethnographic *discovery* we should make maximum use of the native language. In ethnographic *description* we should represent the meanings encoded in that language as closely as possible. As a translation, ethnographic descriptions should flow from the concepts and meanings native to that scene rather than the concepts developed by the ethnographer.

Ethnographers work together with informants to produce a cultural description. This relationship is complex and I will have much to say about it in later chapters. The success of doing ethnography depends, to a great extent, on understanding the nature of this relationship. I use the term *informant* in a very specific way, not to be confused with concepts like subject, respondent, friend, or actor. In this chapter I want to clarify the concept and role of informant.

According to *Webster's New Collegiate Dictionary,* an informant is "a native speaker engaged to repeat words, phrases, and sentences in his own language or dialect as a model for imitation and a source of information." Although derived primarily from linguistics, this definition will serve as a starting point for our discussion. Informants are first and foremost *native speakers,* a fact made clear in the last chapter. Informants are engaged by the ethnographer to speak *in their own language or dialect.* Informants provide a *model for the ethnographer to imitate;* the ethnographer hopes to learn to use the native language in the way informants do. Finally, informants are *a source of information;* literally, they become teachers for the ethnographer.

Most people act as informants at one time or another without realizing it. We offer information to others in response to questions about our everyday lives. "What kind of family did you come from?" "What do you do at school?" "What kinds of problems do you have working as a cocktail waitress?" "You collect comic books? That sounds interesting; what does it involve?" Such questions place us in the role of informant.

An ethnographer seeks out ordinary people with ordinary knowledge and builds on their common experience. Slowly, through a series of interviews, by repeated explanations, and through the use of special questions, ordinary people become excellent informants. Everyone, in the course of their daily activities, has acquired knowledge that appears specialized to others. A shaman knows how to perform magic rituals; a housewife can prepare a holiday meal; a sportsman is an expert in fishing for lake trout; a physician knows her way around a large hospital and can perform open heart surgery; a tramp has acquired strategies for making it; a boy can maneuver with skill on a skate board. Knowledge about everyday life is a common property of the human species. So is the ability to commuicate that knowledge in a native language. This ability makes it possible for almost anyone to act as an informant.

I distinctly recall Laurie, one of my best informants. She answered my questions with all the calm assurance of an expert. She recalled incidents that had happened and told me stories that brought to life the cultural scene she knew so well. It didn't matter that she had just passed her fourth birthday; she had mastered the complex culture of her kindergarten class. She named and described each one of her classmates and identified the criteria by which she distinguished them. She enumerated more than twenty different kinds of "work," everything from *science table* and *home center* to *clay* and *rig-a-jigs*. Like every good informant, she spoke unselfconsciously in her own language—the language of kindergarten children. She didn't realize how much she knew; she had learned this culture in the course of day-to-day activities. Once I discovered the questions to ask, her cultural knowledge flowed out as if some unseen gate in her mind had been flung open.

Another informant who taught me his culture must have been over sixty. He had traveled the length and breadth of the United States as a tramp for more than thirty years. A first or second generation immigrant from France, other tramps called him "Frenchy." Uneducated, unemployed, and unwilling to give up his fierce independence, Frenchy was a first-rate informant. He knew more about places *to make a flop,* more about ways *to beat a drunk charge,* and more about avoiding *bulls* (police) on the street than college-educated men half his age who also lived on skid row. Frenchy seldom analyzed the way of life he had adopted, nor did he try to justify and explain what, to others, looked like a down and out condition. He talked with excitement about the joy of travel. He explained the cultural strategies he had learned over the years to survive without a steady job. He talked about jails and freight trains and friends and how he managed to balance his good days against the bad ones. Once I had gained his confidence, once he knew that I wanted him to be my teacher, he fell into the informant role with great delight.

The informant-ethnographer relationship is frequently confused with other relationships. An anthropologist working in a non-Western society knows the difficulties that arise when he or she is perceived as a missionary, a trader, or a government agent. I interviewed many skid row men at the treatment center for alcoholics operated by a county sheriff's department. I repeatedly explained to the tramps that I was *not* a member of the staff but a faculty member at the University of Washington Medical School. Even so, potential informants often believed I was a *bull* from the sheriff's department. One man who observed that I asked endless questions asked if I was an F.B.I. agent. I soon discovered that until they understood that I was an ethnographer, interested in their culture, they could not easily assume the role of informant.

In our own society, the informant role is often confused with *traditional roles* such as friend or employer, and with *social science roles* such as subject or respondent. It will help to clarify the nature of the informant-ethnographer relationship if we examine these two sources of confusion.

CONFUSION WITH TRADITIONAL ROLES

Sometimes a beginning ethnographer, anxious about conducting ethnographic interviews, decides it will be easier to talk with a friend, relative, or a college roommate. Consider the following example from an undergraduate student's experience.

Joan decided to interview her friend, Bruce, about the culture of the college football team on which he played. "Could you describe a typical football game to me?" she began, asking a good ethnographic question. Bruce looked quizzical; he knew that Joan had never attended the college games, but he also knew that she must have seen at least part of a game on television or in high school. Still, he wanted to cooperate, so he answered her questions but skimmed over the parts he assumed she knew. Without realizing it he looked bored whenever Joan asked a naive question. When a friend asked him how the interviews were going, he replied, "She asks such dumb questions. I'm not sure what she wants to know."

Joan sensed that Bruce was reluctant to talk and many of her questions received brief answers or a comment like, "Oh, you know about that." This forced Joan to repeat some questions in later interviews, questions Bruce knew she had asked previously. More important, Bruce's responses made her ask more complex, analytic questions. Without knowing it, she shifted away from an ethnographic approach and began to analyze why Bruce was so excited about football before she understood the fundamentals of the culture. Both Joan and Bruce felt uncomfortable with the questions and answers demanded by the ethnographic approach. Their uneasiness arose because this new relationship departed from what they had come to expect of each other as friends. But these vague feelings were never expressed or understood.

If Joan had approached Dr. Adams, a retired pharmacist who spent most of his afternoons in lawn bowling tournaments, many of the difficulties would never have arisen. "Could you tell me about lawn bowling?" she could have asked with complete sincerity. Her informant, recognizing Joan's age, would assume she must be completely ignorant of this game and the activities that go on during a tournament. If she asked for more detailed descriptions or repeated questions, her informant would have interpreted these as signs of interest rather than stupidity.

And Bruce would have felt differently with another ethnographer. Assume that he boarded an airplane and sat down next to an elderly Japanese man from a remote village on the island of Hokkaido. After a few questions to get acquainted, Bruce could easily have become a good informant.

"What do you do in school?" the man might ask.

"Well, besides my classes, I'm on the football team."

"Football team? What is that?"

"That's a game we play called *football;* there are two teams, eleven men on each side."

"Football? I've never heard of that. Do you play with your foot?"

"No. Well, yes, sometimes. But mostly it's running and blocking and trying to move the ball on a field." The look of sincere puzzlement on the man's face would tell Bruce that he had taken too much for granted. He would have to go into more detail, to describe the game in the most basic terms. And Bruce would interpret any requests for clarification as an opportunity to further inform an interested stranger.

During the weeks and months that Joan attempted to conduct ethnographic interviews with Bruce, a great many problems arose that had nothing to do with Bruce's culture or the primary task of doing ethnography. They came from the confusion of two roles: informant and friend. Conversation between friends is usually reciprocal: each person asks and answers questions. Conversation between ethnographer and informant is much less balanced; the ethnographer asks the questions and the informant talks about activities and events that make up his lifestyle. A friend does not ask the same question over and over; an ethnographer does. A friend does not ask for endless clarification; an ethnographer does. This does not mean ethnographers cannot be friends with their informants. But that is quite different from trying to make informants out of friends.

I have known undergraduate and graduate students who attempted to make informants out of an employer, a professor, their mother, a roommate, or someone else in a traditional role. In almost every case, their ethnographic interviews met with mixed results. Some, with great patience and ingenuity, managed to describe part of a cultural scene. Others gave up in frustration. Some traditional roles present less difficulties than others to the would-be ethnographer. A skilled, experienced ethnographer can often work with friends, relatives, or acquaintances, but such traditional roles will always create certain difficulties. In learning to do ethnographic interviews most people find that strangers make better informants.

CONFUSION WITH SOCIAL SCIENCE ROLES

By far the greatest barrier to a productive informant relationship occurs when this role is confused with other social science roles. The act of investigation necessarily means that the researcher and the person studied assume roles. Each person in the relationship constructs a definition of what is going on; these definitions have a profound impact on the research. At least three roles that contrast with informant are used in the social sciences:

subject, respondent, and *actor.* Sometimes, within the context of a single project, the same individual will act as subject, actor, respondent, and informant. In order not to confuse these roles, let's look at their most important differences.

Subjects

Social science research that uses subjects usually has a specific goal: to test hypotheses. Investigators are not primarily interested in discovering the cultural knowledge of the subjects; they seek to confirm or disconfirm a specific hypothesis by studying the subject's responses. Work with subjects begins with preconceived ideas; work with informants begins with a naive ignorance. Subjects do not define what it is important for the investigator to find out; informants do.

When I began seeking informants among men arrested for public drunkenness, I *tentatively* thought of them as "alcoholics." But when I began informant interviews, I set aside that definition and allowed my informants to define themselves. I soon discovered that their most salient identity concept was "tramp" rather than alcoholic. Even those confined to an alcoholic treatment center did not think of themselves primarily as alcoholics. I then set about to discover the meaning of this folk concept to my informants. Contrast this ethnographic approach with an excellent study of alcoholic *subjects.*

Godwin, *et al.* (1974), wanted to shed light on the question, "What causes a person to beome an alcoholic? Is it due to social conditioning and environmental factors or is it inherited?" Previous studies showed that when the children of alcoholics became adults, the incidence of alcoholism among them tended to be high. But scholars disagreed as to the cause of this fact. Some argued the cause was genetic; others argued that growing up in a family environment where one parent was a severe alcoholic would produce it.

Godwin and his colleagues found a "natural experiment" with subjects ideally suited to the aims of their research. The subjects were a sample of male identical twins with two important characteristics: (1) they were sons of an alcoholic parent, and (2) one son had been adopted during infancy and raised by nonalcoholic stepparents. Throughout the study the researchers selected the concepts (such as alcoholism) and defined their meaning. They reasoned that if both sons showed a high incidence of alcoholism, this would support the hypothesis that environmental conditioning was *not* a significant factor in the development of alcoholism. Their research confirmed this hypothesis. There was a high incidence of alcoholism among their subjects, and no significant difference occurred between adopted and nonadopted sons. They concluded that the environment contributed little to the development of the alcoholism.

29

It would have been possible to use these same twins as informants rather than as subjects. However, this would have led to an entirely different set of questions and procedures. The major differences can be summarized by noting the fundamental questions asked by each approach.

RESEARCH WITH SUBJECTS	RESEARCH WITH INFORMANTS
1. What do I know about a problem that will allow me to formulate and test a hypothesis?	1. What do my informants know about their culture that I can discover?
2. What concepts can I use to test this hypothesis?	2. What concepts do my informants use to classify their experience?
3. How can I operationally define these concepts?	3. How do my informants define these concepts?
4. What scientific theory can explain the data?	4. What folk theory do my informants use to explain their experience?
5. How can I interpret the results and report them in the language of my colleagues?	5. How can I *translate* the cultural knowledge of my informants into a cultural description my colleagues will understand?

Research with subjects is neither more nor less important than research with informants. The two approaches are simply different. Some social scientists set out to describe a culture (work with informants) and also to test certain hypotheses (work with subjects). They may begin their research with informants but before the ethnographic task is completed, these informants have become subjects with hardly anyone aware of the change. Ethnography thus becomes confused with hypothesis testing and problem-oriented research. When this occurs, a unique and interesting culture becomes recast into the concepts and ideas of social science before anyone has described it in its own terms. This book is designed primarily to circumvent this confusion.

As I pointed out earlier, ethnographic studies can make important contributions to social science research with subjects. For example, ethnography can generate hypotheses for later testing by other research techniques. Consider the following generalization that can easily become a hypothesis about male and female roles. In studying Brady's Bar, we discovered that when men and women employees worked together, an *asymmetrical crossover phenomenon occurred* (Spradley and Mann 1975). In our society, when men and women work together, they sometimes "cross over" and do the tasks traditionally assigned to the other sex. In traditional families, for example, men sometimes care for babies and prepare meals; women sometimes drive the car even when their husbands are riding in that car. In Brady's Bar we found that although women crossed over and performed roles normally assigned to male bartenders, the reverse never occurred. Tasks assigned to female cocktail waitresses were of lower status and the men simply refused to cross over, even though many occasions presented this opportunity. And so we concluded "The rules that regulate the cross-over phenomenon in Brady's Bar are not the same for each sex. They are asymmetrical, functioning in such a way as to put women at a disadvantage in the game of social interaction" (Spradley and Mann 1975:40). This represents, not only a general statement about the culture of Brady's Bar, but also a hypothesis that could be tested by using subjects or respondents in other bars, in other settings, and even in other cultures.

Respondents

A respondent is any person who responds to a survey questionnaire or to queries presented by an investigator. Many people confuse respondents with informants because both answer questions and *appear* to give information about their culture. One of the most important distinctions between these two roles has to do with the language used to formulate questions. Survey research with respondents almost always employs the language of the social scientist. The questions arise out of the social scientist's culture. Ethnographic research, on the other hand, depends more fully on the language of the informant. The questions arise out of the informant's culture.

Let's look at the difference in these approaches. At the time I began my ethnographic research on skid row men, many survey studies had already been published. Some included ethnographic data mixed with survey data; most included information about "employment" and "income," topics of great interest to social scientists. Bahr (1973) summarizes some of these studies: unemployment among skid row men ranges from 50% to 76%. Their typical jobs are as unskilled laborers, farm laborers, railroad workers, restaurant workers, and transportation workers. Only a few men work as craftsmen, clerks, or at other white-collar jobs. In Chicago, only 12% of the employed men held the same job for a year; 33% changed jobs every day, or every two months if they had a steady job. The median income in Chicago for 1957 was just over $1000. Some men reported no earned income at all for the year.

Now these kinds of facts are readily identified as survey information. However, the nature of the questions that elicited this data is not self-evident. They involve concepts from outside the culture, concepts like "employment," "steady job," and "income." Because skid row men know the culture from which investigators come, they can answer questions like "How much did you earn last year?" "What kind of work do you do?" and "Do you have a steady income?" But these questions pre-define what

31

respondents will report and do not necessarily tap the cultural knowledge of tramps.

Because I wanted to discover the tramps's culture and not impose my concepts on them, I began by listening to their conversations. They talked about things that I was often tempted to call "income" and "employment." But instead, like an ethnographer studying some remote tribe, I set aside my concepts and tried to learn their language. I did not assume that because they spoke English, I really did know what they were talking about.

As I listened, one of the folk concepts I discovered was "ways to make it." This concept refers to the strategies that tramps employ to survive, whether on skid row, in tramp jungles, on freight trains, in city jails, or in alcoholism treatment centers. I discovered nearly twenty different terms that informants identified as "ways to make it." They included such things as *making the sally* (mission), *making the V.A.* (Veterans Administration Hospital), *junking* (finding and selling junk items), *making the blood bank* (to sell their blood), *spot jobbing, meeting a live one* (a person who will give them money), and *working*. Income and employment are related only to the last concept, but what about the others? What about all the money a tramp "earns" from *making the blood bank, junking, panhandling* (a form of begging), and *pooling* (sharing money with others to make a purchase)? My goal as an ethnographer was to find out the meaning of all these concepts, not just the ones that seemed to connect with the dominant culture.

Survey research has many values and it generates important information. It even results in descriptions of people, but not in cultural descriptions. For survey research, in general, begins with questions rather than a search for questions. However, it is possible to devise *ethnographic* questions and administer them by means of a questionnaire, but this is not the same as the usual survey questionnaire. I stress the importance of a clear distinction between respondents and informants because it will help the ethnographer to set aside culture-bound questions that prevent discovery of the other person's point of view.

Actors

An actor is someone who becomes the object of observation in a natural setting. An infant sleeping in a hospital nursery or a judge sentencing men for public drunkenness can both be observed as actors. A scholar who watches a group of gorillas is studying actors; however, gorillas can never become informants.

Ethnographers often use participant observation as a strategy for both listening to people and watching them in natural settings. Those they study thus become actors and informants at the same time; informant interviews may even be conducted casually while doing participant observation. But when we merely observe behavior without also treating people as informants, their cultural knowledge becomes distorted. For human beings, what an act means is never self-evident. Two persons can interpret the same event in completely different ways. The father who strikes a child may be "spanking" her as punishment or "teasing" her in play.

When social scientists observe actors in a natural setting, they must decide how to describe what they see. My first contact with tramps came as I observed their being arraigned in the Seattle Criminal Court. As *actors* in this courtroom drama, they stood before the judge, listened to the charge of public drunkenness, made brief statements, offered pleas of guilty or innocent, then walked out of the courtroom. An average of sixty-five men appeared each day and I had an ideal opportunity to observe similar acts over and over again. I watched, listened, and wrote down everything I could. I recorded the way men dressed, how they stood, what they said, how long it took the judge to inform them of their rights, and how long the entire process of arraignment took for each man. But as an observer of *actors,* nearly everything went into my field notes in my language, using my concepts.

Later, when I began informant interviews, I discovered that what I had seen and recorded was not what tramps saw themselves doing. Sometimes the differences were subtle, somethimes striking. But, in all cases, my descriptions tended to distort the culture I sought to describe. For example, in my field notes I recorded the following kinds of things:

1. A man said to the judge, "I have a job if you'll give me a suspended sentence."
2. A man said, "My family is sick and I want to take care of them."
3. A man said, "I request a continuance."
4. A man said, "Guilty."
5. A man said, "Not guilty."
6. A man said, "I need help with my drinking problem; I'd like to go to the treatment center."
7. The clerk called Jim Johnson's name, no one appeared.
8. The clerk read off a list of names for men to appear; none did. He said they forfeited their bail.

These are all actions and events I saw. I believed they were all separate events, ones I could understand. But informants explained that these were all the *same kind of thing.* They called them *ways to beat a drunk charge.* When a tramp says, "Guilty," they told me, he isn't necessarily saying, "I was drunk"; many are not intoxicated when arrested. Saying "Guilty" is one way to beat a drunk charge, as is saying "Not guilty," "I request a continuance," or any of the others. These strategies aim to reduce the difficulties a tramp faces for being poor and living on skid row. Like the counselors from the alcoholism treatment center, I interpreted the request for treatment as a cry for help on the part of a down and out alcoholic. Once I began to see things the way tramps saw them, once I treated tramps as informants, I learned it was a way to escape jail—to beat a drunk charge. Not only did I begin to see the events in court through different eyes, but I also began asking questions to discover the rules for selecting a particular strategy for beating a drunk charge.

Making detached observations of social behavior as an outsider has many values. But because the two perspectives appear so similar and yet lead in such different directions, one must distinguish between treating people as actors and as informants.

Ethnographers adopt a particular stance toward people with whom they work. By word and by action, in subtle ways and direct statements, they say, "I want to understand the world from your point of view. I want to know what you know in the way you know it. I want to understand the meaning of your experience, to walk in your shoes, to feel things as you feel them, to explain things as you explain them. Will you become my teacher and help me understand?" This frame of reference is a radical departure from treating people as either subjects, respondents, or actors.

ETHICAL PRINCIPLES

Informants are human beings with problems, concerns, and interests. The values held by any particular ethnographer do not always coincide with the ones held by informants. In doing field work one is always faced with conflicting values and a wide range of possible choices.[1] Should I tape record what an informant says or merely make a written record? How will I use the data collected and will I tell informants how it will be used? Should I study the kinship terms used by informants or the tactics used by the colonial government to keep them oppressed? If an informant engages in illegal behavior should I make my field notes inaccessible to the police? If informants are children, should teachers or parents have access to my field notes? Should I pay informants for participating in ethnographic interviews? Whenever faced by choices such as these, the decision will necessarily involve an appeal to some set of ethical principles based on underlying values.

In 1971, the Council of the American Anthropological Association adopted a set of principles to guide ethnographers when faced with conflicting choices. These *Principles of Professional Responsibility* begin with the following preamble:

Anthropologists work in many parts of the world in close personal association with the peoples and situations they study. Their professional situation is, therefore, uniquely varied and complex. They are involved with their discipline, their colleagues, their students, their sponsors, their subjects, their own and host governments, the particular individuals and groups with whom they do their field work, other populations and interest groups in the nations within which they work, and the study of processes and issues affecting general human welfare. In a field of such complex involvements, misunderstandings, conflicts and the necessity to make choices among conflicting values are bound to arise and to generate ethical dilemmas. It is a prime responsibility of anthropologists to anticipate these and to plan to resolve them in such a way as to do damage neither to those whom they study nor, in so far as possible, to their scholarly community. Where these conditions cannot be met, the anthropologist would be well advised not to pursue the particular piece of research.

The great variation and complexity of field work situations make it difficult, if not impossible, to adopt a single set of standards for all ethnographers. However, the following ethical principles, based on those adopted by the American Anthropological Association, can serve as a useful guide.

Consider Informants First

In research, an anthropologist's paramount responsibility is to those he studies. When there is a conflict of interest, these individuals must come first. The anthropologist must do everything within his power to protect their physical, social and psychological welfare and to honor their dignity and privacy.
(*Principles of Professional Responsibility,* 1971, para. 1.)

Ethnographic research often involves more than ethnographers and informants. Sponsors may provide funds for the support of research. Gate keepers may have the power to give or withhold permission to conduct interviews. In complex societies, informants' lives are frequently intertwined with other people. For example, in studying cocktail waitresses, the bartenders, customers, and owners of the bar all had certain interests, often in conflict with the waitresses. Tramps were constantly involved with treatment center staff, policemen, and county health officials. The ethnographer cannot assume that informants' interests are the same as those of other people. All ethnography must include inquiries to discover the interests and concerns of informants. And when choices are made, these interests must be considered first.

Safeguard Informants' Rights, Interests, and Sensitivities

Where research involves the acquisition of material and information transferred on the assumption of trust between persons, it is axiomatic that the rights, interests, and sensitivities of those studied must be safeguarded.
(*Principles of Professional Responsibility,* para. 1,a.)

This principle suggests that ethnographers go beyond merely *considering* the interests of informants. We have a positive responsibility to *safeguard* their rights, their interests, and even their sensitivities. We must examine the implications of our research from this vantage point, for it may have consequences unseen by informants.

James Sewid, a Kwakiutl Indian in British Columbia, was an excellent informant, and together we recorded his life history about growing up during the early part of this century (Spradley 1969). When it became apparent that the edited transcripts might become a published book, I decided to safeguard Mr. Sewid's rights by making him a full partner who signed the contract with Yale University Press. He shared equally in all royalties and, with me, had the right to decide on crucial matters of content. I also wanted to safeguard his sensitivities, so before we submitted the final manuscript I read the complete version to both him and his wife. They made deletions and changes that were in their best interests, changes which reflected their sensitivities, not mine.

No matter how unobtrusive, ethnographic research always pries into the lives of informants. Ethnographic interviewing represents a powerful tool for invading other people's way of life. It reveals information that can be used to *affirm* their rights, interests, and sensitivities or to *violate* them. All informants must have the protection of saying things "off the record" which never find their way into the ethnographer's field notes.

Communicate Research Objectives

The aims of the investigation should be communicated as well as possible to the informant.

(Principles of Professional Responsibility, 1971, para. 1,b.)

Informants have a right to know the ethnographer's aims. This does not require a full course on the nature of ethnography. The scholar's aims can often be explained simply: "I want to understand what life at Brady's Bar is like from your perspective as a cocktail waitress. I think this will help us to understand the role of women who work in this kind of job. I'll be writing up my study as a description of the role of cocktail waitresses."

Communicating the aims of research must often become a process of unfolding rather than a once-and-for-all declaration. The ethnographer must decide to whom the aims will be explained. Certainly anyone who participates in ethnographic interviews deserves an explanation. In our study of Brady's Bar we explained our goals to the cocktail waitresses; our study focused on their role. We did not talk with all the customers and all the bartenders, although their behavior certainly entered into our study. In this particular study, communicating the aims was made more difficult because one of the researchers assumed the role of a cocktail waitress and had difficulty convincing others to take her role as a researcher seriously. In a detailed analysis of that role, Brenda Mann has discussed the ethical problems connected with communicating the aims of research.[2]

For the beginning ethnographer, especially those who are students, the primary aim may be to learn how to study another culture. One might communicate this goal quite simply: "I want to find out what it's like to be a student in the fourth grade. As a university student myself, I'm learning how to interview and discover things from your point of view. I'll be writing a paper on what you and other children in this fourth-grade classroom do each day, the things you like best, and just what it's like to be in the fourth grade."

However, as discussed in the first chaper, the aims of research often need to go beyond the mere accumulation of knowledge. Every ethnographic research project should, to some extent, include a dialogue with informants to explore ways in which the study can be useful to informants. The *Principles of Professional Responsibility* include a specific statement in this regard (para. 1,h): "Every effort should be exerted to cooperate with members of the host society in the planning and execution of research projects." This not only means planning with teachers and administrators, if one is studying a fourth-grade classroom for instance, but also with students. In many cases, since informants do not yet understand the nature of ethnography, the aims of research will have to develop during the study. This means the ethnographer, in consultation with informants, must be willing to direct the investigation into paths suggested by informants. I began my research with skid row tramps by explaining, "I want to understand alcoholism from the perspective of men like yourself who are repeatedly arrested for being drunk." But as I progressed, informants' interests led to a change in goals. I communicated my new aims to each informant I interviewed, explaining that my investigation of life in jail could perhaps improve conditions there for incarcerated alcoholics.

Protect the Privacy of Informants

Informants have a right to remain anonymous. This right should be respected both where it has been promised explicitly and where no clear understanding to the contrary has been reached. These strictures apply to the collection of data by means of cameras, tape recorders, and other data-gathering devices, as well as to data collected in face-to-face interviews or in participant observation. Those being studied should understand the capacities of such devices; they should be free to reject them if they wish; and, if they accept them, the results obtained should be consonant with the informant's right to welfare, dignity and privacy. Despite every effort being made to preserve anonymity it should be made clear to informants that such anonymity may be compromised unintentionally.

(*Principles of Professional Responsibility*, 1971, para. 1,c.)

Protecting privacy extends far beyond changing names, places, and other identifying features in a final report. These are minimal requirements of anonymity. However, every ethnographer must realize that field notes can become public knowledge if subpoenaed by a court. In doing research on illicit drug use, one student made lengthy interviews with local drug dealers.[3] One day she discovered that her primary informant's "contact" in the illicit marketing system had been arrested, placing her informant in immediate jeopardy. It became apparent that her field notes and transcribed interviews might become of interest to law enforcement officials. She immediately eliminated all names and initials from her field notes. Even so, it probably would have been impossible to protect the identity of her informant unless she had taken the further step of destroying the field notes, an act that may well have been an illegal destruction of evidence. In another case, an ethnographer studying a local school system collected data about a teacher's strike. A suit between the union and the school board developed and the possibility arose that his field notes would be subpoenaed by the court. Although neither of these cases materialized, each threat placed the ethnographers in an ethical dilemma. One must continually ask"How can I maintain the anonymity of my informants?" A serious consideration of this ethical principle might, in some cases, lead to the selection of an alternate research project. At a minimum, it should mean use of pseudonyms in both field notes and final reports.

Don't Exploit Informants

There should be no exploitation of individual informants for personal gain. Fair return should be given them for all services.
(Principles of Professional Responsibility, 1971, para. 1,d.)

Personal gain becomes exploitative when the informant gains nothing or actually suffers harm from the research. Every ethnographer bears a responsibility to weigh carefully what might constitute a "fair return" to informants. In some cases they can be paid an hourly wage; in others this would insult an informant. Sometimes an informant will gain directly from the results of the investigation; this possibility increases to the extent that informants have some say in the aims of the research. An ethnography often describes some part of an informant's culture in a way that gives the informant new insight and understanding. A copy of the ethnographic description might be fair return to many informants. But there are also less direct ways in which a project can have value to an informant. Students who study the culture of the elderly inevitably find that their informants relish the opportunity to reminisce about the past and talk to a younger, interested listener. An obvious value to many informants is the opportunity to assist a student in learning about another way of life. Even the simple gain of participating in a research project can be sufficient reason for many informants to talk to an ethnographer. Although "fair return" will vary from one informant to the next, the needs of informants for some gain from the project must not be ignored.

Make Reports Available to Informants

In accordance with the Association's general position on clandestine and secret research, no reports should be provided to sponsors that are not also available to the general public and, where practicable, to the population studied.

(*Principles of Professional Responsibility*, 1971, para. 1,g.)

When students in my classes follow the steps in this book to interview an informant, I encourage them to make their papers available to their informants. This undoubtedly influences the way in which a report is written. For informants who would not understand the report, as in the case of a first-grade class, an oral presentation may be in order. This principle does not mean we should insist informants read our reports; it does mean that what is written for teachers, colleagues, or the general public, should also be available to informants.

This brief list of ethical principles does not exhaust the issues that will arise when doing research. The ethnographer has important responsibilities to the public, and to the scholarly community. The full statement of *Principles of Professional Responsibility* adopted by the Council of the American Anthropological Association offers a rich source of additional principles for guiding our decision making. Every ethnographer should study this document as well as those developed by other associations involved in social science research.

Part Two
THE DEVELOPMENTAL RESEARCH SEQUENCE

This part of the book is based on an important assumption: *the best way to learn to do ethnography is by doing it*. This assumption has influenced the design of the remainder of this book. Each chapter contains the following elements:

Objectives: A brief statement of the learning goals at each particular stage in the ethnographic process.

Concepts: A discussion of the basic concepts necessary to achieving the learning goals at each particular stage.

Tasks: A specific set of tasks, which when completed enable one to achieve the objectives.

It is no accident that each chapter title is an activity—"Locating an Informant," "Interviewing an Informant," "Making an Ethnographic Record," etc. These activities are steps in the larger Developmental Research Process. They lead to an original ethnographic description.

I cannot emphasize too strongly that each successive chapter depends on having read the preceding chapter and *having done the tasks* identified in that chapter. If you read the remainder of this book in the same way as the first part, it will tend to result in a distorted understanding of ethnographic interviewing. In short, each step in Part II is designed to be *done* as well as *read*.

Finally, I want to remind the reader that Part II focuses exclusively on conducting ethnographic interviews. This focus will enable the reader to acquire a higher degree of mastery than is possible when using multiple research techniques. I also limit the discussion to interviewing a single informant for the same reason. Depending on available time and the reader's background, one can easily combine the tasks that follow with participant observation and interviewing more than one informant.

It is well to keep in mind from the beginning of a research project that the end result will be a written cultural description, *an ethography*. An ethnographer may only describe a small segment of the culture in a brief article or paper for a course in ethnographic research. On the other hand, the ethnographer may end up writing a book or several books to describe the culture. In Step Twelve I will discuss some strategies for writing an ethnography. One of the most important ones is to *begin writing early*. The major reason for beginning early is that writing, in addition to being an act of communication, involves a process of thinking and analyzing. As you write, you will gain insights, see relationships, and generate questions for research. If the ethnographer waits until after all the data are collected to begin writing, it will be too late to follow the leads that writing creates. Another reason to begin writing early is to simplify the task. Most people contemplate the task of writing a thirty-page report as formidable; writing ten three-page reports seems much less difficult.

In order to facilitate the writing task and make it a part of the research process, I have made a list of brief topics that an ethnographer can write about while conducting research. These are listed separately in Appendix B at the end of the book. Each writing task is designed to fit in with a particular stage of research. I envision a few pages written in a rough draft. Then, when you sit down to write the final ethnography, the task will be simplified as you revise these brief papers. It may be useful to read Step Twelve and review the writing tasks in Appendix B before starting the D.R.S. steps.

OBJECTIVES
1. To identify the characteristics of a good informant.
2. To locate the best possible informant for learning ethnographic interviewing skills and doing ethnographic research.

Although almost anyone can become an informant, not everyone makes a good informant. The ethnographer-informant relationship is fraught with difficulties. One of the great challenges in doing ethnography is to initiate, develop, and maintain a productive informant relationship. Careful planning and sensitivity to your informant will take you through most of the rough seas of interviewing. However, successful interviews depend on so many things it is impossible to plan for, or control, them all. For one thing, interviews are influenced by the identity of both parties. One young female ethnographer set out to interview an elderly man who seemed willing to talk; he proved to be a poor informant because he made sexual advances during most interviews. If a male student had been the ethnographer, the relationship might have easily developed into a productive one.

Sometimes unknown aspects of the informant's culture influence the relationship. One beginning ethnographer set out to investigate the culture of antique dealers. She made an initial contact with an eighty-year old woman who ran her own antique shop. After the first interview, their relationship began to deteriorate until finally, in desperation, she asked the woman why she didn't want to answer any more questions. "You should be paying me fifteen dollars an hour for all this," the woman said, clearly irritated. "I've taught others before and that's what they paid me for what I told them." This ethnographer, without knowing it, had encountered a cultural practice among antique dealers that became an unseen barrier to successful interviews. In some cultures, tacit rules act as a kind of taboo on asking questions. One student found his locksmith informant reluctant to talk for fear of revealing trade secrets.

The interaction of the personalities of informant and ethnographer also has a profound influence on the interviews. One assertive, talkative student found it difficult to listen to others talk. He located an informant who worked as a tugboat captain on the Mississippi River. This quiet, unassuming man willingly agreed to serve as an informant about his life on the river. During the first interview, the student felt bothered by the long lulls in the conversation and unwittingly began to fill these gaps by talking too much. He asked more pointed questions and said things his informant interpreted as being pushy. The interviews went from bad to worse; the tugboat captain became noticeably uncooperative. Without realizing it, the student became a threat to his informant who began to feel, "If you know so much, why are you asking me?" Personality differences cannot always be anticipated. I have contacted tramps for ethnographic interviews and then, after one or two sessions, found it difficult to maintain a productive relationship with them. These same men would have made excellent informants for someone else.

Interviewing informants depends on a cluster of interpersonal skills. These include: asking questions, listening instead of talking, taking a passive rather than an assertive role, expressing verbal interest in the other person, and showing interest by eye contact and other nonverbal means. Some people have acquired these skills to a greater degree than others; some learn them more quickly than others. I recall one novice ethnographer who felt insecure about interviewing an urban planner. During the interviews she kept thinking about the next question she should ask and often looked down at a list she had prepared. Each time she lost eye contact with her informant, he interpreted it as lack of interest. She seldom nodded her head or encouraged her informant with such statements as, "That's really interesting," or "I never realized urban planners did so much!" Although she continued the interviews, rapport developed slowly because she lacked this specific skill of showing interest.

During the past ten years I have listened to hundreds of students discuss their relationships with informants. Many of their difficulties resulted from identity differences, cultural barriers, incompatible personalities, and lack of interpersonal skill. But the most persistent problems came from their *failure to locate a good informant*. By "good" informant, I mean someone who can assist the novice ethnographer in learning about that informant's culture while at the same time learning the interviewing skills. Based on the experience of undergraduate and graduate students, long discussions with professional ethnographers, and my own ethnographic interviewing, I have identified five minimal requirements for selecting a good informant: (1) thorough enculturation, (2) current involvement, (3) an unfamiliar cultural scene, (4) adequate time, and (5) nonanalytic. In the field, a skilled ethnographer uses many different informants and some will not meet these five requirements. But, in order to learn to conduct informant interviews, it is essential that the first informants selected meet all of these five requirements.

THOROUGH ENCULTURATION

Enculturation is the natural process of learning a particular culture. Potential informants vary in the extent of their enculturation: good ones know their culture well. Sandy took a job as a cocktail waitress at Brady's Bar. On the first night everything seemed strange and she had to depend on others to guide her. "You'll work the lower section and give orders at this station," the bartender told her. "Here's the best way to arrange your tray," a waitress explained. "Change goes here, keep your bills under the ash tray." Late in the evening, the bartender told her, "It's time to make last call. Check your tables and see if anyone wants another drink." As Sandy encountered new situations and problem customers, the others continued to help enculturate her. "I had a table of guys like that once; I just ignored them." "If those jocks give you any trouble, just let me know." As the months passed, the number of unfamiliar situations decreased. Sandy no longer had to think when she took orders, repeated them to the bartender, or made change for customers. Even on the busiest nights her work became routine. She knew what to anticipate; she understood the language of this cultural scene; she could even instruct new girls who became waitresses. She had become thoroughly enculturated.

As a novice learning the role of waitress, Sandy did not know as much about this cultural scene. She was not able to identify all the range of customers, the kinds of hassles waitresses encountered, or the pecking order among bartenders. She was a good informant about only one thing: *the experience of learning to be a cocktail waitress*. But this information only made sense against the larger pattern of waitress culture. When Sandy became thoroughly enculturated she could talk about this culture in detail.

One of the great advantages (often unrecognized) in doing ethnography in small, traditional societies has been that informants were almost always thoroughly enculturated. Sometimes a marginal person would volunteer as an informant and his or her view of life might contrast with others in a village. But most of the time adults who spoke the native language could be counted on to know the culture well. In complex societies, with greatly increased communication and mobility, that changes. When ethnographers set out to study a cultural scene, they cannot assume that those they talk with actually know the culture well enough to act as informants.

Good informants know their culture so well they no longer think about it. They do things automatically from years and years of practice. The mail carrier who has delivered his route for sixteen years knows every name, street, and address so well he can carry on a conversation while sorting the mail. He is thoroughly enculturated. The substitute carrier who is learning a new route is not a good informant.

Some cultural scenes are learned through formal instruction as well as informal, on-the-job experience. The new policeman goes through an intensive training program; the pilot attends flight school. But formal instructions alone do not constitute a high level of enculturation. A good informant is one who has had years of informal experience as well.

One way to estimate how thoroughly someone has learned a cultural scene is to determine the length of time they have been in that scene. I discovered tramps who were novices as well as those who had become veterans. George seemed like an experienced tramp; he was in his late sixties. I interviewed him several times about making a flop. He answered many of my questions but sometimes seemed confused and frequently admitted his ignorance. Finally, after several questions that he could only partially answer, he said, "Would you like to talk to my friend Bob? I've only been learning to be a tramp for four years—since I retired from the railroad. Bob, he's been teaching me to be a tramp." George introduced me to Bob, a thoroughly enculturated tramp, who became an excellent informant. After that, one of my first questions to a potential informant was "How long have you been a tramp?" or "How long have you been on the road?" or "How long have you been making the bucket in Seattle?"

In general, an informant should have at least a year of full-time involvement in a cultural scene. If it is a part-time interest, such as membership in the League of Women Voters or a hobby of collecting beer steins, at least three or four years of involvement is needed. But, these are only minimum time periods. The more thoroughly enculturated an informant, the better. A man who has worked for twenty-five years as a railroad engineer is a better choice than one who has been on the job for only two years. A fifth grader who has gone through each grade at her school is a better choice than one who transferred in during the fifth grade.

CURRENT INVOLVEMENT

"I've found a great informant," a student ethnographer told me one afternoon, pleased to have located someone so easily. "He lives across the street and has worked as a milkman for seventeen years." The first few interviews progressed smoothly, but then she came to me with problems. "I asked him questions but he makes excuses and says he can't remember. When I ask for stories or examples, he can't think of any." After several minutes of discussion, I asked, "Can you visit his place of work or ride with him while he delivers milk?" Oh, he doesn't work as a milkman now," she said. "He changed jobs three years ago." This student had assumed that because her informant had been thoroughly enculturated at one time, it didn't matter that he didn't currently deliver milk. Her final description of this cultural scene reflected her informant's lack of involvement.

When people are currently involved in a cultural scene, they use their knowledge to guide their actions. They review what they know; they make interpretations of new events; they apply their knowledge to solving everyday problems. When people stop using some part of their cultural knowledge, it becomes less accessible, more difficult to recall. Informants who leave a cultural scene forget the details and can only remember general outlines of the activities that went on. Most important, they stop speaking the language they once used. When asked about a former cultural scene, they may talk about it but do so using terms and phrases from a different scene.

Sometimes leaving a cultural scene involves a major change in perspective. An informant not currently involved may greatly distort that former culture. I encountered a dramatic example of this possibility not long after *You Owe Yourself a Drunk* was published. A sociologist sent me an unpublished review of my book he had written. He was sharply critical of the conclusions I had drawn from my study of tramp culture. Whereas my description rested heavily on the language of tramps, he believed it was inappropriate to accept their terms, phrases, insights, and definitions. "Drunks are notorious liars and manipulators," he wrote. "Spradley unfortunately takes the lies as facts and bases his conclusions on them." Near the end of the review, after disagreeing with my report that tramps did not like the coercive aspects of the jail, his perspective became clear. "Looking back," he wrote, "across my long career as a drunk, I believe I would have changed my irresponsible way of life much earlier had I been forced to." Even though this person once lived and traveled like many tramps do, he had left that way of life and now saw it in a very different light.

The ethnographer must look closely at the *kind* of current involvement a potential informant has. I met several men who had been tramps and were presently involved in trying to help tramps. But these potential informants now considered themselves to be "recovered alcoholics;" they had taken jobs as counselors in alcoholic treatment centers. Although they spent a great deal of time with tramps, the tramp way of life was *not* part of their present selves; it was a cultural scene they rejected.

In a similar sense, a young teacher a few years out of high school is not a good informant for the student culture. And a college student who lives in a dormitory cannot act as a good informant on the culture of women who work as maids cleaning the same dormitory. Individuals who live and work in close proximity often believe they share the same way of looking at the world. The ethnographer wants to interview people who have expert knowledge, informants who have a first-hand, current involvement in the cultural scene.

AN UNFAMILIAR CULTURAL SCENE

As I said earlier, much of our cultural knowledge is tacit, taken for granted, and outside our awareness. When ethnographers study unfamiliar cultures, this unfamiliarity keeps them from taking things for granted. It makes them sensitive to things that have become so commonplace to informants that they ignore them. For this reason, many ethnographers begin their ethnographic studies on cultures very different from their own. The most productive relationship occurs between a thoroughly enculturated informant and a thoroughly *un*enculturated ethnographer.

In urban society, some cultural scenes are completely known to the ethnographer; others appear strange and exotic. Scenes range from those shared with family members or close friends all the way to immigrants who continue traditional customs and speak a foreign language. An experienced ethnographer with adequate time for research can select informants anywhere along this continuum. However, if you set out to learn to do ethnography following the steps in this book, it is another matter. When differences become too great, the field work problems can become overwhelming. Such is the case if you select someone who only speaks a foreign language you don't understand. When differences are not great enough, other problems emerge.

In the first place, when researching a familiar cultural scene, the language differences seem to be slight and are easily overlooked. I knew less about tramp culture than Brady's Bar which attracted mostly college students. When my tramp informants started using strange terms like *mission stiffs, airedales, dings, nose divers* and *making a frisco circle,* they immediately caught my attention. When waitresses, on the other hand, talked of *employers, customers, jocks, businessmen,* and *bouncers,* the terms did not catch my attention. Research at Brady's Bar took a great deal more careful analysis to discover its social organization.

The second problem that comes from studying a familiar cultural scene is that the analysis of field data becomes more difficult. I recall one beginning ethnographer, a physical education major, who against my advice chose a member of the swim team as an informant. "I'm not a swimmer," he said. "I know hardly anything about the swim team." But soon he brought in his field notes with the common complaint: "I can't find anything in what my informant says. There are different kinds of strokes and things they do at swim meets, but not much else." Looking at his field notes I quickly saw things he had missed because they were so familiar to him. Later, when he had completed his study, the cultural description was superficial and offered few insights. This student lived too close to the culture he had studied to really understand it. He took too much for granted because it was part of his own cultural knowledge.

Finally, an informant from a familiar cultural scene creates problems for interviewing. At the same time you study an informant's culture, your informant is gathering information about what you know. If informants believe your background has already taught you the answer to your own questions, they will feel you are asking dumb questions and that you may be trying to test them in some way. When informants believe you are really ignorant, that you don't know anything about their way of life, these problems do not arise.

Many ethnographers do study familiar cultures. Anthony Wallace, an anthropologist, even used himself as an informant and produced an outstanding cultural description of driving an automobile.[1] Jeff Nash, a long-distance runner, has written about the culture of distance runners with great insight.[2] But, if you are starting out to learn informant interviewing, you can eliminate many difficulties by finding someone who knows about a cultural scene that is unfamiliar to you.

ADEQUATE TIME

The approach presented in this book requires a series of ethnographic interviews interspersed with careful analysis. At a minimum, it will take six to seven one-hour interviews, so it is important to estimate whether a potential informant has adequate time to participate. The willingness or lack of it exhibited by a potential informant does not always give a good clue to whether that person has adequate time.

One student, a junior anthropology major, wanted to study the cultural scene of executives, so she approached a director for the Northern States Power Company. He seemed willing and interested but from the start she found it difficult to schedule appointments. When she phoned, she couldn't reach him; when she did, she had to schedule appointments far in advance and even then, he occasionally cancelled. Inadequate time for interviews continued to create problems throughout the project. Another student selected an informant who lived in a high-rise apartment for the elderly. She was seventy-five years old and spent her time visiting with friends, reading, and painting. She was available whenever this student wanted to schedule an interview and often invited him for tea and a visit.

Children usually make good informants and they have adequate free time. One ethnographer contacted a first-grade boy and interviewed him about his matchbox car collection. Her informant was eager to talk whenever she came and even brought his friends along who contributed important information. She not only carried out a sufficient number of interviews, but often observed her informants playing matchbox cars.[3]

Most of my informants among skid row men were confined to an alcoholism treatment center and had a great deal of free time. Interviews helped to break the monotony of incarceration. But when these informants went back to skid row they were busy trying "to make it"; they had much less time for interviews. Furthermore, their mobile style of life meant I never knew if I would see the same informant again.

In estimating the amount of time someone might give to interviews, it is well to keep in mind that a busy informant keenly interested in the project will often *make* time. Because interviews involve the informant as an expert witness, they generate considerable enthusiasm. When one student decided to interview a college maid who had worked cleaning dormitories and campus houses for many years, this woman didn't know if she would have enough information to help him. But once in the role of informant, she realized that this student actually wanted her to teach him about her work. She grew excited about the interviews and gave freely of her time.[4] Sometimes a busy informant can be interviewed on the job, thus reducing the amount of extra time required. When the student interviewed the executive from the power company, she partially resolved the difficulties by traveling with him as he visited plants under his supervision.

One solution to the problem of inadequate time is to use *tandem informants*. A beginning ethnographer approached a young salesman in Len's Camera Store and he agreed to become an informant. But soon it became difficult to schedule interviews, so this ethnographer asked, "Could you suggest someone else I could talk to?" His informant introduced him to another salesman who had more time and also more experience. Without repeating the first steps in the interview series, he began where he had left off with the first informant. I have known others who completed a series of ethnographic interviews by using several informants in tandem. This required careful selection to insure that each informant shared the same cultural scene. If you select the president of a local company for interviews, it will be impossible to utilize additional informants since only one person fills that role. A member of a hot air balloon club, on the other hand, does not present such limitations; other members could also serve as informants.

In considering potential informants, then, high priority should be given to someone who has adequate time for the research. This criteria can be ignored if you select someone who will make time because of their interest in the project. If neither of these criteria can be met, select the kind of cultural scene in which you can easily contact and interview a series of different persons who share the same knowledge.

NONANALYTIC

Some informants use their language to describe events and actions with almost no analysis of their meaning or significance. Other informants offer insightful analyses and interpretations of events from the perspective of the native "folk theory." Both can make excellent informants.

However, there is one type of analytic informant that is best avoided. An example will make clear the kind of analysis which can make interviewing difficult. My first encounter with this type of informant came unexpectedly. I had interviewed numerous tramps and was constantly on the lookout for new informants who could talk about "making the bucket" in Seattle. Each week new patients from the city jail arrived at the treatment center and I reviewed their arrest records. Anyone arrested fifty to one hundred times suggested a man who could talk with authority about the jail. "You can't be a tramp if you don't make the bucket," I had learned from more than one informant.

Bob Johnson had a long arrest record. He had spent the last four years on skid row in Seattle, a good part of that time going through the revolving door of the jail. But something else struck me about Bob: he was a graduate of Harvard University and had gone on to do some graduate work in anthropology. I immediately contacted him and he agreed to an interview. His knowledge of life in the Seattle City Jail was detailed and current. I became excited about the possibilities of working with Bob as a key informant and at the end of our first interview I asked for his assistance.

"Could you think about the men who are at this center," I said, "and next week we can talk about the different *kinds* of men who are arrested and sent to the center."

On my next visit to the treatment center I invited Bob into my office. We chatted casually for a few minutes, then I started asking him some ethnographic questions. "What kind of men go through the Seattle City Jail and end up at this alcoholism treatment center?" I asked. "I've been thinking about the men who are here," Bob said thoughtfully. "I would divide them up first in terms of race. There are Negroes, Indians, Caucasians, and a few Eskimo. Next I think I would divide them on the basis of their education. Some have almost none, a few have some college. Then some of the men are married and some are single." For the next fifteen minutes he proceeded to give me the standard analytic categories that many social scientists use.

"Have you ever heard men referred to as tramps?" I asked. From numerous informants I knew this identity was the most important. "Oh, yes," Bob said, "some guys use that term."

"Are there different kinds of tramps?" I asked.

"I suppose so, but I'm not up on what they would be." Bob then proceeded to talk about intelligence, education, race, and other categories that usually interested social scientists. In later interviews Bob tended to analyze the motives men had for drinking and other behavior, but his analysis always reflected his background in college. He had great difficulty recalling how most other tramps would refer to things.

The ethnographer wants to discover patterns of meaning in what an informant says. This requires constant *analysis* of utterances, taking them apart to find the tacit relationships and patterns. Some informants can assist in analyzing their own culture—provided it is always from the perspective of the insider. In our society, many persons draw from psychology and the social sciences to analyze their own behavior. They mistakenly believe they can assist the ethnographer by offering these analytic insights. Such individuals make poor informants for the novice ethnographer. Even the experienced interviewer must take special precautions such as using frequent "native language questions."

One student, a junior majoring in psychology, decided to study the culture of clinical psychologists. He approached someone who agreed to serve as an informant. But soon he discovered it was almost impossible for his informant to talk in his native language, the way he would talk to *other psychologists*. Instead, he constantly interpreted, analyzed, and explained to the student what psychologists are supposed to do.

Informants who are sophisticated in the social sciences can learn to respond to questions in a nonanalytic fashion. In studying cocktail waitresses, I collaborated with Brenda Mann who worked as a waitress during the study and served as a primary informant. She managed to set aside her social science background and respond from the perspective of Brady's Bar. In general, the beginning ethnographer will do well to locate informants who do not analyze their own culture from an outsider's perspective.

These criteria do not exhaust the ones that will make a good informant. However, if these criteria are met, the beginning ethnographer will eliminate some of the most vexing problems of learning to conduct ethnographic interviews. Having identified these general characteristics, we are now ready to undertake those tasks that will result in locating a good informant.

Tasks

1.1. Make a list of potential informants (or cultural scenes). (A beginning ethnographer seeking a scene to study should list 40–50 possibilities.)
1.2. Identify five or six of the most likely informants (or cultural scenes).
1.3. Compare this list of potential informants on the five minimal requirements for a good informant. Place the selections in rank order.

OBJECTIVES
1. To identify the basic elements in the ethnographic interview.
2. To formulate and use several kinds of ethnographic explanations.
3. To conduct a practice interview.

An ethnographic interview is a particular kind of *speech event*.[1] Every culture has many social occasions identified primarily by the kind of talking that takes place; I refer to these as speech events. In our society most of us quickly recognize when someone gives us a *sales pitch* for a used car or a set of encyclopedias. We recognize Johnny Carson's *monologue* on the Tonight Show. We can easily tell the difference between a *lecture,* a *job interview,* or a *friendly conversation*. Many of the cues to distinguish among these speech events remain outside our awareness, but we use them nonetheless. All speech events have cultural rules for beginning, ending, taking turns, asking questions, pausing, and even how close to stand to other people. In order to clarify the ethnographic interview, I want to compare it with a more familiar speech event, the friendly conversation.

THE FRIENDLY CONVERSATION

Let's consider a brief example of a friendly conversation between two businessmen. Then we can identify some of the features of this speech event. Fred and Bob have known each other since college days; they live in the same city and see each other occasionally at the Rotary Club. It has been several months since they have talked. This conversation takes place in a large department store where they have by chance encountered one another.

BOB: "Hi Fred! How are you?" (Bob extends his hand while Fred hurriedly shifts a package to his left hand so he can respond.)
FRED: "Fine. It's good to see you." (A firm handshake is now underway, one that goes on for several seconds as they continue to talk.)
BOB: "How's the family? I haven't seen you since March. Did you have a good summer?"
FRED: "They're all doing fine. Jean just left for college a few weeks ago."

BOB: "That's right! How does it feel to have your oldest gone? Hardly seems possible. Billy's talking about the University of North Carolina for next year."

FRED: "Did you have a good summer?"

BOB: "Well things were pretty hectic at the office. We did get away for a couple weeks to the Smokies. Then Barbara and I had a long weekend up in D.C."

FRED: "The Smokies? That sounds great. We've never been to that part of the country."

BOB: "It was beautiful. But hot in August. We camped out for part of the time. If we go again I think we'd try to make it in September, maybe even after the leaves have started to turn. How about you? Did you get away?"

FRED: "Yes, we spent three weeks in July up in Wisconsin."

BOB: "Really! Where did you stay?"

FRED: "Rented a cabin up in the northwest corner of the state. Did a lot of fishing. Best time was canoeing on the Brule River—nice rapids, but not too much for the kids. Had to rent two canoes, but we spent several days doing that river."

BOB: "What kind of fish did you get?"

FRED: "Bass, mostly, and panfish. John caught a musky and I think I had a northern pike on my line but he got away."

BOB: "Say, how are things at the company?"

FRED: "In May Al was transferred to Fort Lauderdale and that took a lot of pressure off. And since then sales have been up, too. Had a really productive week in early June—all the field men came in and I think that helped. How about you, still thinking of a transfer?"

BOB: "Well, they keep talking about it. I've told them I'd rather wait till Danny finishes high school, but I don't think I could turn down a regional if it came along."

FRED: "Look, I've got to meet Joan up the street in a few minutes; I'd better be off. It was really good to see you."

BOB: "Yeah, let's get together sometime. I know Barbara would love to see Joan."

FRED: "O.K. Sounds good. Take it easy now."

BOB: "You too. Have a good day."

It is not difficult to recognize this exchange between Fred and Bob as a friendly conversation rather than a lecture, a sales presentation, or an interview for employment. The greeting, the casual nature of the encounter, the speech acts they used, and certain cultural rules they followed, all clearly define this speech event as a friendly conversation. In this example we can see at least the following elements:

1. *Greetings*. "Hi" and "It's good to see you," as well as the questions, serve as verbal markers to start the conversation. Physical contact expresses their friendship. When such people meet, they almost never begin talking without some form of greeting, usually both verbal and nonverbal. Some physical contact frequently emphasizes the closeness of their relationship.

2. *Lack of explicit purpose*. People engaging in friendly conversations don't have an agenda to cover, at least not an explicit one. They almost never say, "Let's talk about the vacations we each took this summer," or "I

want to ask you some questions about your work." They don't care where they are going in the talk as long as they *get somewhere*. Either person can bring up a wide range of topics; either person can signal they want to change the subject; either person can end the conversation. Both parties know the rules that make for this kind of purposelessness and flexibility.

3. *Avoiding repetition*. One of the clearest rules in friendly conversations is to avoid repetition. Friends will often say things like " Did I tell you about Al Sanders?" or "Have I told you about our summer?" This allows the other person to save us from the embarrassment of repeating ourselves without knowing it. Both friends assume that once something has been asked or stated, repetition becomes unnecessary. Repetition in the same conversation is especially avoided. We don't say, "Could you clarify what you said by going over it again?" This assumption, that it is good to avoid repetition, is not part of the informant interview.

4. *Asking questions*. Both Bob and Fred made inquiries about the other person. "How's the family?" "Did you have a good summer?" These questions allow them each to talk about personal matters; they also make it appropriate for the other person to ask similar kinds of questions in return. None of the questions required a lengthy answer, though some did elicit descriptions of their experiences.

5. *Expressing interest*. The questions themselves indicated interest in the other person. But both went beyond this to make statements like "That sounds great" and "Really!" Undoubtedly, friendly conversations are almost always filled with expressions of nonverbal interest. Frequent smiles, listening with eye contact, and various body postures all say, "I find what you're talking about very interesting, keep talking."

6. *Expressing ignorance*. People who repeat things we already know are considered bores. One way to protect friends from boring us or repeating themselves is to give messages that say, "Go on, I'm not bored, you're not telling me something I already know." These messages function in the same way as asking questions and expressing interest. "We've never been to that part of the country" is an expression of ignorance and an important means to encourage the other person to go on talking.

7. *Taking turns*. An implicit cultural rule for friendly conversations, turn taking helps keep the encounter balanced. We all have experienced violations of this rule and know how it leads to a sense of uneasiness or even anger. In other speech events, such as a sales presentation or interview, people do not take turns in the same way. Turn taking in friendly conversations allows people to ask each other the same kind of questions, such as "What did you do this summer?"

8. *Abbreviating*. Friendly conversations are filled with references that hint at things or only give partial information. It is as if both parties are seeking an economy of words; they avoid filling in all the details on the assumption that the other person will fill them in. This assumption leads to

abbreviated talk that is extremely difficult for outsiders to understand. Long-time friends have come to share a vast number of experiences and can fill in much of what is left unstated. They find it unnecessary to make explicit many of their meanings; the other person understands. Al Sanders refers to the name of Fred's boss. The "trouble" occurred when Al threatened to fire Fred from his job as sales manager if he didn't increase each salesman's quota, something an outsider would not know. Bob does not need to say, "You really mean that Al, the Vice President for sales, had called you in four times to talk about quotas and was putting pressure on you to put pressure on the sales force, something you were reluctant to do." A chief characteristic of this kind of conversation, then, is leaving out details that you think the other person will know without further explanation.

9. *Pausing*. Another element is the brief periods of silence when neither person feels it necessary to talk. The length of the silence depends on many personal factors. Pauses may function to indicate the parties wish to discontinue talking; they may be thinking in order to answer a question; they may wish to change the topic of conversation.

10. *Leave taking*. Friendly conversations never stop without some verbal ritual that says "The end." The parties must account for what they intend to do—stop talking. They must give some socially acceptable reason for ending. Such rituals are never direct except with very close friends. For example, we don't usually say, "I don't want to talk any more." Leave taking often occurs just before actual physical separation when the parties will not be able to talk further. However, sometimes they do remain together, as when friends ride the same bus; then the verbal leave taking might be "I'm going to catch 40 winks" or "I think I'll read a little."

There are other features of friendly conversations we could examine in this example. However, for understanding the ethnographic interview, these are sufficient to make the comparison.

THE ETHNOGRAPHIC INTERVIEW

When we examine the ethnographic interview as a speech event, we see that it shares many features with the friendly conversation. In fact, skilled ethnographers often gather most of their data through participant observation and many casual, friendly conversations. They may interview people without their awareness, merely carrying on a friendly conversation while introducing a few ethnographic questions.

It is best to think of ethnographic interviews as a series of friendly conversations into which the researcher slowly introduces new elements to assist informants to respond as informants. Exclusive use of these new *ethnographic elements*, or introducing them too quickly, will make interviews become like a formal interrogation. Rapport will evaporate, and informants may discontinue their cooperation. At any time during an interview it is possible to shift back to a friendly conversation. A few minutes of easygoing talk interspersed here and there throughout the interview will pay enormous dividends in rapport.

The three most important ethnographic elements are its *explicit purpose, ethnographic explanations,* and *ethnographic questions.*

1. *Explicit purpose.* When an ethnographer and informant meet together for an interview, both realize that the talking is supposed to go somewhere. The informant only has a hazy idea about this purpose; the ethnographer must make it clear. Each time they meet it is necessary to remind the informant where the interview is to go. Because ethnographic interviews involve purpose and direction, they will tend to be more formal than friendly conversations. Without being authoritarian, the ethnographer gradually takes more control of the talking, directing it in those channels that lead to discovering the cultural knowledge of the informant.

2. *Ethnographic explanations.* From the first encounter until the last interview, the ethnographer must repeatedly offer explanations to the informant. While learning an informant's culture, the informant also learns something—to become a teacher. Explanations facilitate this process. There are five types of explanations used repeatedly.

a. *Project explanations.* These include the most general statements about what the project is all about. The ethnographer must translate the goal of doing ethnography and eliciting an informant's cultural knowledge into terms the informant will understand. "I am interested in your occupation. I'd like to talk to you about what beauticians do." Later one might be more specific: "I want to know how beauticians talk about what they do, how they see their work, their customers, themselves. I want to study beauticians from your point of view."

b. *Recording explanations.* These include all statements about writing things down and reasons for tape recording the interviews. "I'd like to write some of this down," or "I'd like to tape record our interview so I can go over it later; would that be OK?"

c. *Native language explanations.* Since the goal of ethnography is to describe a culture in its own terms, the ethnographer seeks to encourage informants to speak in the same way they would talk to others *in their cultural scene.* These explanations remind informants *not* to use their translation competence. They take several forms and must be repeated frequently throughout the entire project. A typical native language explanation might be, "If you were talking to a customer, what would you say?"

d. *Interview explanations.* Slowly, over the weeks of interviewing, most informants become expert at providing the ethnographer with cultural information. One can then depart more and more from the friendly conversation model until finally it is possible to ask informants to perform tasks such as drawing a map or sorting terms written on cards. At those times it becomes necessary to offer an explanation for the type of interview that will take place. "Today I'd like to ask you some different kinds of questions. I've written some terms on cards and I'd like to have you tell me which ones are alike or different. After that we can do the same for other terms." This kind of interview explanation helps informants know what to expect and to accept a greater formality in the interview.

e. *Question explanations.* The ethnographer's main tools for discovering another person's cultural knowledge is the ethnographic question. Since there are many different kinds, it is important to explain them as they are used. "I want to ask you a different type of question," may suffice in some cases. At other times it is necessary to provide a more detailed explanation of what is going on.

3. *Ethnographic questions.* Throughout this book I have identified more than thirty kinds of ethnographic questions (Appendix A). They will be introduced by stages; it is not necessary to learn all of them at once. The design of this book allows a person to master one form of ethnographic question and make it a part of their interviews; then the next form will be presented and explained. For now, I only want to identify the three main types and explain their function.

a. *Descriptive questions.* This type enables a person to collect an ongoing sample of an informant's language. Descriptive questions are the easiest to ask and they are used in all interviews. Here's an example: "Could you tell me what you do at the office?" or "Could you describe the conference you attended?"

b. *Structural questions.* These questions enable the ethnographer to discover information about *domains,* the basic units in an informant's cultural knowledge. They allow us to find out *how* informants have organized their knowledge. Examples of structural questions are: "What are all the different kinds of fish you caught on vacation?" and "What are all the stages in getting transferred in your company?" Structural questions are often repeated, so that if an informant identified six types of activities, the ethnographer might ask, "Can you think of any other kind of activities you would do as a beautician?"

c. *Contrast questions.* The ethnographer wants to find out what an informant *means* by the various terms used in his native language. Later I will discuss how meaning emerges from the contrasts implicit in any language. Contrast questions enable the ethnographer to discover the dimensions of meaning which informants employ to distinguish the objects and events in their world. A typical contrast question would be, "What's the difference between a *bass* and a *northern pike?*"

Let's turn now to an example of an ethnographic interview based on my own research on the culture of cocktail waitresses in a college bar. This example gives an overview of all three types of questions to be discussed in later steps where I begin with descriptive questions, then move on to structural questions, and finally contrast questions.

ETHNOGRAPHIC INTERVIEW	ANALYSIS
ETHNOGRAPHER: Hi, Pam. How are you? PAM: Good. How are things with you? ETHNOGRAPHER: Fine. How's school going? PAM: Pretty slow; things are just getting started in most classes.	*Greetings.* This exchange of questions and words like "Hi," is a bit more formal than what might occur between close friends.
ETHNOGRAPHER: I'm really glad you could talk to me today. PAM: Well, I'm not sure if I can help you. I just don't know what you want to know. ETHNOGRAPHER: Well, as I told you on the phone, I'm interested in understanding your work as a cocktail waitress. You've had quite a bit of experience, haven't you? PAM: Oh, yes! (laughs) But I don't know if that qualifies me to tell you very much.	*Giving ethnographic explanations.* This begins here in recognizing they are going to "talk." Pam expresses doubts about her ability; she is unsure of the purpose of the interview.
ETHNOGRAPHER: How did you get the job at Brady's Bar? PAM: Well, it was July, a couple years ago. I didn't have any waitress experience before. It was really a fluke that I got the job at all. I went to Brady's one night with some friends and they bet me I couldn't get a job so I just walked up to the bartender and asked for it and I got it! Started the very next week. I've only worked part time during school but full time during the summer.	*Asking friendly question.* This is not strictly an ethnographic question, but one that might be asked in a friendly conversation. It does provide information and helps relax the informant.
ETHNOGRAPHER: You know, Pam, I've seen waitresses working in bars and restaurants, but as a customer. I'm sure my impressions of what they do is far different from the way that waitresses see the same things. Don't you think that's true? PAM: Oh, yes! Very different. I found that out when I started.	*Expressing cultural ignorance.* This can be done in many ways. Here the ethnographer places himself in the position of seeing waitresses but *not knowing* what their work is like. This paves the way for an ethnographic explanation. The ethnographer asks the informant to agree that the ethnographer is *truly* ignorant.

ETHNOGRAPHER: Well, let me explain what I'm interested in. I would like to find out what it's like to work as a waitress. I guess what I want to know is if I got a job at Brady's Bar and worked there for a year or two, how would I see things? What would I have to know to do a good job and survive and make sense out of what goes on? I'd like to know what you do each night, the problems you have, just everything that goes into being a cocktail waitress.

PAM: Well, I could tell you some things, but I'm not sure I can answer all your questions.

ETHNOGRAPHER: Well, let me begin with a simple question. I've never been to Brady's Bar and I don't know what takes place there on a typical night. Even when I've been to other bars, it's usually for an hour or so, never an entire evening as a waitress would spend. Could you start at the beginning of an evening, say a typical night at Brady's Bar, and describe to me what goes on? Like, what do you do when you first arrive, then what do you do next? What are some of the things you would have to do on most nights, and then go on through the evening right up until you walk out the door and leave the bar?

PAM: Well, first I should say that there's no typical night at Brady's.

ETHNOGRAPHER: Well, that's fine, just go through any night and tell me what you think might usually happen.

Pam: It depends if I go on at 7 or 9 o'clock. I usually start at 9, at least lately.

ETHNOGRAPHER: O.K. Why don't you tell me what you would usually do, from the beginning of the evening at 9 o'clock when you come in, until the end when you go home.

Giving ethnographic explanations. He conveys the nature of the project without using technical terms like culture, ethnography, science, or cultural knowledge. It is put in everyday language that the informant will understand. Another important ethnographic element here is *repeating*. In several different ways the project explanation is repeated.

Asking ethnographic questions. Before asking, he states that he is going to ask one, thus preparing the informant. Then, *repeating* occurs in which the ethnographer asks the question in several different ways.
Expressing cultural ignorance prefaces the repetition of questions.
Asking descriptive questions. This is a special kind of descriptive question called a "grand tour question." It is asked, not in a simple statement, but with repeated phrases, expanding on the basic question. Expanding allows the informant time to think, to prepare her answer.

Pam's response gives the ethnographer an opportunity to *repeat* the grand tour question, thus giving Pam more time to think.

Pam's short answer gives the ethnographer another chance for repeating the descriptive question.

PAM: I usually get there at about 8:45. I'll go to the kitchen and hang up my coat or sweater, then go back to the bar and sit for a while. I might ask for a coke and then pass the time joking with the bartender or some regular who is sitting nearby. If it's real busy, I'll punch in and go right to work. Anyway, by 9 o'clock I punch in and go to my waitress station and set up my tray. I'll take either the upper section or the lower depending on what the other waitress wants. Depending on what bartenders are working I might say, "Bob's on tonight, can I have the upper section?" But she has first choice since she came in at 7. The upper section is smaller and you get different types of people than in the lower section. You get more dates. My section was really popular last night. It was jammed. I couldn't even take my tray with me by the end of the evening, just carried one drink at a time.

ETHNOGRAPHER: Really! That must make it difficult.

PAM: (Nods her head)

ETHNOGRAPHER: You said that you would go to your waitress station and set up your tray. Could you describe for me what you do when you set up your tray?

PAM: Sure. You have a little round tray, like a pizza tray, two ash trays on it, one on top and one on the bottom. My tips go in the bottom and my loose change goes in the top ash tray. And the bills go under the ash tray, with the big bills on the bottom and the ones on top so you don't make the mistake of handing out a five or a ten.

Pam now begins to answer the grand tour question, easily describing the things she does at the bar each night. Some informants will talk for fifteen or twenty minutes without stopping; others pause to be sure they are doing the right thing. *Pausing* provides the ethnographer with a chance for *expressing interest.*

Expressing interest. In long responses to grand tour questions it is important to watch for every opportunity to verbally express interest.

Restating. The ethnographer begins to use Pam's words; this tells her it is important for her to use them.

Incorporating. As soon as possible, the ethnographer wants to move from questions that use his words to ones that incorporate native terms. Restating and incorporating are two of the most important elements and they often occur together in this way.

Mini-tour question. The phrase "set up your tray" was incorporated into a mini-tour question. This is a descriptive question that asks the informant to describe some smaller unit of an event or activity. Mini-tour questions can be asked almost any time, even before the grand tour question has been fully answered.

ETHNOGRAPHER: Oh, that's interesting and probably important for not losing money. I'd never thought of that.

Expressing interest.

Expressing cultural ignorance.

PAM: Yeah, it gets dark and can be really hard to see.

ETHNOGRAPHER: O.K. Now, let's go back to my earlier question. You've punched in, gone to your section, set up your tray, and started to work. Could you describe what that would involve?

Restating. The ethnographer picks up a whole series of terms the informant has used to describe what she's doing and repeats them. This serves to jog the memory of the informant, it helps return to the original question, and it helps her expand on the description. The ethnographer could have said, "What do you do next?" but by expanding the question and restating native terms, the informant will have an easier time answering it.

PAM: Well, first I'd look around and see if anyone wants anything. If someone is looking my way or looks like they want me, I'd go right to their table. Otherwise I'd just walk through the section, picking up empty bottles, emptying ash trays, cleaning up any empty tables. Then I'd watch and take orders and clean tables and all evening I'd be serving orders until finally I'd make last call and that would end the evening.

ETHNOGRAPHER: You've mentioned quite a number of things you do during a typical evening. You punch in, set up your tray, pick up empty bottles, take orders, clean tables, serve orders, and make last call. Now, would you say that these are all the things you do at Brady's Bar?

Asking structural questions. The ethnographer wants to introduce a structural question and begins by restating a list of activities that Pam has already mentioned. These make up a domain—things a waitress does at work—and the ethnographer wants to elicit a complete list of the terms in this domain. This question sequence begins with a *verification question,* then after Pam agrees, the structural question is asked.

PAM: Oh, yes. Every night. That's about all I do.

ETHNOGRAPHER: Can you think of any other things you would do?

PAM: Well, I make change and sometimes I mix drinks.

ETHNOGRAPHER: You do? I thought only the bartender did that.

Expressing ignorance. The ethnographer takes every opportunity to express his ignorance, to let the informant know he really doesn't know about the world of cocktail waitresses.

PAM: Well, if he has to go somewhere for a few minutes and it isn't too busy, he might ask me to get behind the bar and mix drinks for a few minutes. And another thing I do is help the other girl, if she wants.

ETHNOGRAPHER: I'm interested in the way waitresses would talk to each other at work. Could you give me a sentence a waitress might use to let you know she wants help?

Ethnographic explanation. The ethnographer reminds the informant that he wants to know how she would use her native language (so she won't use her translation competence). *Asking a native language question.* This descriptive question asks for an expression related to what the informant is talking about—but in her native language.

PAM: Well, she might say, "Could you catch that table of guys over there?" but usually, if I'm not busy and I see her real busy in her section, I'd just go down and say, "Can I give you a hand?" Some girls will say, "Oh, thanks, I've really had a rush." But sometimes they'll say, "That's O.K., I'm almost caught up."

ETHNOGRAPHER: Now, I'd like to ask a different kind of question. I'm interested in the differences between some of your activities. What is the difference between *taking orders* and *serving orders*?

Explaining a question. The ethnographer merely introduces it and says it will be different.
Asking a contrast question. All contrast questions restate and incorporate terms.

PAM: Well, for one thing, you get more hassles taking orders than serving orders.

ETHNOGRAPHER: Oh, really? Now that's something that as a customer I'd never know. But it's probably something every cocktail waitress knows?

PAM: Oh, yeah.

Expressing interest.
Expressing cultural ignorance. Here the ethnographer not only indicates it is something he wouldn't know, but something that every cocktail waitress would, i.e. it is common cultural knowledge to insiders.

ETHNOGRAPHER: You know, you've mentioned several places in Brady's Bar, like the bar itself, the waitress station, the upper section, the lower section. I wonder if you could describe the inside of the bar to me. For instance, if I were blind and you took me into Brady's and took me

Restating. In leading up to another question, the ethnographer uses the informant's language again to remind her of its importance.

throughout the bar telling me each place we were standing or you were looking at, what would it be like?

PAM: Well, when we first came in the front door, you'd be standing in front of a large horseshoe bar. On the left of the bar are a row of stools and behind the stools is a wall. On the right side of the bar are other stools and along that side are the two waitress stations. Then, on the right side of the bar, at the front is the lower section, to the back is the upper section. On the far side, against the wall, are the two restrooms and the door to the kitchen. And that's about it.

Mini-tour question.
Creating a hypothetical situation. This element is used frequently to place the informant in the scene and help her to use terms and phrases from her own language.

ETHNOGRAPHER: Well, that's great. I've really learned a lot today, but it also makes me aware that you know a great deal more. We didn't get to discuss the details of taking orders or any of the different kinds of drinks. I'm sure there are a lot of other things. I'd like to go over my notes and I'm sure I'll think of other questions. It's really an interesting place and a lot more goes on there than meets the eye.

Expressing ignorance. This is a prelude to taking leave.
Taking leave. This element is very different from the friendly conversation. After expressing interest and that there is much more to learn, the ethnographer identifies topics he doesn't know about, things he wants to find out in the future. This helps the informant realize she knows more than she may think she knows, that she can teach the ethnographer a great deal more.

PAM: Yes, it's more complex than most people realize. In fact, I didn't realize there was so much that went on! (laughs)

ETHNOGRAPHER: Well, could we meet again next week at this time?

PAM: Sure, that would be fine.

ETHNOGRAPHER: O.K. Thanks for coming today. This has really been interesting and I'm looking forward to learning a great deal more.

Expressing interest.

PAM: Well I enjoyed talking about it.

ETHNOGRAPHER: Well, I'll see you next week, then. Bye.

PAM: Fine. Bye.

This brief ethnographic interview illustrates most of the elements that make up this kind of speech event. However, in order to include them in a short space, the example distorts the normal course of such interviews. In particular, it appears that the ethnographer is jumping around from one topic to another, rather than allowing the informant to continue talking about what she does, about the difference between taking orders and serving orders, or about the spatial dimensions of the bar. In most ethnographic interviews, the informant would go on at much greater length on most topics and the ethnographer would not ask so many questions in such a short space of time.

More important for those learning to interview by following the steps in this book, the example includes many elements one would not use until after several interviews. So, rather than introducing descriptive questions, structural questions, and contrast questions into the first interview, each kind is slowly introduced over a number of interviews. This example had a specific purpose: to give an overview of the elements in an ethnographic interview. Later we will come back to the most important elements and explore them more fully. In Figure 2.1 I have summarized the basic elements.

In contrast to a friendly conversation, some striking alterations appear. In addition to an explicit purpose, the use of ethnographic explanations, and the use of ethnographic questions, we can identify the following changes.

1. *Turn taking is less balanced.* Although the informant and ethnographer take turns, they do not take turns asking the same kinds of questions or reporting on their experience. The relationship is asymmetrical: the ethnographer asks almost all the questions; the informant talks about her experience.

2. *Repeating replaces the normal rule of avoiding repetition.* Not only

FIGURE 2.1 Elements in the Ethnographic Interview

1. Greetings
2. Giving ethnographic explanations
   2.1 Giving project explanations
   2.2 Giving question explanations
   2.3 Giving recording explanations
   2.4 Giving native language explanations
   2.5 Giving interview explanations
3. Asking ethnographic questions
   3.1 Asking descriptive questions
   3.2 Asking structural questions
   3.3 Asking contrast questions
4. Asymmetrical turn taking
5. Expressing interest
6. Expressing cultural ignorance
7. Repeating
8. Restating informant's terms
9. Incorporating informant's terms
10. Creating hypothetical situations
11. Asking friendly questions
12. Taking leave

does the ethnographer repeat things the informant has said, restating them in her language, but questions are repeated. In a more lengthy interview, the ethnographer would ask similar questions over and over, such as, "Can you think of any other things you do on a typical night?"

3. *Expressing interest and ignorance occur more often but only on the part of the ethnographer.* Again, this aspect of the relationship is more asymmetrical than in friendly conversations. Especially at first, most informants lack assurance that they know enough, that the ethnographer is really interested, and these two elements become very important. Each can occur nonverbally as well as verbally.

4. *Finally, in place of the normal practice of abbreviating, the ethnographer encourages expanding on what each person says.* His questions are phrased and rephrased, expanding into paragraph length. And these very questions encourage the informant to tell more, not less, to go into more detail, not less. It takes many reminders for some informants to overcome the long-established practice of abbreviating.

In this chapter I have identified the major elements of the ethnographic interview. Because it involves a complex speech event, ethnographic interviewing requires practice to acquire the necessary skills. Practice also reduces the anxiety which all ethnographers experience when they begin interviewing a new informant. The tasks which follow are designed to reduce anxiety by making careful preparation and conducting a practice interview.

Tasks

2.1 Conduct a practice ethnographic interview. (If you are in a group with others, interview a beginning ethnographer, then act as informant for that person.)

2.2 Identify in writing the skills you managed well and those that need improvement.

2.3 Write out several different project explanations to be used with one of the potential informants identified earlier. These explanations can reflect (1) a first contact, (2) beginning of the first interview, and (3) beginning of the second interview.

OBJECTIVES
1. To understand the nature of an ethnographic record.
2. To set up a field-work notebook.
3. To contact an informant and arrange for the first interview.

The next step in the Developmental Research Sequence is to begin compiling a record of research. Even before contacting an informant, the ethnographer will have impressions, observations, and decisions to record. When undertaking research in a foreign community, many weeks or months may pass before systematic interviews with informants occur. When studying a cultural scene within our own society, the ethnographer has at least made a selection and has probably visited the scene; recording these first impressions will prove of great value later. Certainly the first contact with an informant deserves documentation. In this step we will examine the nature of an ethnographic record and discuss practical steps for making it the most useful for analysis and writing.

LANGUAGE AND THE ETHNOGRAPHIC RECORD

An ethnographic record consists of field notes, tape recordings, pictures, artifacts, and anything else which documents the cultural scene under study. As Frake has pointed out, "A description of a culture, an *ethnography,* is produced from an *ethnographic record* of the events of a society within a given period of time, including, of course, informants' responses to the ethnographer and his queries, tests, and apparatus" (1964b:111).

In my study of skid row men, many different things went into the ethnographic record. During the first week I wrote down what took place in the Seattle Criminal Court on the seventh floor of the Public Safety Building. I copied off the name of the court, names of judges, and room numbers from the large wall directory on the first floor. I described the physical layout of the courtroom as I saw it. I counted the number of visitors who came to watch the court proceedings. Each morning in the courtroom an average of sixty-five men were arraigned for public drunkenness. The city attorney read aloud part of each man's arrest record and I wrote it down. These arrest records were used by the judge to determine the length of a man's sentence. Later I acquired the complete arrest records from the police department and they also become part of my ethnographic record.

Within a few weeks of beginning this particular project, I began to conduct interviews with informants. I tape recorded these interviews and made transcriptions of them. I also made notes on my experiences as I went to the criminal court, walked up and down the streets of Seattle's skid row, visited the alcoholism treatment center, and talked with various informants. Bill Tanner, a longtime tramp, called me from the Seattle City Jail after one of his arrests for public drunkenness, and I asked him to keep a diary on his stay in jail. A few weeks later, Bill gave me an odd assortment of entries made on the only paper he could find—the title pages torn from books in his jail cell. I added these torn pages to my growing file of information.

Once I discovered the importance of *making a flop* and *avoiding the bulls* (police officers), I visited skid row and made observations of men actually making a flop and encountering the police. I photographed these events and the pictures became part of my data.

Some of my informants left Seattle and we corresponded for many months. All these letters went into my files. In addition I collected newspaper clippings, police department reports, and bulletin board notices posted at the alcoholism treatment center. I held interviews with judges, social workers, the alcoholism counselors. And always, I made notes about my experiences while I was actually doing the research. This record became the basis for writing an ethnography of tramp culture.[1]

The major part of any ethnographic record consists of written field notes, whether observations, interviews, records, diaries, or other personal documents. This means that, from the first entry, every ethnographer must come to grips with the problem of language. Earlier I pointed out that language influences *ethnographic discovery* and *ethnographic description*. However, the easy distinction between discovery and description, and the way language enters into these processes, represents an oversimplification. In practice, they often take place simultaneously. Making an ethnographic record acts as a bridge between discovery and description, linking them into a single, complex process. Discoveries find their way into the field notes; rereading this record while in the field leads to additional discoveries. Early field-note descriptions will find their way into the final ethnographic monograph. There is even feedback while writing the ethnography that leads to new discoveries and additions to the ethnographic record. This process is represented in the diagram below.

These feedback relationships underscore the fact that each step in the

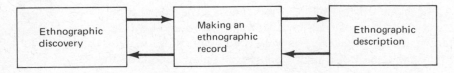

ethnographic enterprise involves *translation*. We have already seen how talking with informants to find out their view of the world (discovery) and writing the final ethnography (description) require a careful consideration of the translation process. Now we must raise the central question faced by all ethnographers when taking field notes: *what language shall be used in making an ethnographic record?*

Consider, for a moment, the various languages that became part of my ethnographic record studying tramps:

1. *Investigators' language*. Many of my field notes were written in the ordinary language I used as a social scientist. Obviously, this included meanings drawn from as far back as childhood as well as specialized concepts learned within the culture of anthropology.

2. *The language of tramps*. I recorded what tramps said in court, during informal conversations at the treatment center, and also during interviews.

3. *Courtroom languages*. A specialized way of talking was used by the city attorney, court clerks, and the judge who presided over the daily arraignment and sentencing. The languages in the courtroom also included the testimony of police officers who spoke in a language that usually reflected their culture outside the courtroom.

4. *The language of the alcoholism treatment center*. The staff at the center came from three distinct cultural scenes: social work, law enforcement, and Alcoholics Anonymous. In order to carry out their tasks, staff members frequently translated their meanings into terms that the others could understand. However, the distinct language usage of each cultural group emerged in almost every conversation. For example, a social worker would refer to tramps as "patients," a guard from the Sheriff's Department would call them "inmates," and an alcoholic counselor would call them "alcoholics." Each term conveyed a distinct meaning with enormous implications for the tramps assigned to the treatment center.

Although this research situation may appear linguistically complex, even in the simplest situations ethnographers must deal with their own language and that of informants. More important, they must deal with their own tendency to translate and simplify. Two principles must be kept in mind when making an ethnographic record: (a) the language identification principle, and (b) the verbatim principle. These principles have a single purpose, to reduce the influence of the ethnographer's translation competence when making an ethnographic record. Let us look at each briefly.

Language Identification Principle

This principle can be simply stated: *identify the language used for each field-note entry*. Because it is necessary to select a language, whenever the ethnographer writes something down in the field notes, some method of identification must be used. This might involve setting things off in parentheses, quotation marks, or brackets. It must include identification of the speaker. The goal is to have an ethnographic record *that reflects the same differences in language usages as the actual field situation.*

When I first began fieldwork on skid row, I failed to follow the language identification principle. My record of events contained an unidentified mixture of language usages, some picked up from tramps, some from the languages in the courtroom, some from the treatment center staff, and some from my own enculturation. From long discussions with other ethnographers, I have found that this is not an uncommon experience. Ethnographers fall back on their own translation competence, taking the things spoken by others and fitting them into a composite picture of the cultural scene. The process of the ethnographer's translation competence can be diagrammed in Figure 3.1.

The use of an amalgamated language for recording field notes has the apparent virtue of simplification. However, when the ethnographer returns to these notes to make a more careful analysis of cultural meanings, it becomes difficult, if not impossible, to do. Cultural meanings have become distorted during the process of making an ethnographic record. One of the most important payoffs in doing field work in an alien society with a completely new language is that this process of translation can hardly occur without the ethnographer's becoming keenly aware of it.

FIGURE 3.1. Ethnographer's Translation Competence

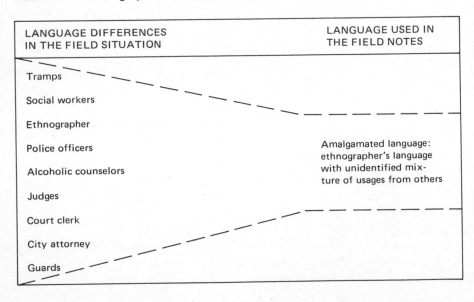

Verbatim Principle

In addition to identifying the various language usages in the field situation, the ethnographer must *make a verbatim record of what people say*. This obvious principle of getting things down word for word is frequently violated. Whether recording things people say in natural contexts or in more formal ethnographic interviews, the investigator's tendency to translate continues to operate. When I began research with tramps I did not realize the importance of the verbatim principle. I freely summarized, restated, and condensed what informants said without realizing it.

Consider the following example: (a) Informant's actual statement: "I made the bucket in Seattle one time for pooling; I asked a guy how much he was holding on a jug and he turned out to be a ragpicker and he pinched me." (b) Field notes entry: "I talked to Joe about his experience of being arrested on skid row when he wasn't drunk." At the time, this condensed entry appeared sufficient; I certainly did not feel it was a distortion of what Joe said. I didn't fully understand all his words but I thought I knew roughly what they meant. However, this entry lost some of the most important clues to the informant's culture. These clues came from such folk terms as *pooling* (a complex routine for contributing to a fund for purchasing something), *the bucket* (city jail), *ragpicker* (a certain kind of policeman), and *pinched* (arrested). Joe's phrases were leads to further questions; my summary was not. As my research progressed, I became aware that the words informants spoke held a key to their culture and so I began to make a verbatim record.

It may seem wiser, under the pressure of an interview situation, or in some natural context, to make a quick and more complete summary rather than a partial verbatim record. Such is not the case. In the previous example it would have been more valuable to make a partial, but verbatim, record such as the following:

> "made the bucket"
> "holding on a jug"
> "a ragpicker . . . pinched me"

These scattered phrases could then have been used to generate ethnographic questions; the summary could not.

Both *native terms* and *observer terms* will find their way into the field notes. The important thing is to carefully distinguish them. The native terms must be recorded verbatim. Failure to take these first steps along the path to discovering the inner meaning of another culture will lead to a false confidence that we have found out what the natives know. We may never even realize that our picture is seriously distorted and incomplete.

The best way to make a verbatim record during interviews is to use a tape recorder. It is especially valuable to tape record the first two or three interviews in order to quickly acquire a large sample of informant statements. However, tape recorders are not always advisable, especially during the first few interviews when rapport is beginning to develop. The use of a tape recorder may threaten and inhibit informants. Each ethnographer must decide on the basis of the willingness of informants and their feelings about using a tape recorder. When interviewing tramps, I often did not use a tape recorder because it aroused suspicion. When I interviewed cocktail waitresses, I always used a recorder with the full cooperation of waitress-informants. Here are some general rules for making a decision:

1. Always take a small tape recorder in case the opportunity arises to use it. One ethnographer decided not to tape record his first interview with an encyclopedia saleswoman. But when he started the interview, she asked, "Don't you want to tape record this?" If he had brought a recorder, he could have easily brought it out and started the tape.

2. Go slowly on introducing a tape recorder immediately. Often the first interview is likely to be a time to get acquainted, a time to develop rapport and trust. Informants will not know what kind of questions to expect. With an enthusiastic and eager informant, it is possible to ask casually, "How would you feel about tape recording this interview?" If the informant shows any hesitation, one might want to say, "Well, maybe it would be best to wait, perhaps later when we get into things." Sometimes it is necessary to wait until the second or third interview or even discard the idea entirely. It is possible to do good ethnography without a tape recorder; it is not possible to do good ethnography without rapport with key informants.

3. Watch for opportunities to tape record even a small part of an interview. After talking for half an hour, it might be appropriate to say, "This is so interesting and I'm learning so much, I wonder if you would mind if I tape recorded some of this. I can turn it off any time you want." Most informants will be more than willing to oblige.

Whether or not the ethnographer tape records interviews, it is still necessary to take notes during each interview. Sometimes tape recorders do not work; often some information from the interview is needed before it can be transcribed. Let's look more closely at how to take field notes.

KINDS OF FIELD NOTES

There are several different kinds of field notes that will make up an ethnographic record. Each investigator will develop a unique way to organize a file and field notebook. The following suggested format reflects the organization I have found most useful.

The Condensed Account

All notes taken during actual interviews or field observations represent a condensed version of what actually occurred. It is not humanly possible to write down everything that goes on or everything that informants say. Condensed accounts often include phrases, single words, and unconnected sentences. Consider the experience of one ethnographer who decided to interview a policeman. After making contact, her informant wanted her to ride in the squad car for a four-hour shift. However, it would be impossible to tape record in the car. In the squad car, she began to make notes of things that occurred, the places they drove, calls that came over the radio, and many of the phrases and terms used by her informant. During the four hours she recorded several pages of *condensed notes* in her notebook. She left the first interview with a feeling that she had only recorded a fraction of what she had experienced. Still, this condensed account was of enormous value because it had been recorded on the spot.

It is advisable to make a condensed account during every interview. Even while tape recording, it is good to write down phrases and words used by your informants. The real value of a condensed account comes when it is expanded after completing the interview or field observation.

The Expanded Account

The second type of field notes represents an expansion of the condensed version. As soon as possible after each field session the ethnographer should fill in details and recall things that were not recorded on the spot. The key words and phrases jotted down can serve as useful reminders to create the expanded account. When expanding, different speakers must be identified and verbatim statements included.

Much of my research among skid row men took place at the alcoholism treatment center where I mingled informally with informants while they worked, ate meals, played cards, and sat around talking. Occasionally, I jotted down condensed notes on small cards carried in my pocket. After several hours of listening and watching, I would slip away to a private office and expand my notes with as many details as I could remember. Like most ethnographers, I discovered my ability to recall events and conversations increased rapidly through the discipline of creating expanded accounts from condensed ones.

Tape-recorded interviews, when fully transcribed, represent one of the most complete expanded accounts. Despite the tedious and time-consuming nature of the work, making a full transcription becomes invaluable for conducting the series of ethnographic interviews discussed in this book. However, some investigators transcribe only parts of an interview or listen to the tape to create an expanded account, marking all verbatim phrases and words. Short of a complete transcription, an "index" of the tape can aid in locating relevant topics for later transcription.

Field Work Journal

In addition to field notes that come directly from observing and interviewing (the condensed account and expanded account), ethnographers should always keep a journal. Like a diary, this journal will contain a record of experiences, ideas, fears, mistakes, confusions, breakthroughs, and problems that arise during field work. A journal represents the personal side of field work; it includes reactions to informants and the feelings you sense from others.

Each journal entry should be dated. Rereading at a later time shows how quickly you forget what occurred during the first days and weeks of field work. Months later, when the ethnographer begins to write up the study, the journal becomes an important source of data. Doing ethnography differs from many other kinds of research in that *the ethnographer* becomes a major research instrument. Making an introspective record of field work enables a person to take into account personal biases and feelings, to understand their influence on the research.

Analysis and Interpretation

The fourth type of field notes provides a link between the ethnographic record and the final written ethnography. Here is the place to record analyses of cultural meanings, interpretations and insights into the culture studied. Most of the tasks in the remaining steps involve detailed analysis and can be recorded in this category of field notes.

Analysis and interpretation notes often represent a kind of brainstorming. Ideas may come from past reading, from some particular theoretical perspective, from some comment made by an informant. It is important to think of these field notes as a place to "think on paper" about the culture under consideration.

Tasks

3.1. Set up a field-work notebook or file with sections for
    a. condensed accounts
    b. expanded accounts
    c. journal
    d. analysis and interpretation
3.2. Begin making an ethnographic record with entries in each section for field work completed to date.
3.3. Contact an informant and arrange for the first ethnographic interview.

ASKING DESCRIPTIVE QUESTIONS

OBJECTIVES
1. To conduct the first ethnographic interview.
2. To understand the process of developing rapport with an informant.
3. To collect a sample of an informant's speech by asking descriptive questions.

Ethnographic interviewing involves two distinct but complementary processes: *developing rapport* and *eliciting information*. Rapport encourages informants to talk about their culture. Eliciting information fosters the development of rapport. In this step we will examine rapport and discuss the nature of ethnographic questions, particularly descriptive questions.

THE RAPPORT PROCESS

Rapport refers to a harmonious relationship between ethnographer and informant. It means that a basic sense of trust has developed that allows for the free flow of information. Both the ethnographer and the informant have positive feelings about the interviews, perhaps even enjoy them. However, rapport does not necessarily mean deep friendship or profound intimacy between two people. Just as respect can develop between two people who do not particularly like one another, rapport can exist in the absence of fondness and affection.

It is impossible to identify universal qualities that build rapport because harmonious relationships are culturally defined in every society. And so the ethnographer must pay particular attention to friendly relationships in each cultural scene to learn local, culture-bound features that build rapport. For example, when I interviewed Kwakiutl informants in British Columbia, I observed that friends and kinsmen sat together in long periods of silence. Although difficult, I learned to sit in silence and to converse more slowly. The rapport I gained through adopting these local patterns of interaction contributed to successful interviews. What follows regarding rapport must be taken as general suggestions. Some will work well within our own society in many cultural scenes; other suggestions must be modified to fit local cultural situations as well as the peculiarities of individual informants.

Probably the only universal characteristic of rapport is that it changes and fluctuates over time. On first encounter a potential informant may appear eager and cooperative. During the first interview this same informant appears uncomfortable, anxious, and even defensive. A different informant, after several interviews conducted in a harmonious fashion, becomes suspicious and bored, even discontinuing further contact. Laura Bohannon, in her classic anthropological novel, *Return to Laughter,* graphically describes the fluctuating rapport she experienced with her informants. Yabo, an old man who showed initial antagonism, became the first informant to reveal the secrets of witchcraft. Kako, the chief, took the anthropologist into his homestead and expressed willingness to help from the start. However, circumstances changed and he soon refused to talk of anything significant, influencing others to ignore the anthropologist. Finally, this phase in the relationship passed and Kako again became a willing and helpful informant.

Although sometimes unpredictable, rapport frequently does develop in a patterned way. I want to suggest a model of the *rapport process* in ethnographic interviewing. This model will provide the beginning ethnographer with a kind of compass for recognizing when rapport is developing well and when it has wandered off course. It can provide a basis for identifying and correcting problems that arise in the ethnographer-informant relationship.

The rapport process, in cases where it develops successfully, usually proceeds through the following stages:

APPREHENSION $\longrightarrow$ EXPLORATION $\longrightarrow$ COOPERATION $\longrightarrow$ PARTICIPATION

I want to discuss these stages by focusing on the interaction that goes on *during* interviews. In doing this, however, we should not lose sight of the wider context of field work. Most ethnographers will conduct participant observation at the same time, thus encountering key informants when they are working, visiting friends, enjoying leisure time, and carrying out ordinary activities. These encounters contribute to rapport as much as, or more than, the encounters during actual interviews. Under such conditions, the relationship may move more quickly to full cooperation. However, rapport still goes through a sequence of stages. Many times an ethnographer may want to conduct interviews with people not encountered during participant observation; rapport can still develop in a positive manner.

Apprehension

Ethnographic interviews always begin with a sense of uncertainty, a feeling of *apprehension*. This is true for both experienced ethnographers and the beginner. Every time I contacted a tramp and asked if we could talk, I felt apprehensive and sensed that each potential informant had similar feelings. Sometimes apprehension is slight; at other times informants express deep anxiety and suspicion. I recall one tramp who seemed overly anxious. I

79

explained my purpose and began asking questions but received only brief, curt replies. I felt increasing discomfort and made further attempts to put my informant at ease. "Are you with the F.B.I.?" he finally blurted out. I assured him I was a professor at the nearby medical school and had no connection with the F.B.I. or the local police department. He made me promise that I would not divulge his name to anyone, that all his statements could only be used anonymously.

Such extreme apprehension is rare, but some degree of uncertainty starting with the first contact through one or two interviews is common. The informant doesn't know what to expect, doesn't really understand the purposes and motives of the ethnographer. Both researcher and informant are unsure how the other person will evaluate responses. Informants may fear that they will not meet the expectations of the ethnographer. They may comment: "I don't know if I know enough," or "I'm not sure I can really help you, maybe you ought to talk to someone else about this."

The realization that ethnographic interviews begin with some uncertainty in the relationship can help the beginning ethnographer relax and accept this fact. At the same time, several things can help move the interviews through the stage of apprehension. The most important thing is to get informants talking. As we shall see later in this step, *descriptive questions* are especially useful to start the conversation and keep an informant freely talking. It does not usually matter what a person talks about; it does matter that the informant does most of the talking during the first couple of interviews. When an informant talks, the ethnographer has an opportunity to listen, to show interest, and to respond in a nonjudgmental fashion. These kinds of responses represent the most effective way to reduce an informant's apprehension. They communicate acceptance and engender trust. One of the most important principles, then, for the first interviews is to *keep informants talking*.

Exploration

Apprehension usually gives way quickly to *exploration*. In this stage of the rapport process, both ethnographer and informant begin trying out the new relationship. Together they seek to discover what the other person is like, what the other person really wants from the relationship. Exploration is a time of listening, observing, and testing. What does he want me to say? Can she be trusted? Is she going to be able to answer my questions? What does she really want from these interviews? Am I answering questions as I should? Does he really want to know what I know? These questions often go unspoken but exist nonetheless.

Apprehension, the first stage, arises in part from simple unfamiliarity with the terrain of ethnographic interviews. Exploration is the natural process of becoming familiar with this new landscape. Although each party begins exploring immediately, there comes a point where they leave behind the feelings of uncertainty and anxiety to enter the fullblown stage of exploration. It may occur when each laughs at something said, when the informant seems to go off on an interesting tangent, or when the ethnographer mentally sets aside prepared questions to talk about something. When a sense of sharing occurs, a moment of relaxation comes. Both can then begin to explore the territory with greater freedom.

Informants need the opportunity to move through the stage of exploration without the pressure to fully cooperate. It takes time to grasp the nature of ethnographic interviews. It takes time to see if the ethnographer's actions will match the explanation offered during the first interview. Valuable data can be collected during this stage if the ethnographer is willing to wait for full cooperation. During this stage a certain tenseness exists and both parties may find the interviews exhausting.

Three important principles facilitate the rapport-building process during this stage. First, *make repeated explanations*. A simple statement may suffice: "As I said earlier, I'm interested in finding out how you talk about things, how you see things. I want to understand things from your point of view." One dare not assume that informants appreciate the nature of ethnographic interviews based only on the first explanation. Repetition before each interview, during interviews, and at the end of each will pay great dividends.

Second, *restate what informants say*. Using this principle, the ethnographer selects key phrases and terms used by an informant and restates them. Restating in this fashion reinforces what has been said by way of explanation. Restating demonstrates an interest in learning the informant's language and culture. Here are three examples of restatements typical of my interviews with tramps:

1. "Then you would say, 'I made the bucket in Seattle.' "
2. "So, if a man was a trustee, he'd do easy time."
3. "Then I might hear another tramp saying, 'He's a bindle stiff.' Is that right?"

Restating embodies the nonjudgmental attitude which contributes directly to rapport. When the ethnographer restates what an informant says, a powerful, unstated message is communicated—"I understand what you're saying; I am learning; it is valuable to me." Restatement must be distinguished from reinterpreting, a process in which the interviewer states *in different words* what the other person said. Reinterpreting prompts informants to translate; restating prompts them to speak in their own ordinary, everyday language.

The third principle states, *don't ask for meaning, ask for use*. Beginning ethnographers often become overconcerned with meanings and motives. They tend to press informants with questions like, "What do you mean by that?'' and "Why would you do that?'' These questions contain a hidden judgmental component. Louder than words, they seem to shout, "You haven't been clear; you haven't explained adequately; you are hiding the true reasons for what you told me.'' Ethnographic interviewing differs from most other approaches by the absence of probing "why" and "what do you mean" questions.

Let me contrast the use of *why questions* and *meaning questions* with the strategy of asking informants how they use their ordinary language. An unfamiliar term emerged in my interviews with tramps; it was called "days hanging." I heard an informant say, "I had twenty days hanging so I pled guilty and asked the judge for the alcoholism treatment center.'' Another recalled, "Well, I left town because I had a lot of days hanging." Tramps could respond to direct questions and at first I asked things like, "Why did you have twenty days hanging?" "Why did you leave town?" and "What do you mean you had twenty days hanging?" However, this kind of questioning led directly to translations for my benefit. "Well, I had twenty days hanging because I'd made the bucket four times in a row." "I left town 'cause I knew I'd do hard time." And such translations required still more probing "why" questions—"*Why* did you have twenty days?" "What do you *mean*, did hard time?" Such questions communicated to my informants that they had not been clear. In a subtle, unspoken way, these questions pressured informants to use their translation competence.

As time went on I learned that instead of asking for meaning, it worked best to ask for use. Cultural meaning emerges from understanding how people *use* their ordinary language. With tramps, I would restate, then ask how the phrase was used. For example, I would say, "You had twenty days hanging. Could you tell me what you would say to the judge if you had ten or thirty or sixty days hanging?" Or I might ask for the way others used this phrase: "Would tramps generally talk about the days they had hanging before they went into the courtroom? What kinds of things would I hear them saying?" I might be more direct: "What are some other ways you could talk about days hanging?" or "Would someone ever say, 'I had twenty days hanging so I pled *not* guilty?' '' Asking for use is a guiding principle that underlies all ethnographic interviewing. When combined with restating and making repeated explanations, ethnographic interviews usually move quickly through the stage of exploration.

Cooperation

In time, the rapport process moves into the next stage—cooperation. Informants often cooperate from the start of the first interview, but this stage involves more complete cooperation based on mutual trust. Instead of uncertainty, the ethnographer and informant know what to expect of one another. They no longer worry about offending each other or making mistakes in asking or answering questions. More and more, both persons find satisfaction in meeting together to talk. Informants may offer personal information and feel free to ask the ethnographer questions. Most important, both share in the definition of the interviews; they both know the goal is to discover the culture of the informant in the language of the informant. Now informants may spontaneously correct the ethnographer: "No, I wouldn't say 'the police arrested me,' but that 'a bull pinched me.' "

Participation

The final stage in the rapport process is *participation*. After many weeks of working closely with an informant, sometimes a new dimension is added to the relationship, one in which the informant recognizes and accepts the role of teaching the ethnographer. When this happens there is a heightened sense of cooperation and full participation in the research. Informants begin to take a more assertive role. They bring new information to the attention of the ethnographer and help in discovering patterns in their culture. They may begin to *analyze* their culture, but always from their own frame of reference. Between interviews they are on the lookout for information relevant to the ethnographic goals. Not all informants progress to this last stage of participation. If they do, they increasingly become participant observers in their own cultural scene. The ethnographer's role is then to help informant/participant-observers record what they know.

Building rapport is a complex process, one that every ethnographer must monitor when doing field work. In conducting ethnographic interviews, this process is facilitated by following certain principles: keep informants talking; make repeated explanations; restate what informants say; and don't ask for meaning, ask for use. When combined with asking ethnographic questions, rapport will usually develop in a smooth way from apprehension through cooperation and even into the stage of participation.

ETHNOGRAPHIC QUESTIONS

In most forms of interviewing, questions are distinct from answers. The interviewer asks the questions, someone else responds with answers. This separation often means that questions and answers come from two different cultural meaning systems. Investigators from one cultural scene draw on their frame of reference to formulate questions. The people who respond are from a different cultural scene and draw on another frame of reference to provide answers. This kind of interviewing assumes that questions and answers are separate elements in human thinking. In the study of other cultures it frequently leads to distortions.

Ethnographic interviewing, on the other hand, begins with the assumption that the question-answer sequence is a single element in human thinking. Questions always imply answers. Statements of any kind always imply questions. This is true even when the questions and answers remain unstated. In ethnographic interviewing, *both questions and answers must be discovered from informants*. Mary Black and Duane Metzger have summarized this point of view:

It is basic to communications theory that you don't start getting any information from an utterance or event until you know what it is in response to—you must know what question is being answered. It could be said of ethnography that until you know the question that someone in the culture is responding to you can't know many things about the responses. Yet the ethnographer is greeted, in the field, with an array of *responses*. He needs to know what question people are *answering* in their every act. He needs to know which questions are being taken for granted because they are what "everybody knows" without thinking. . . . Thus the task of the ethnographer is to discover questions that seek the relationship among entities that are conceptually meaningful to the people under investigation (1965:144).

There are three main ways to discover questions when studying another culture. First, the ethnographer can record the questions people ask in the course of everyday life. An ethnographer on a university campus in the United States might hear students asking the following questions about motion pictures: "Who stars in that one?" or "Is it rated R?" Other questions would probably be asked about particular courses such as: "Is that a sluff course?" or "When does it meet?" Some settings offer unique opportunities for discovering questions, as Frake has pointed out:

The ethnographer can listen for queries in use in the cultural scenes he observes, giving special attention to query-rich settings, e.g., children querying parents, medical specialists querying patients, legal authorities querying witnesses, priests querying the gods (1964a:143).

Second, the ethnographer can inquire directly about questions used by participants in a cultural scene. Black and Metzger have suggested three strategies:

1. To ask the informant, "What is an interesting question about _____?"
2. To ask the informant, "What is a question to which the answer is _____?"
3. To ask the informant to write a text in question-and-answer form on some topic of interest to the investigator (1965:146).

In my ethnographic research with tramps and cocktail waitresses I found it useful to create a hypothetical situation and then ask for questions. For example, I would ask a waitress-informant, "If I listened to waitresses talking among themselves at the beginning of an evening, what questions would I hear them ask each other?" To which they might answer, "Who's the other bartender tonight?" or "Which section would you like to work?"

A third strategy for discovering questions simply asks informants to talk about a particular cultural scene. This approach uses general *descriptive questions* that are less likely to reflect the ethnographer's culture. Answers can be used to discover other culturally relevent questions. This approach is like offering informants a frame and canvas and asking them to paint a word-picture of their experience. "Could you tell me what the jail is like?" and "Could you describe a typical evening at Brady's Bar?" are examples of such *descriptive questions*. A variation on this approach developed by Agar (1969) in his study of heroin addicts in prison, is to ask two or more informants to role-play typical interactions from the cultural scene under consideration. As informants talk to each other, the ethnographer can record questions and answers. In the rest of this chapter I want to discuss in detail several kinds of descriptive questions.

DESCRIPTIVE QUESTIONS

Descriptive questions take "advantage of the power of language to construe settings" (Frake 1964a:143). The ethnographer does need to know at least one setting in which the informant carries out routine activities. For example, I needed to know my informants spent much of their time in jail to be able to ask, "Could you tell me what the jail is like?" I needed to know that cocktail waitresses worked evenings in Brady's Bar to be able to ask, "Could you describe a typical evening at Brady's Bar?" Because ethnographers almost always know *who* an informant is, they almost always know at least one appropriate setting to be used in a descriptive question. If one is studying air-traffic controllers, it is easy to ask, "What do you do as an air-traffic controller?" If one is studying the culture of housewives, it is easy to ask an informant, "Could you describe a typical day? What do you do as a housewife?"

There are five major types of descriptive questions and several subtypes (Figure 4.1). Their precise form will depend on the cultural scene selected for investigation. Descriptive questions aim to elicit a large sample of utterances in the informant's native language. They are intended to encourage an informant to talk about a particular cultural scene. Sometimes a single descriptive question can keep an informant talking for more than an hour.

One key principle in asking descriptive questions is that *expanding the length of the question tends to expand the length of the response*. Although a question like, "Could you tell me what the jail is like?" qualifies as a descriptive question, it needs expansion. Instead of this brief form, I might say, "I've never been inside the jail before, so I don't have much of an idea

FIGURE 4.1 Kinds of Descriptive Questions

1. Grand Tour Questions
   1.1. Typical Grand Tour Questions
   1.2. Specific Grand Tour Questions
   1.3. Guided Grand Tour Questions
   1.4. Task-Related Grand Tour Questions
2. Mini-Tour Questions
   2.1. Typical Mini-Tour Questions
   2.2. Specific Mini-Tour Questions
   2.3. Guided Mini-Tour Questions
   2.4. Task-Related Mini-Tour Questions
3. Example Questions
4. Experience Questions
5. Native-Language Questions
   5.1. Direct Language Questions
   5.2. Hypothetical-Interaction Questions
   5.3. Typical-Sentence Questions

what it's like. Could you kind of take me through the jail and tell me what it's like, what I would see if I went into the jail and walked all around? Could you tell me what it's like?'' Expanding descriptive questions not only gives informants time to think, but it says, ''Tell me as much as you can, in great detail.''

1. Grand Tour Questions

A grand tour question simulates an experience many ethnographers have when they first begin to study a cultural scene. I arrived at the alcoholism treatment center and the director asked, ''Would you like a grand tour of the place?'' As we walked from building to building, he named the places and objects we saw, introduced me to people, and explained the activities in progress. I could not ask tramps to give me a grand tour of the Seattle City Jail, so I simply asked a grand tour question: ''Could you describe the inside of the jail for me?'' In both situations, I easily collected a large sample of native terms about these cultural scenes.

A grand tour usually takes place in a particular locale: a jail, a college campus, a home, a factory, a city, a fishing boat, etc. Grand tour questions about a locale almost always make sense to informants. We can now expand the idea of ''grand tour'' to include many other aspects of experience. In addition to *space,* informants can give us a grand tour through some *time* period: ''Could you describe the main things that happen during the school year, beginning in September and going through May or June?'' They can take an ethnographer through a sequence of *events*: ''Can you tell me all the things that happen when you get arrested for being drunk, from the first moment you encounter the police, through going to court and being sentenced, until you finally get out of jail?'' An informant can give the ethnographer a grand tour through some group of *people*: "Can you tell me the names of all your relatives and what each one is like?" Some large events such as a ceremony are made up of *activities* that can become the basis for a grand tour question: "What are all the things that you do during the initiation ceremony for new members who join the fraternity?" Even a group of *objects* offers an opportunity for a grand tour: "Could you describe all the different tools and other equipment you use in farming?" Whether the ethnographer uses *space, time, events, people, activities,* or *objects*, the end result is the same: a verbal description of significant features of the cultural scene. Grand tour questions encourage informants to ramble on and on. There are four different types which vary the way such questions are asked.

1.1. Typical Grand Tour Questions. In this form, the ethnographer asks for a description of how things usually are. "Could you describe a *typical* night at Brady's Bar?" One might ask a secretary informant: "Could you describe a *typical* day at the office?" In studying Kwakiutl salmon fishing, I asked, "Could you tell me how you *usually* make a set?" Typical grand tour questions ask the informant to generalize, to talk about a pattern of events.

1.2. Specific Grand Tour Questions. A specific question takes the most recent day, the most recent series of events, or the locale best known to the informant. "Could you describe what happened at Brady's Bar last night, from the moment you arrived until you left?" An ethnographer might ask a secretary, "Tell me what you did yesterday, from the time you got to work until you left?" "Tell me about the last time you made a set, fishing for salmon." Some informants find it difficult to generalize to the *typical* but can easily describe a recent situation.

1.3. Guided Grand Tour Questions. This form asks the informant to give an actual grand tour. A secretary might be asked: "Could you show me around the office?" The ethnographer might ask a Kwakiutl fisherman, "The next time you make a set, can I come along and could you explain to me what you are doing?" Some subjects, such as a typical year or month, do not lend themselves to a guided tour.

1.4. Task-Related Grand Tour Questions. These questions ask the informant to perform some simple task that aids in the description. For example, I frequently asked tramps, "Could you draw a map of the inside of the Seattle City Jail and explain to me what it's like?" While performing this task, they added a great deal of verbal description. The map helped informants to remember and gave me a better understanding of the jail as they saw it. In studying the cultural scene of backgammon players, I asked, "Could you play a game of backgammon and explain what you are doing?" When informants perform tasks in the context of grand tour questions, the ethnographer can ask numerous questions along the way, such as, "What is this?" and "What are you doing now?"

2. Mini-Tour Questions

Responses to grand tour questions offer almost unlimited opportunities for investigating smaller aspects of experience. Because grand tour questions lead to such rich descriptions, it is easy to overlook these new opportunities. One ethnographer, investigating the culture of directory assistance operators working for Bell Telephone Co., began with a grand tour question: "Could you describe a typical day in your work as a directory assistance operator?" After a lengthy description, she discovered that one recurrent activity was "taking calls." Each call lasted an average of 37 seconds. This led to a mini-tour question: "Could you describe what goes on in taking a call?" The informant was able to break down that brief period of time into more than a dozen activities, ones that were far more complex than the ethnographer realized when she asked the question.[1]

Mini-tour questions are identical to grand tour questions except they deal with a much smaller unit of experience. "Could you describe what you do when you take a break at Brady's Bar?" "Could you draw me a map of the trusty tank in the Seattle City Jail?" "Could you describe to me how you take phone calls in your work as a secretary?" The four kinds of mini-tour questions (typical, specific, guided, task-related) use the same approaches as their counterparts do with grand tour questions.

3. Example Questions

Example questions are still more specific, in most cases. They take some single act or event identified by the informant and ask for an example. A tramp, in responding to a grand tour question, says, "I was arrested while pooling," and so I would ask, "Can you give me an example of pooling?" A waitress states, "There was a table of guys who really gave me a hard time last night." An example question: "Could you give me an example of someone giving you a hard time?" This type of question can be woven throughout almost any ethnographic interview. It often leads to the most interesting stories of actual happenings which an ethnographer will discover.

4. Experience Questions

This type merely asks informants for any experiences they have had in some particular setting. "You've probably had some interesting experiences in jail; can you recall any of them?" "Could you tell me about some experiences you have had working as a directory assistance operator?" These questions are so open ended that informants sometimes have difficulty answering them. They also tend to elicit atypical events rather than recurrent, routine ones. They are best used after asking numerous grand tour and mini-tour questions.

5. Native-Language Questions

Native-language questions are designed to minimize the influence of informants' translation competence. Because descriptive questions are a first step to discovering more culturally relevant questions, they sometimes contain words and phrases seldom used by informants. This encourages informants to translate. Native-language questions ask informants to use the terms and phrases most commonly used in the cultural scene.

When I first began studying tramps, I only knew they were often incarcerated in the Seattle City Jail. "Could you describe the jail?" was a useful grand tour question, but I still was not sure that "jail" was a commonly used term. And so I asked a native-language question: "How would you refer to the jail?" When informants uniformly said, "Oh, most guys would call it *the bucket*," I was able to use this term in future questions. "How would you talk about getting arrested?" led to the term "made the bucket." Only then could I ask more meaningful descriptive questions like "Could you describe in detail what happens from beginning to end when you make the bucket?"

Native-language questions serve to remind informants that the ethnographer wants to learn their language. They can be used whenever one suspects an informant is translating for the ethnographer's benefit. They should be employed frequently in early interviews until an informant begins to state voluntarily, "The way we would say it is _____," or "Our term for that is _____." Every ethnographer can develop ways to insert native-language queries into each interview. I want to identify three useful strategies.

5.1. Direct-Language Questions. This type of native-language question simply asks "How would you refer to it?" when an informant uses a term. Sometimes it may take the form "Is that the way most people would say it?" For example, tramps often spoke of trying to find a place to sleep at night, so I would ask: "Would you say, 'I was trying to find a place to sleep?' " "No," they responded. "Probably I would say I was trying to *make a flop*." An ethnographer studying the culture of secretaries might ask the following native-language question:

SECRETARY: When I type letters I have to watch out for mistakes.
ETHNOGRAPHER: How would you refer to *mistakes*?
SECRETARY: Oh, I would call them *typos*.

The more familiar the informant and ethnographer are with each other's cultures, the more important native-language questions become. I asked many direct-language questions of cocktail waitresses for this reason. An informant would say, "These two customers were really hassling me," and I would ask, "How would you refer to them, as *customers*?" To which she would reply: "I'd probably say those two *obnoxos*."

5.2. Hypothetical-Interaction Questions. Speaking takes place between people with particular identities. When an informant is talking to an ethnographer, it may be difficult to recall ways to talk to other people. The ethnographer can help in this recall by creating a hypothetical interaction. For example, an ethnographer could ask, "If you were talking to another directory assistance operator, would you say it that way?" Tramps not only interact among themselves but with policemen, or *bulls*. I often phrased hypothetical-interaction questions to discover how tramps talked to bulls as well as to other tramps.

Hypothetical-interaction questions can be used to generate many native-language utterances. I have interviewed children about school who could easily recall native usages when placed in situations such as the following: "If I were to sit in the back of your classroom, what kinds of things would I hear kids saying to each other?" "If a friend called on the phone to ask if you were going to bring your lunch, what would that person say?" It is even possible to construct the situation in more detail, as in the following question to a waitress: "Imagine yourself at a table of four male customers. You haven't said anything yet, and you don't know any of them. What kinds of things would they likely say to you when you first walked up to their table?" By being placed in a typical situation and having the identities of speaker and listener specified, most informants overcome any tendency to translate and recall many phrases used in ordinary talk.

5.3. Typical-Sentence Questions. A closely related kind of native-language question, this one asks for typical sentences that contain a word or phrase. "What are some sentences I would hear that include the phrase *making the bucket*," or "What are some sentences that use the term *flop*?" are two examples. The typical-sentence question provides an informant with one or more native terms and then asks that informant to use them in typical ways.

Descriptive questions form the basis of all ethnographic interviewing. They lead directly to a large sample of utterances that are expressed in the language used by informants in the cultural scene under investigation.

All ethnographic questions can be phrased in both personal and cultural terms. When phrasing questions *personally,* the ethnographer asks, "Can *you* describe a typical evening you would have at Brady's Bar?" or "How would *you* refer to the jail?" This tells the informant to present his own point of view or her own particular language usage. When phrasing questions *culturally*, the ethnographer asks, "Can you describe a typical evening for most cocktail waitresses at Brady's Bar?" or "How would most tramps refer to the jail?" An informant is someone who can tell about patterns of behavior in a particular scene, not merely his or her own actions. I recall one novice ethnographer who asked a letter carrier about lunch. "I don't eat lunch" was the reply. The ethnographer later rephrased the question in cultural terms: "What do letter carriers do at lunch time?" This query brought a long response which included those who didn't eat lunch, those who brought lunches and ate together, those who ate at restaurants, and several other variations. The various things letter carriers did at lunch turned out to be important cultural information. But eliciting this information depended on phrasing the question in cultural terms.

In this chapter we have examined the rapport process and some of the principles that will facilitate the development of rapport. In addition, we have examined the nature of ethnographic questions and descriptive questions in particular. Descriptive questions form the backbone of all ethnographic interviews. They will make up most of the questions asked in the first interview and their use will continue throughout all subsequent interviews. With practice, a beginning ethnographer can easily gain skill in asking this type of ethnographic question.

Tasks

4.1. Review the examples given of the various kinds of descriptive questions and prepare several of each type for Informants in the cultural scene you are studying.

4.2. Conduct and record an ethnographic interview with an informant, using descriptive questions.

4.3. Transcribe the recorded interview (or expand the condensed notes taken during the interview).

OBJECTIVES
1. To understand the nature of ethnographic analysis.
2. To learn how meaning is created with cultural symbols.
3. To begin a domain analysis by making a preliminary domain search.

The last step brought us through the first ethnographic interview with an informant. Before proceeding to the next interview it becomes necessary to analyze the data collected. This analysis will enable you to discover questions to ask in future interviews. It will also lead to finding out what things mean to your informant. In order to achieve our goal of describing a cultural meaning system in its own terms, the ethnographer must analyze cultural data in a way that is distinct from other forms of analysis used in social science research. In this step I want to consider ethnographic analysis as a tool for discovering cultural meaning.

ETHNOGRAPHIC ANALYSIS

Analysis of any kind involves a way of thinking. It refers to the systematic examination of something to determine its parts, the relationship among parts, and their relationship to the whole. One can search for the component parts of a tree, a butterfly, a painting, a symphony, a community, or anything else in human experience. Even a joke can be analyzed into (1) the opening line, (2) the topic, (3) the characters, and (4) the punch line. We can analyze the parts of a day into categories like dawn, forenoon, noon, early afternoon, evening, and midnight. We can then examine the relationship among these parts of a day and their relationship to the whole day. In each case, analysis proceeds by examining some phenomenon, dividing it into its constituent parts, then identifying the relationships among the parts and their relationship to the whole.

At the outset we must recognize that it is possible to analyze any phenomenon in more than one way. One person may identify four parts to a joke; another might see seven or eight. A day can be analyzed into large units like evening and morning or divided into 86,400 seconds. And every culture can be analyzed in numerous ways. But most important for ethnography is the fact that informants have already learned a set of categories into which their culture is divided. An informant's cultural knowledge is more than random bits of information; this knowledge is organized into categories, all of which are systematically related to the entire culture. Our goal is to employ methods of analysis that lead to discovering this organization of cultural knowledge. We especially want to avoid imposing categories from the outside that *create* order and pattern rather than discover it. *Ethnographic analysis* is the search for the parts of a culture and their relationships *as conceptualized by informants*. Most of the time this internal structure as it is known to informants remains tacit, outside their awareness. The ethnographer has to devise ways to discover this tacit knowledge.

How does analysis fit into the overall research endeavor? Let's answer this question by looking first at the research sequence as it is usually conceived of in social science.[1] Then we can contrast it with the sequence of research in ethnography.

Most social science research follows a well-known sequence:

1. *Selecting a problem.* The investigator usually begins by reviewing the relevant theoretical literature to discover an area that appears interesting and in need of further research.

2. *Formulating hypotheses.* They will be stated in a form that can be tested. They represent a further refinement of the problem and they function to guide the investigator in gathering data.

3. *Collecting data.* At this point in the sequence the research or data-collecting phase begins. Usually one or more methods of research have been selected to gather the necessary data.

4. *Analyzing the data.* Only after collecting all the data does one begin to analyze it. The analysis is always done with respect to the original problem and the specific hypotheses. In social science research, the investigator would not change hypotheses or the problem under consideration while collecting data, for this would contaminate the results.

5. *Writing up the results.* This final phase of the study is done after all others have been completed.

Ethnography differs from this social science sequence in several ways. Most important, instead of discrete stages, ethnographic research requires constant feedback from one stage to another. Although we can identify five tasks in sequence, they must all go on at the same time.

1. *Selecting a problem.* Ethnography all begins with the same general problem: What are the cultural meanings people are using to organize their behavior and interpret their experience? This problem is based on a general theory of culture which shares many similarities with symbolic interactionism. Sometimes an ethnographer might narrow the problem after reviewing the ethnographic literature on a particular group. But it would still take

the same form: What are the cultural meanings people are using to organize their *kinship* behavior and interpret this aspect of their experience?

2. *Collecting cultural data.* This phase begins before any hypotheses have been formulated (unless they have been generated by prior ethnographic research in that society).[2] The ethnographer begins asking descriptive questions, making general observations, and recording these in field notes.

3. *Analyzing cultural data.* Within a short time after beginning to collect data, analysis begins. It consists of reviewing field notes to search for cultural symbols (usually encoded in native terms) and to search for relationships among those symbols. For example, not long after beginning our study of Brady's Bar, we identified several terms such as *setting up the tray, punching in,* and *making last call* (Spradley and Mann, 1975). Then we began searching for relationships among these terms.

4. *Formulating ethnographic hypotheses.* Although ethnographers formulate hypotheses to test, these hypotheses arise from the culture studied. They are ethnographic hypotheses that must be formulated after collecting initial data. They propose relationships to be tested by checking what informants know. For example, we proposed that the terms noted above from Brady's Bar were all *stages in a night's work,* that they were related in some kind of temporal sequence. Most of the ethnographic hypotheses arise from the various forms of analysis to be discussed in this and later chapters. Now, before going on to any new phase of research, the ethnographer must go back and collect more cultural data, analyze it, formulate new hypotheses, and then repeat these stages over and over again.[3]

5. *Writing the ethnography.* Although writing a cultural description will come near the end of research, it can well stimulate new hypotheses and send the investigator back for more field work. Writing, in one sense, is a refined process of analysis.

In this book I will discuss four kinds of ethnographic analysis. Together with the various types of ethnographic questions, these strategies have a single purpose: to uncover the system of cultural meanings that people use. *Domain analysis* involves a search for the larger units of cultural knowledge called domains (considered in Step Five and Step Six). In doing this kind of analysis we will search for cultural symbols which are included in larger categories (domains) by virtue of some similarity. *Taxonomic analysis* involves a search for the internal structure of domains and leads to identifying contrast sets (considered in Step Eight). *Componential analysis* involves a search for the attributes that signal differences among symbols in a domain (considered in Step Nine). *Theme analysis* involves a search for the relationships among domains and how they are linked to the culture as a whole (considered in Step Eleven). All these types of ethnographic analysis lead to the discovery of cultural meaning, and therefore it is necessary to discuss briefly the nature of meaning.

A RELATIONAL THEORY OF MEANING[4]

From the first chapter I have stressed the central importance of cultural *meaning*. People everywhere order their lives in terms of what things mean. All of us make use of meanings most of the time without thinking about it. Walk into a room and the furniture has a variety of meanings. Someone is sitting in a chair with his eyes closed and we take it to mean he is tired or sleeping. Someone laughs in our presence and we seek its meaning; did she laugh at us or with us? A friend across the street raises her hand in our direction and her gesture means a greeting. A bell rings and we know its meaning: to end a class. The noon hour means eating lunch; certain foods mean breakfast or dinner or a holiday celebration. A friend appears in shorts and brightly colored shoes that tell us he plans to run. And even the way he runs tells us other things about him. Most important, people constantly exchange words, sometimes with lightning rapidity for hours at a time, conveying elaborate meanings. Meaning, in one form or another, permeates the experience of most human beings in all societies. But what is meant by meaning itself? How do words and behavior and objects become meaningful? And how do we find out what things mean? These are some of the questions we will begin to answer in this chapter.

Symbols[5]

All cultural meaning is created by using symbols. All the words your informant used in responding to your questions in the first interview were symbols. The way your informant dressed was also a symbol, as were your informant's facial expressions and hand movements. *A symbol is any object or event that refers to something.* All symbols involve three elements: the symbol itself, one or more referents, and a relationship between the symbol and referent. This triad is the basis for all symbolic meaning.

The symbol itself consists of anything we can perceive or experience. The symbols we will deal with in this book are the *folk terms* used by your informant. We perceive these folk terms as *sounds* of one sort or another. No less a symbol are the *analytic terms* from the culture of anthropology, terms such as *ethnography, descriptive question,* and *culture.* You have perceived these terms as written words, but they also are based on vocal sounds. But the range of things that can become symbols goes far beyond speech sounds. A shiver runs down your spine; it can be perceived and it can also become a symbol of fear, excitement, or anything else. Clench your teeth, wink an eye, nod your head, bow forward from the waist, or make any other possible movement; these movements could all become symbols. Because we can experience colors, sounds, objects, actions, group activities, and complex social situations, they can all become symbols. Every society has a limitless supply of material for creating symbols.

A referent is the thing a symbol refers to or represents. It can be anything conceivable in human experience. We can refer to trees and stars as symbols, but we can also represent mythical creatures never before experienced. We can refer to dreams we never had, places that do not exist, people who will live in the future, and always to the ordinary things around us. We can even refer to other symbols, making them into referents in a never-ending chain of meaning.

The relationship between a symbol and a referent is the third element in meaning. It is an arbitrary relationship in which the referent becomes encoded in the symbol. Once this encoding takes place we cease to think of the symbol itself and focus our attention on what it refers to. Once learned, we take our symbolic codes for granted, often treating them as if equivalent to what they referred to.

We have now partially answered our question about the nature of meaning. At a minimum, meaning involves symbols and referents. We call this *referential meaning*. Although important, it does not take us very far toward understanding a culture. It only begins to scratch the surface of meanings encoded in the symbols people use. Consider a symbol from our own culture, the term *mouse*. Referentially, this symbol represents a small mammal, a rodent with four legs and a pink nose. But this referential definition does not say anything about children's longing for pet mice or the fear and repulsion some adults have for mice. It doesn't tell us that corporations produce and sell mouse poison, mouse traps, mouse cages, animated mouse films, and Mickey Mouse shirts and hats. It doesn't even hint at the fact that mice are used in scientific experiments or that our economy is based on myths about building a better mousetrap. It doesn't tell us when it is appropriate to call someone a *mouse*. A full cultural definition of this symbol would include all these things and many more.

One way that scholars have considered this larger sphere of meaning is by distinguishing *denotation* from *connotation*. Denotative meaning involves the things words refer to (what I have called referential meaning). *Mouse* denotes a small rodent. Connotative meaning includes all the suggestive significance of symbols, over and above their referential meaning. *Mouse* connotes a great many suggestive ideas.

Although this is a useful distinction, it tends to oversimplify the empirical situation faced by ethnographers. Take the case of a tramp who says that he "made a flop" on the previous night. We inquire, "What is a flop?" And in a cooperative mood he responds with a typical referential definition. "A flop is a place to sleep." *Flop*, then, in the culture of tramps, is a symbol that *denotes* a place to sleep. But on further inquiry we discover that the term flop appears to denote more than one hundred different kinds of places—everything from graveyards to stairwells are called flops. We could simply say that this symbol (the folk term *flop*) has more than one hundred referents. The problem with this is that it tells us nothing about the differences among them.

For purposes of ethnographic research, I think it is more useful to look at cultural meaning systems from the perspective of a relational theory of meaning. This will shift our attention away from what a particular symbol denotes and connotes to *the system of symbols that constitute a culture*.

Meaning Systems

Cultural knowledge is more than a collection of symbols, whether folk terms or other kinds of symbols. It is, rather, an intricately patterned *system* of symbols. All symbols, whether a spoken word like *flop*, an object such as a flag, a gesture like waving one's hand, a place like a church, or an event like a wedding, are parts of a system of other symbols.

A relational theory of meaning is based on the following premise: *the meaning of any symbol is its relationship to other symbols*. Rather than asking, "What does *flop* refer to?" we must examine how this symbol is related to others in the culture of tramps. The meaning of *flop* lies in its relationship to other symbols, including *stairwell, graveyard flop, all-night theater, ways to make a flop, policemen*, and many others. The ethnographer who wants to discover the meaning of *flop* must find out the nature of these relationships. A system of symbols can be likened to the stars that make up the Big Dipper. To the uninformed observer, these stars are merely pinpoints of meaningless light in the night sky. It is only by seeing the relationships among these stars that they take on the meaning we call the Big Dipper. Decoding cultural symbols involves far more than finding their referents; it requires that we discover the relationships that occur among these symbols.

You will recall that in the last chapter I introduced an important principle of ethnographic interviewing: *don't ask for meaning, ask for use*. This principle is based on the relational theory of meaning. When the ethnographer asks for meaning ("What does *days hanging* mean?"), the informant almost always responds with brief, referential definitions. But when the ethnographer asks for use ("What are some sentences in which you might use the term *days hanging*?"), informants reveal relationships between one term and many others. When I asked tramps to give me examples of how they used the term *days hanging*, they revealed relationships between this term and others like *suspended sentence, dead time, beating a drunk charge, rabbit*, etc. Listen for use, not meaning; this principle leads directly to decoding the full meaning of symbols in any culture. It also applies to participant observation and the study of nonverbal symbols: watch the way people use symbolic objects instead of merely inquiring about their meaning.

It is through the use of symbols that relationships are revealed, and these enable us to decode the rich meaning of the symbol.

Let us look at one of the most important ways that folk terms (and other symbols) are related to each other. Many symbols in all cultures *include* other symbols. Thus we can use a general term like *flop* or *tree* to refer to hundreds of specific types. When symbols are related by *inclusion,* we speak of them as categories.[6] Indeed, categories are so important in conveying cultural meaning that I will often use the terms *category, symbol,* and *folk term* interchangeably. Cultural symbols are cultural categories; folk terms are simply the primary type of cultural symbol under investigation in this book.

A category is an array of distinct things that we treat as if they were equivalent. I can distinguish the six trees in my backyard, but I also treat them all as equivalent by calling them *elms.* A Kwakiutl fisherman points to several silvery objects in the water, each slightly different in color, size, and shape; he calls them *fish,* thus treating them as equivalent. Three of them are *chums,* two are *silvers,* indicating the use of still other categories. The folk terms *fish, chums,* and *silvers* are thus related by inclusion; part of their meaning derives from this relationship. A child holds five metal objects in her hand, each of minutely different weight, size, and shape, yet she calls them all pennies and treats them as if they were equivalent. A Trobriand Islander points to four unique individuals, each different from the other in many ways, but he calls them all "my mother's brothers." Even large abstract chunks of experience can be treated as equivalent as when we refer to "the years of my childhood," or "the gods in heaven."

When symbols function as categories they serve to reduce the complexity of human experience. We can distinguish nearly one million colors but people in every society manage with less than a couple of dozen categories. They simplify the complexity of experience by using symbols that treat different shades as if they were all red, yellow, blue, etc. Without symbolic categories for everything we experience, we would become hopelessly enslaved to the particular. One of the most important functions of every human language is to provide people with ready-made categories for creating order out of the complexity of experience.

Perhaps the most confusing feature of symbolic categories is their variation in size. A simple category like *1876 flintlock rifles* includes a fairly small set of objects. Consider, on the other hand, the category *rifles,* which includes all the different kinds that have ever existed. And we can easily make *rifles* seem like an extremely small category by introducing *weapons,* a category that includes all rifles, handguns, spears, knives, bombs, brass knuckles, nuclear warheads, etc. When people talk, they convey meaning by bringing symbols into this relationship of inclusion with great ease. "I looked around for a *weapon.* I had no *knife* or *gun,* but then I picked up a small *piece of chipped quartz.*"

When you talk to your informant, it is difficult to tell which categories are included in others. The folk terms are arranged in sentences and usually there is little in the way of clues to this relationship of inclusion. Yet, if meaning is based on the relationships that symbols have to one another, it is necessary to identify this relationship of inclusion and other relationships. Many of the strategies that are discussed in the remainder of this book are designed to sort out the varying sizes or degrees of inclusiveness among categories.

Symbolic categories not only vary in size, they are related to each other in many other ways. Some categories include others, which, in turn, include still others. *Tree* includes *deciduous tree,* which includes *oak,* which includes *pin oak.* This kind of relationship suggests an image of a large box; when it is opened a smaller box appears inside; when that one is opened a still smaller box appears, and so on until we discover the last tiny container. But other categories are related by opposition with each other: *sun* and *moon, light* and *dark, male* and *female.* Still other categories belong to a larger set but contrast with each other inside that larger set. *Boys* and *girls* are both included in the category *children*; it's as if a large box were opened and inside were two smaller boxes, side by side. Sometimes symbols are related in a sequence, like children lined up for lunch in the cafeteria. The categories into which we divide our year—January, February, March, etc.—are related in this sequential manner. Many of the activities in which humans engage are symbols linked in sequence. For example, a traditional Protestant wedding ceremony involves a sequence of the *wedding march, giving away the bride, saying the vows, exchanging rings, kissing,* etc.

Let me summarize briefly the basic assertions of a relational theory of meaning:

1. Cultural meaning systems are encoded in symbols.
2. Language is the primary symbol system that encodes cultural meaning in every society. Language can be used to talk about all other encoded symbols.
3. The meaning of any symbol is its relationship to other symbols in a particular culture.
4. The task of ethnography is to decode cultural symbols and identify the underlying coding rules. This can be accomplished by discovering the relationships among cultural symbols.

In the rest of this chapter and the next we will examine ways to conduct a domain analysis. Then, in the remainder of this book, we will focus increasingly on strategies for discovering the relationships among the folk terms you collect from your informant.

DOMAINS[7]

Any symbolic category that includes other categories is a domain. All the members of a domain share at least one feature of meaning. In the process of discovering domains we will look especially for the similarities that exist among folk terms. Domains are the first and most important unit of analysis in ethnographic research.

Consider an example of a domain from the Tausug culture in the Philippines (Kiefer 1968). The category "friend" (*kabagayan*) includes eight other categories for different types of friends: ritual friend, close friend, casual friend, opponent, personal enemy, follower, ally, and neutral. In our culture we do not include enemies in the domain of friends, but for the Tausug, it is meaningful to do so. One reason that personal enemies (*bantah*) may be included in this domain is that through a special ceremony they can be transformed into ritual friends.

Domain Structure

The first element in the structure of a domain is a *cover term*. Cover terms are names for a category of cultural knowledge. *Tree,* for example, is a cover term in English for a larger category of knowledge, the various types of trees such as oak, pine, and yew. *Kabagayan,* in the Tausug language, is a cover term for the eight types of friends a person may have in Tausug society. *The bucket* is a cover term for dozens of places inside the Seattle City Jail, each named with a folk term known to tramps. In any sample of language collected through an ethnographic interview there will be numerous cover terms.

Second, all domains have two or more *included terms*. These are folk terms that belong to the category of knowledge named by the cover term. In searching for domains, the ethnographer often notices that informants use several different terms in the same way, thus suggesting they might be included terms. For example, an English-speaking informant might say, "We planted an elm, an oak, and three pines in our yard last summer." This usage suggests that elm, oak, and pine might all go together as included terms in some domain. I often overheard tramps talking about all the time they had spent in the *drunk tank* before they went to a *lock-up cell,* and then were transferred to the *trusty tank.* I tentatively grouped them together as members of a domain and later verified this by asking, "Are these all parts of *the bucket?*"

The third feature of all domains is a single *semantic relationship.*[8] When two folk categories are linked together, we refer to this link as a semantic relationship. Almost all simple definitions seem to be constructed by linking two concepts with a semantic relation. A child asks, "What is a Volkswagen?" and we define it by saying, "A Volkswagen is a kind of car," or "A

Volkswagen is a kind of foreign car." In each case the term to be defined (Volkswagen) has been linked by a semantic relation (*is a kind of*) to the term *car* and *foreign car*.

In a simple definition a semantic relationship links only two terms. In a domain the semantic relationship links a cover term to all the included terms in its set. For example, we can define an oak by saying, "An oak is a kind of tree." This is a simple definition. But if we go further to consider *oak* and *tree* as members of a domain, *tree* becomes the cover term and *oak* becomes one included term along with pine, spruce, elm, and hundreds of others. This, of course, is the semantic relationship of *inclusion* discussed earlier. The cultural knowledge of every society is made up of many such domains.

Finally, every domain has a *boundary*. This feature often goes unrecognized until an informant says something line, "No, that's not a tree, its a bush." The informant has called attention to the fact that some folk terms belong *inside* the domain and others belong *outside* the domain. The decision as to whether a term is a member of one domain or another must always be made by native informants. In studying tramps, for example, I began with the idea that the jail and the court were two different places. I treated these as symbols for places but did not see these symbols related by inclusion. I had visited the court on numerous occasions; it was a large room in the public safety building. The jail was somewhere else in that building, but clearly not part of the court. However, when I asked informants to tell me all the folk terms included in the domain *parts of the bucket,* I was surprised to discover that the *court* was a member of this domain along with places like the *delousing tank,* the *trusty tank,* and *the lock-up cell.* The boundary to this domain was quite different from what I would have thought as an outsider.

Another brief example will help to make this structure clear. The following statement was recorded in my field notes from an interview with a waitress-informant who worked at Brady's Bar:

A table of about seven guys deliberately gave me a lot of grief, each ordering separately instead of in a round like most guys do. They all wanted to pay with large bills, too. I ordered four Buds with and passed the glasses out and they decided they didn't want the glasses after all. I was mad but I kept smiling and saying, I'm sorry.

If we examine this statement, the following folk terms appear to fit the basic elements for a possible domain:

possible included terms:	"ordering separately" "paying with large bills"
possible cover term:	"give waitresses grief"
possible semantic relationship:	(X) is a way to (Y)

The basic structure can be stated in a single sentence: *Ordering separately* is a way to *give waitresses grief*. We can show the basic elements in the structure of a domain in the form of a diagram using these two examples (Figure 5.1).

Making a Preliminary Domain Search

The task of identifying and analyzing folk domains is one of the most difficult faced by ethnographers. For one thing, informants do not talk in domains but in sentences which skip rapidly from one domain to another. They do not, when speaking, arrange words in categories based on the relationship of inclusion, but arrange them in linear fashion, one word after another. In addition, although informants know the domains (including cover terms, included terms, and the relationship of inclusion) of their culture well, this knowledge is tacit, outside everyday awareness. It is often difficult to ask directly about domains. But by far the greatest barrier to discovering domains comes from the ethnographer's cultural background. Every investigator comes to the research with a large repertoire of analytic categories that are difficult to set aside. As one begins to search through interview transcriptions and field notes for clues to domains, it is like looking for something that is unknown. The temptation is to find a few folk terms, then, instead of pursuing the analysis completely through native terms, to organize most of the data into analytic categories from the professional culture of social science. Much ethnographic research suffers from what I call *shallow domain analysis*. In a sense, the ethnographer has changed horses in the middle of research—from the analysis of folk terms to imposition of analytic terms. Indeed, because of the difficulty of domain analysis, investigators who write about doing research suggest lists of analytic categories to use for organizing native cultures. As an example of such lists, I

FIGURE 5.1. Basic Elements in a Domain

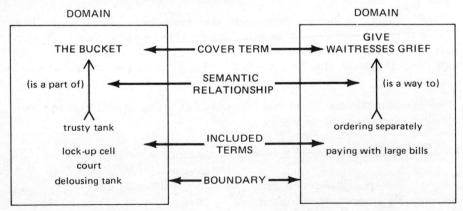

have presented one in Figure 5.2 prepared by another author. This list is not offered to guide your research, but to show how strong the temptation is to create order out of other cultures by imposing your own categories.

Because domain analysis is so difficult, I have found it best to begin with a preliminary search. This familiarizes the ethnographer with possible domains and helps us look at interview data in a different way. After making a preliminary search, it is easier to move on to a systematic search based on an understanding of semantic relationships. The next chapter discusses this more detailed procedure for domain analysis.

The first step in a preliminary domain search is to select a sample of verbatim notes from an ethnographic interview. (Verbatim notes of what people say, collected through participant observation, may also be used.) It is possible to make the search by using a single paragraph or even a few sentences or sentence fragments. The following description taken from my own field notes will provide a good sample for making a preliminary search.

This guy ordered a tequila and lime and that's all he said. So, I said I wanted a tequila and lime and the bartender said, "Fine." And he fixed it and I took it and the guy

FIGURE 5.2 Analytic Categories from Social Science[9]

TOPIC CATEGORIES

Life Cycle	*Travel and Transportation*
birth	paths and roads
naming	halting places
weaning	mode of travel
betrothal	
marriage	*Politics*
	methods of governance
Household Habits	figurehead, chieftain, leader
food	warfare
personal hygiene	
cleaning	*Economics*
	sources of income
Everyday Round	method of production
language	organization of work
division of labor	
	The Supernatural
Instructions to Children	fate of the dead
danger	spirits
taboos	prophets
customs	shrines
beliefs	sacred objects
fears	
	Forms of Ritual
Material Culture	prayer
styles of dress	offerings
kind of dwelling unit	ordeals
cultivation	oaths
manufacture	divinations

From *Notes and Queries in Anthropology.*

said, "No! I want tequila with a twist of lime and a salt shaker or a shot of tequila." So I had to take the drink back and the bartender was a little upset about it but he knew it wasn't my fault so he fixed the other drink. Then this one girl ordered a beer and tomato juice. She said, "I want a red beer." I said, "What?" I'd never heard of it before and it sounded really awful to me and I went up to the bartender and I said, "Could I have a tomato juice and beer?" And he looked really strange. "She wants it mixed together?" "Yes," I said, smiling. And so he got out a beer and a tomato juice. "Oh! Forget it! I'm not going to mix this stuff together!" And he put it on the tray and he didn't know how much to charge me because it's not a standard drink. Beer's fifty so he said, "Make it 75¢." So I took that over there and I said, "I'm sorry, but you'll have to mix it yourself, the bartender didn't know how you liked it."

The second step in a preliminary search is to look for *names for things*. This involves reading through the sample to look for folk terms that name things. It is usually easiest to search for nouns that label objects. These folk terms should be underlined and written on a separate sheet of paper. It is important *not* to identify all names for things on the first time through the sample, but to select only the names that seem to stand out. From the above interview sample with a cocktail waitress the following names for things seem quite obvious:

tequila and lime	beer
bartender	guy
drink	girl
beer and tomato juice	standard drink

The next step in a preliminary search is to see if any of these folk terms might be cover terms. Because cover terms are names for domains, and because they include many other folk terms, one clue is the use of the plural form. For example, if this informant had talked about *bartenders,* it would suggest that there *might* be more than one kind. As it turns out, the folk terms we have identified are all singular forms.

Another way to tentatively identify a possible cover term is to ask if any folk terms are being used for more than one thing. In this sample, the term *drink* is used several times, once to refer to the first tequila and lime, once to refer to the second tequila and lime, and once to refer to the beer and tomato juice by saying it was not a standard *drink*.

When a domain involves *names for things*, the nouns in that domain can usually be related as *kinds of* something (the cover term). In the example, the tequila and lime does seem to be a *kind of drink,* as does the beer and tomato juice. And so we have formulated an ethnographic hypothesis about a possible folk domain which we can state and represent in a diagram on page 105.

The final step in the preliminary search is to test the hypothesis by reading over additional interview data. For example, I would read through the entire

Ethnographic hypothesis: *tequila and lime and beer and tomato juice are kinds of drinks.*

interview from which the sample of statements came looking for additional *kinds of drinks*. Very soon I would come across *fancy drinks, screwdriver,* and *Hamms,* all terms which appear to be used in a way that suggests they are drinks. I would look for any references to the two hypothesized, included terms which might confirm they are kinds of drinks. For instance, I might discover that a customer had ordered saying, "Bring me two drinks: a tequila and lime and a screwdriver." In addition, every place where informants explicitly stated that something was a *kind of drink* would be underlined and transferred to a separate analysis page. The preliminary search ends when I have identified as many included terms as possible.

To summarize briefly, making a preliminary search for domains involves the following analytic tasks:

1. Selecting a sample of verbatim interview notes.
2. Looking for names for things.
3. Identifying possible cover terms and included terms from the sample.
4. Searching through additional interview notes for other included terms.

Having completed a preliminary search for one domain, the same process can be used to find additional domains which name things in the informant's world. In the next chapter we will discuss further how to expand the domain analysis and how to test the hypotheses with informants by using structural questions.

Tasks

5.1 Make a preliminary domain search to locate several domains which are names for things.

5.2 List the tentative cover term and included terms for each of the domains identified.

5.3 Conduct, record, and transcribe an ethnographic interview using primarily descriptive questions.

OBJECTIVES
1. To understand the nature of semantic relationships and their role in making a domain analysis.
2. To identify the steps in conducting a domain analysis.
3. To carry out a systematic domain analysis on all interview data gathered to date.
4. To introduce one or two structural questions into the ethnographic interview.

In the last step I presented the analytic procedures for making a preliminary domain search which focused on domains that are *names for things*. This preliminary search served only to introduce a beginning ethnographer to finding folk domains. Now we can move on to more systematic procedures called *domain analysis*, which will lead to finding other kinds of domains. Once the ethnographer has tentatively identified domains in a culture, it is necessary to test them with informants. This is done by asking structural questions to confirm or disconfirm hypothesized domains. In this chapter I will discuss *domain analysis* and in the next, *structural questions*.

DOMAIN ANALYSIS

Every culture has an enormous number of cover terms and an even larger number of included terms. Moreover, it is often difficult to tell from the way informants talk whether a particular folk term falls into one or the other class. This makes it difficult to search for new domains by merely looking for cover terms.

A more efficient procedure in identifying domains makes use of the semantic relationship as a starting point. From a growing body of research, it appears that the number of semantic relationships in any culture is quite small, perhaps less than two dozen. In addition, certain semantic relationships appear to be universal.[1] These remarkable facts make semantic relationships an extremely useful tool in ethnographic analysis. Using these relational concepts, the ethnographer can discover most of a culture's principles for organizing symbols into domains. Furthermore, because cultural meaning depends on the relationships among symbols, using these relational concepts leads directly to decoding the meaning of these symbols. Domain analysis begins by using semantic relationships rather than cover terms to discover domains. We want to look more closely at the nature of semantic relationships before identifying the steps in domain analysis.

Semantic Relationships

Every language contains a vast number of folk terms people can use to refer to things they experience. These names for things, events, qualities, processes, and actions make up most of the words that go into a typical dictionary. We all use such folk terms to convey meaning to others when we talk. However, most of the time we do not merely utter an isolated folk term or random lists of folk terms. Rather, we carefully select two or more and place them in a well-planned relationship to each other. For example, although in some special context someone might merely say *legs,* this term will more likely be spoken in relationship to other folk terms like *walk* (walk on your legs), *the body* (legs are part of the body), and *broken* (his legs were broken). When people talk, they almost always express themselves by using terms that are linked together by means of semantic relationships.

Semantic relationships are not the most obvious part of any utterance. In fact, they usually lie beneath the surface, hidden by the more apparent folk terms for things and actions. Listening to and analyzing talk, including what informants say during interviews, can be compared to observing people together. A man and woman are walking down the street and, as observers, we immediately note their sex. We also notice that the man is tall, the woman short. We observe that the woman walks evenly, the man limps. We easily recognize that these two people are distinct, animate objects (man, woman); we note their qualities (tall, short); we see their actions (walk, limp). However, it is much more difficult to recognize the relationship between this man and woman. Are they husband and wife? Mother and son? Grandmother and grandson? Colleagues who work together? Spies meeting for some clandestine purpose? Or merely strangers who happened, at that moment, to walk together? We would have to observe them closely in many different situations over a long period of time in order to grasp the relationship that links these two people together. In the same way, semantic relationships often seem much less obvious than the words they link together in ordinary speech.

Semantic relationships allow speakers of a particular language to refer to all the subtleties of meaning connected to its folk terms. *Her leg was broken* links an object and a condition, thus enabling a speaker to convey more meaning than by using either folk term alone. One of the first systematic studies to demonstrate the role of semantic relationships in the creation of meaning was done by Casagrande and Hale (1967). Working with Papago Indian informants in the Southwest, they started from a rather simple observation about how people acquire meaning. In every society, people learn the meaning of most words by hearing them used in everyday speech. However, Casagrande and Hale observed, "there will inevitably be occasions when the meanings of particular words must be explained to language learners, whether children or adults" (1967:165). This fact gives rise to a universal linguistic need for definitions. In literate societies dictionaries have, in part, filled this need. In nonliterate societies, people frequently make use of *folk definitions* to explain the meaning of words.

Casagrande and Hale set out to study Papago folk definitions. They collected a sample of about 800 definitions for objects, events, processes, qualities, and actions from many areas of Papago culture. One of the first things they discovered was that informants did not always respond with the *referential meaning* of a folk term. Instead, the definitions stated a variety of different relationships between the term being defined and other symbols. For example, an informant defined *leg* as that "with which we walk" and *throat* as that "through which we cause things to go while eating."

When Casagrande and Hale examined all these definitions in search of common characteristics, they did find an important similarity. All the definitions linked two or more folk terms together by means of a semantic relationship. They concluded that "a definition can be regarded as a statement of a semantic relationship between a concept being defined and one or more concepts, presumed to be known to the hearer (reader), and having properties considered relevant to the term being defined" (1967:167).

The next step in their research was to see if they could find similarities among the various semantic relationships used in the Papago folk definitions. They discovered thirteen types of semantic relationships from which all 800 definitions were constructed. For example, when an informant said that "a leg is that with which we walk," this implies the embedded relationship of *function*. The leg is being defined by its function of walking. Defining *key* as "that with which a door is opened" also makes use of the semantic relationship of function. The definition tells us what the key *does*. A complete list of the semantic relationships discovered by Casagrande and Hale is shown in Figure 6.1.

A number of other investigators have proposed similar types of semantic relationships as a result of their work in other cultures.[2] All agree that the number of semantic relationships is quite limited. In order to identify types, one must reduce what people actually say to a basic structure of two terms and a relationship. Depending on the analysis, one can enlarge or reduce the number of proposed semantic relationships. Oswald Werner has suggested, for example, that many if not all semantic relationships discovered to date can be reduced to three types: (1) taxonomy or inclusion (an oak is a kind of tree); (2) attribution (an oak has acorns); and (3) queueing or sequence (an oak goes through the stages of acorn, seedling, sapling, mature tree, etc.)[3] My interest here is not to discuss the evidence for a certain number of

FIGURE 6.1 Papago Semantic Relationships

RELATIONSHIP	EXAMPLES
1. *Attributive*: X is defined with respect to one or more attributes of Y.	A *scorpion* has a tail with a stinger; a *bee* makes honey; a *star* comes out at night.
2. *Contingency*: X is defined with relation to an antecedent or concomitant of Y.	*To wash*: If a person gets dirty, he washes himself; *to get mad*: when we do not like something, we get mad.
3. *Function*: X is defined as the means of effecting Y.	*Tooth*: that with which we chew things; *hat*: that with which we shade ourselves.
4. *Spatial*: X is oriented spatially with respect to Y.	*Bridge*: built across a wash or gully; *stinger*: stands on the end of scorpion's tail.
5. *Operational*: X is defined with respect to an action Y of which it is a goal or recipient.	*Pipe*: that which is smoked; *shirt*: that which we wear.
6. *Comparison*: X is defined in terms of its similarity and/or contrast with Y.	*Bat*: that which looks like a mouse; *willow*: that which looks like a cottonwood but its leaves are rather narrow.
7. *Exemplification*: X is defined by citing an appropriate co-occurrent Y.	*To shine on*: as when the sun goes over and gives us light; *red*: like our blood.
8. *Class inclusion*: X is defined with respect to its membership in a hierarchical class Y.	A *crane* is a bird; a *whale* is supposed to be a fish.
9. *Synonymy*: X is defined as an equivalent to Y.	*Thirsty* is wanting a drink; *amusing* is funny.
10. *Antonymy*: X is defined as the negation of Y, its opposite.	*Low* is not high; *rough* is not smooth.
11. *Provenience*: X is defined with respect to its source, Y.	*Milk*: we get it from a cow; *gold*: it comes out of a mountain.
12. *Grading*: X is defined with respect to its placement in a series or spectrum that also includes Y.	*Monday*, the one following Sunday; *yellow*, when something is white, but not very white.
13. *Circularity*: X is defined as X.	*To teach*: when someone teaches us something, we call it to teach.

Adapted from Casagrande and Hale (1967).

semantic relationships or their universality. Rather, I want to show how to use them as a tool for discovering folk domains. For this purpose, we can usefully divide semantic relationships into two types: *universal* and *informant expressed*.

Universal Semantic Relationships

Universal semantic relationships include all the general types proposed by Casagrande and Hale or anyone else. It has been proposed that these are types that occur in all human cultures. For example, all known languages employ the relation of *strict inclusion* (X is a kind of Y; a crane is a kind of bird).[4] The ethnographer can take any proposed list of universal relationships and use them to search for domains. For example, I took the relationship of strict inclusion and looked for folk terms used by tramps that might fit that relationship. I heard informants using the term *tramp* and I formulated the hypothesis that they might recognize different *kinds of tramps.* I then tested this hypothesis by asking, "Are there different kinds of tramps?" Informants responded with more than fifteen folk terms for the various kinds.

In my own research and in working with other ethnographers, I have found the following proposed universal semantic relationships the most useful for beginning an analysis of semantic domains.

1. Strict inclusion	X is a kind of Y
2. Spatial	X is a place in Y, X is a part of Y
3. Cause-effect	X is a result of Y, X is a cause of Y
4. Rationale	X is a reason for doing Y
5. Location for action	X is a place for doing Y
6. Function	X is used for Y
7. Means-end	X is a way to do Y
8. Sequence	X is a step (stage) in Y
9. Attribution	X is an attribute (characteristic) of Y

Informant-Expressed Semantic Relationships

Sometimes an informant will express a semantic relationship in a form identical to one on this list. A waitress-informant said, "A regular is a kind of customer." At other times, a phrase or sentence clearly uses one of these universal relationships, but it is embedded in a longer sentence and must be abstracted from that sentence. For example, a waitress said, "The worst kind of hassle is when people pay separately." Embedded in this statement is the following semantic relationship: "Paying separately (is a kind of) hassle." When there is little ambiguity about the underlying relationship, the ethnographer can proceed by using one of the universal relationships.

However, at other times, it is not so easy to identify one or another universal semantic relationship in what an informant says. In these cases it is best to work directly with some informant-expressed semantic relationship. For example, my tramp-informants would say something like, "You can make the Sally," or "Tramps often make the Sally." This informant-expressed relationship can be stated as "X (is something done by) Y" (Making the Sally (is something done by) tramps). This led to hypothesizing that tramps had customary things they did, one of which was to *make the Sally.* Rather than try to reduce this relationship to one that clearly fit the form of a universal relationship, I simply treated this as one form of a universal relationship expressed in my informant's idiom. I then went ahead and

111

searched for other members of this domain—things done by tramps. Later, as more terms were collected, this domain was formulated as *ways to make it used by tramps*. *Making the Sally, making the V.A.* (hospital), *junking*, and *making the blood bank*, were some of the included terms in this domain.

Ethnographic research as presented in this book is based on a relational theory of cultural meaning which I introduced in Step Five. Semantic relationships provide the ethnographer with one of the best clues to the structure of meaning in another culture. They lead directly to the larger categories (folk domains) that reveal the organization of cultural knowledge learned by informants. By keeping in mind a basic list of *universal relationships* and by searching for *informant-expressed relationships,* the ethnographer can find a doorway into the system of meaning of another culture. Now we can examine the specific steps that will unlock that doorway to meaning.

STEPS IN DOMAIN ANALYSIS

The following steps represent a set of tools for identifying folk domains. It is well to keep in mind that one can discover domains without such tools; children in every society make such discoveries with little difficulty. They merely listen to adults, ask questions, and observe the way people use language. However, like most adults, many of these domains remain part of their tacit knowledge. Ethnographic tools simply make the learning process faster, more explicit, and more systematic. However, all ethnographers will want to use the less formal approaches some of the time.

Step One: Select a single semantic relationship. In order to facilitate the discovery process it works best to begin with a universal semantic relationship. Then, after locating a number of domains, you can move to the use of informant-expressed semantic relationships discovered in your field notes. The two semantic relationships I suggest for making a start in domain analysis with English-speaking informants are *strict inclusion* (X is a kind of Y) and *means-end* (X is a way to Y). The former relation focuses your attention on nouns; the latter one on verbs. For purposes of illustration I will begin the analysis with strict inclusion.

Step Two: Prepare a domain analysis worksheet. Some ethnographers underline folk terms directly in their field notes or write in the margins to identify domains. Because it is necessary to review field notes repeatedly in search of new domains, I have found a separate worksheet a distinct advantage. It also helps to visualize the structure of each domain: cover term, semantic relationship, included terms, and boundary (see Figure 6.2).

Each domain analysis worksheet requires you to enter certain information before beginning the search: (1) the semantic relationship selected; (2) a statement of the form in which it is expressed; and (3) an example from your own culture of a sentence that has an included term, the semantic relation-

FIGURE 6.2. Domain Analysis Worksheet

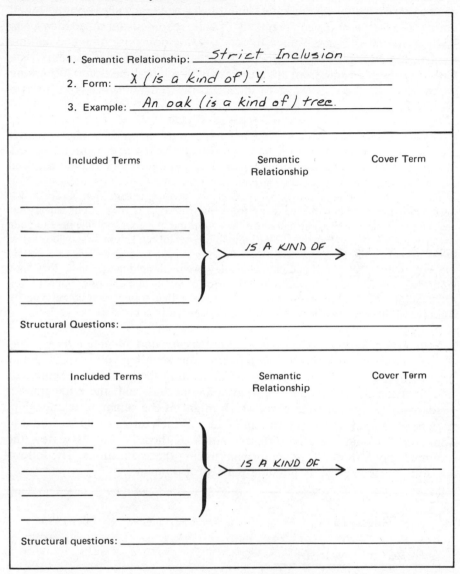

1. Semantic Relationship: *Strict Inclusion*
2. Form: *X (is a kind of) Y.*
3. Example: *An oak (is a kind of) tree.*

Included Terms   Semantic Relationship   Cover Term

} *IS A KIND OF* →

Structural Questions: _____

Included Terms   Semantic Relationship   Cover Term

} *IS A KIND OF* →

Structural questions: _____

ship, and a cover term (see Figure 6.2). The worksheet is divided into empty domains with blank spaces for immediately entering the semantic relationship you have selected. Then, both cover term and the included terms will be written in as you identify them from interviews and field notes. Making systematic use of this kind of worksheet will help to uncover domains embedded in the sentences spoken by your informants.

Step Three: Select a sample of informant statements. To begin with, one need only select a few paragraphs from transcribed interviews or notes taken during an interview. Even fragments of talk recorded during participation will provide an adequate source for discovering domains. As noted earlier, discovering domains always requires a verbatim sample of statements. The following sample came from an interview with a long-time tramp discussing where to flop. We can use it to illustrate the remaining steps in domain analysis.

You can take papers and stuff and flop in a box car. There's a lot of angles you can use to get a flop. Travelers Aid will help you. Hitchhiking to Chattenooga I slept in an old filling station in an old mortar box; picked up some grass they had just cut. You can make a bed with newspapers, cardboard on top. Cover up with newspapers. You can make a bed with rolled brown paper, dry grass, leaves, cotton from old seats, dry rags, and sponge rubber thrown away from mattresses. It's best to put newspaper next to you, a sheet under you and one over you, put it at a cold spot like next to your shoulders. I've slept in toilets in hotels, and in a hotel lobby. I slept on the floor in the Puget Sound and nobody spotted me. A flophouse runs from fity cents to a dollar. The bulls will bother you if you flop in an alley or an all-night laundromat, they spot you. They vag you or book you for drunk or for breaking and entering. Some places are a call job, like an orchard or under a bridge. Other tramps can bother you by snoring, telling you their troubles, just getting on your nerves.

Step Four: Search for possible cover terms and included terms that appropriately fit the semantic relationship. This search involves reading, but reading in a different manner. Instead of reading the *meaning* of sentences and focusing on the *content* of what someone has said, the ethnographer reads with an eye for folk terms which might fit the semantic relationship. You have to read with a question in mind: "Which terms could be a kind of something? Could there be different kinds of those?" Let us review the example above from a tramp informant asking these questions. The following folk terms emerge as possible parts of a domain.

Included Terms		Semantic Relationship	Cover Term
all-night laundromat	box car		
filling station	toilets		
mortar box	hotel lobby	is a kind of	flop
flophouse	alley		
orchard	under bridge		

Most of the time, especially when small samples of interview material are used, not more than two or three included terms emerge. Indeed, often this approach leads to folk terms which appear important but only fit one side of the semantic relationship. For example, we could enter the following term for a possible domain from the last sentence:

Included terms	Semantic Relationship	Cover Term
?	is a kind of	trouble

Or we could hypothesize the following relationship:

Included terms	Semantic Relationship	Cover Term
Tramp	is a kind of	?

It is important not to overlook such terms because they still provide the basis of structural questions like "Are there different kinds of troubles that tramps talk about?" and "Is a tramp a kind of something?" Let's look at one other possible domain, this time using a different semantic relationship.

---

1. Semantic relationship: means-end

2. Form: X (is a way to) Y

3. Example: Reviewing notes (is a way to study)

Included terms		Semantic Relationship	Cover Term
vaging you	snoring		
booking you			
telling you	troubles	is a way to	bother you
getting on	your nerves		

It should be pointed out that all references to *who* bothers a tramp were eliminated. The domain consists of *actions,* or things people do that bother tramps. Later, when we discuss componential analysis, we will see that the other information (such as who bothers tramps and where they are bothered) will become important.

The first four steps in domain analysis lead directly to a set of ethnographic hypotheses. In the first example we have generated the following hypotheses about tramp culture:

1. That tramps recognize a folk domain (category) called *kinds of flops.*
2. That each of the included terms (box car, mortar box, etc.) is recognized by tramps as a member of this domain (kinds of flops).
3. That this domain has additional included terms yet to be discovered.

In cases where the ethnographer only identifies a cover term or included terms, but not both, the first or second hypotheses above can still be made, but in modified form. From earlier examples, I would hypothesize that tramps recognize a folk domain that includes *tramp,* but that the name of that domain remains to be discovered. Also, that tramps recognize a folk domain, *kinds of trouble,* but any included terms are yet to be discovered.

Hypotheses such as these must be tested. The ethnographer cannot assume the truth of such assertions without reviewing field notes, making observations, and checking with informants. But before any of these hypotheses can be tested, we must carefully formulate the questions that can either confirm or disconfirm them. This leads us to the next step in domain analysis.

Step Five: Formulate structural questions for each domain. Structural questions were first identified in Step Two as tools for discovering information about a folk domain. These specially designed ethnographic questions enable the ethnographer to elicit from an informant such items as cover terms and included terms. Eventually we can discover the boundary of any particular folk domain. Structural questions are also specifically designed to test the ethnographic hypotheses that have emerged from domain analysis. In the next chapter we will discuss the major types of structural questions.

A structural question makes use of the semantic relationship of a domain and terms from either one side or the other of the relationship (either the cover term or an included term). In order to formulate a structural question, the ethnographer must first know the way in which questions are asked in the culture studied. Then, taking the basic information from domain analysis, we simply rewrite it as a question. Let's look again at our examples from tramp culture. I hypothesized that *kinds of flops* was the name of one domain. This can be rewritten as a question: "Are there different kinds of flops?" If an informant responds positively to this question (yes, there are different kinds of flops) then the hypothesis is confirmed. If an informant responds negatively, it has been disconfirmed (with this informant). If confirmed, I would formulate a second kind of structural question: "What are all the different kinds of flops?" By repeatedly asking this question, I could elicit all the included terms known to informants.

When the ethnographer begins to rewrite *statements about domains* into *questions about domains* (structural questions), it often becomes necessary to revise earlier formulations. For example, I hypothesized the domain *ways to bother you.* But when we try to rewrite this as a structural question ("Are there different ways to bother you?") it is immediately apparent that it lacks contextual information. It can be rewritten in more meaningful ways, each of which implies a revision of how the domain is stated: (1) Are there different ways that tramps bother tramps? (X is a way to bother tramps) and (2) Are there different ways that people bother tramps? (X is a way that people bother tramps.) Although I have the intuitive feeling that these additional questions will tap my informants' knowledge of the original domain, I will also have to test these questions to see if they are meaningful to informants.

Step Six: Make a list of all hypothesized domains. The goal of a domain analysis is twofold: to identify native categories of thought and to gain a preliminary overview of the cultural scene you are studying. The first five steps in making a domain analysis should be repeated to expand the list of domains. At first this appears to be an endless task, but the number of domains are limited and soon you will have identified many of the major domains your informant has talked about thus far. In order to gain an overview of the cultural scene and select domains for more intensive study, make a separate list of all the domains you have hypothesized. The following list is an example of some domains from an ethnographic study of Collier's Encyclopedia salespeople.[5]

DOMAIN	SEMANTIC RELATION	STRUCTURAL QUESTION
Kinds of presentations	X is a kind of Y	Are there different kinds of presentations?
Kinds of training classes	X is a kind of Y	What are all the different kinds of training classes?
Kinds of Welcome Colliers signs	X is a kind of Y	What are all the kinds of Welcome Colliers signs?
Parts of an area	X is a part of Y	What are all the parts of an area?
Parts of a presentation	X is a part of Y	What are all the parts of a presentation?
Parts of a contract	X is a part of Y	What are all the parts of a contract?
Results of missing the wife	X is a result of Y	What are all the results of missing the wife?
Results of getting enthused	X is a result of Y	What are all the results of getting enthused?
Results of getting negative	X is a result of Y	What are all the results of getting negative?
Reasons for getting negative	X is a reason for Y	What are all the reasons for getting negative?
Reasons for summer contest	X is a reason for Y	What are all the reasons for the summer contest?
Reasons for keeping a door record	X is a reason for Y	What are all the reasons for keeping a door record?
Reasons for cherry picking	X is a reason for Y	What are all the reasons for cherry picking?

117

Places to find hidden clues	X is a place to Y	What are all the places to find hidden clues?
Places to get a triple	X is a place to Y	What are all the places to get a triple?
Places for pickup points	X is a place for Y	What are all the places for pickup points?
Uses for briefcases	X is a use for Y	What are all the uses for briefcases?
Uses for broadsides	X is a use for Y	What are all the uses for broadsides?
Ways to get enthused	X is a way to Y	What are all the ways to get enthused?
Ways to give a qualifier	X is a way to Y	What are all the ways to give a qualifier?
Ways to do a close	X is a way to Y	What are all the ways to do a close?
Ways to knock	X is a way to Y	What are all the ways to knock?
Stages in retraining	X is a stage in Y	What are all the stages in retraining?
Stages in closing a deal	X is a stage in Y	What are all the stages in closing a deal?
Stages in a year	X is a stage in Y	What are all the stages in a year?
Stages in selling books	X is a stage in Y	What are all the stages in selling books?

In this chapter we have examined procedures for discovering domains and culturally relevant structural questions. These procedures, called domain analysis, consist of six interrelated steps:

1. Selecting a single semantic relationship
2. Preparing a domain analysis work sheet
3. Selecting a sample of informant statements
4. Searching for possible cover terms and included terms that appropriately fit the semantic relationship.
5. Formulating structural questions for each domain
6. Making a list of all hypothesized domains

In order to proceed with the next steps in the Developmental Research Sequence it is necessary to carry out a systematic domain analysis using all interview data collected to date. Domain analysis is not a once-for-all procedure; it must be repeated as new data are collected through interviews. Every few weeks throughout a research project, the ethnographer will want to use these procedures to find new domains.

TASKS

6.1 Following the steps presented in this chapter, conduct a thorough domain analysis on all material collected from ethnographic interviews to date.

6.2 Make a summary list of all hypothesized domains discovered and review it to ascertain possible domains for further research.

6.3 Conduct an ethnographic interview using primarily descriptive questions, but introduce several structural questions to further explore several domains.

OBJECTIVES
1. To identify the various kinds of structural questions.
2. To learn how to use structural questions in ethnographic interviews.
3. To test hypothesized domains and discover additional included terms for those domains by asking structural questions.

Let us review briefly where the Developmental Research Sequence has brought us. We began with three preparatory steps: (1) Locating an informant; (2) Interviewing an informant; and (3) Making an ethnographic record. With Step Four the actual ethnographic interviews began by (4) Asking descriptive questions. Using the sample of language collected from this interview, we went on to the next step, which introduced strategies for (5) Analyzing ethnographic interviews. This was followed by (6) Making a domain analysis, following the steps outlined in the last chapter. This analysis resulted in structural questions which will be employed in future interviews. By following the steps thus far, you have selected an informant, conducted three ethnographic interviews, and undertaken an in-depth analysis to discover the folk categories into which the culture is divided. We are now ready to test these hypothesized folk categories (domains) and discover additional included terms. In the last interview with an informant you introduced several structural questions. In this chapter I want to examine several important interviewing principles the ethnographer should follow in asking this type of question. Then I will present all the different types of structural questions.

PRINCIPLES FOR ASKING STRUCTURAL QUESTIONS

Structural questions need to be adapted to each individual informant, meshed with other kinds of questions, and skillfully repeated over and over again. Each of the following principles will serve as guides for using structural questions.

Concurrent Principle

Ask structural questions *concurrently* with descriptive questions. They complement rather than replace descriptive questions. Although the Developmental Research Sequence goes from descriptive questions to structural questions to contrast questions, the ethnographer never proceeds from descriptive to structural to contrast *interviews*. Descriptive questions will make up part of every interview. From this point on, structural questions will also find their way into every interview. And beginning with Step Nine, contrast questions will become part of each interview. Indeed, with new informants from the same cultural scene, an experienced ethnographer will make use of all types of ethnographic questions almost from the start.

The concurrent principle means that it is best to *alternate* the various types of questions in each interview. For example, the following sequence shows how this might occur:[1]

ETHNOGRAPHER: You mentioned that the deaf use different ways to communicate. What are some of these? (Structural question)

INFORMANT: Yes, they can use writing, lipreading, sign language like ASL or signed English, and pantomiming. (Included terms)

ETHNOGRAPHER: Can you give me an example of signed English? (Descriptive question)

INFORMANT: Oh, yes. Like you might sign, I will go to the store, using signs for all the words in English and also indicating the future tense, will go.

ETHNOGRAPHER: Can you tell me more about signed English: when people use it, how deaf people feel about it, and maybe your experience using it? (Descriptive question)

INFORMANT: Well, most really deaf people learn ASL and some have trouble with signed English. Most times you can tell when it's a hearing person using sign because they use Signed English. That's what they always used when I went to school with hearing kids, but at home we used ASL.

ETHNOGRAPHER: Let's go back to the other ways to communicate. You said that ASL, signed English, writing, lipreading, and pantomiming were all ways to communicate. Can you think of any other ways the deaf use to communicate? (Structural question)

INFORMANT: Oh, yes. There's speaking. Some deaf use that, and then there's Qued Speech, that's something developed by a professor at Gallaudet College. (Included terms)

Alternating questions is different from simply including each type of question in an interview; they are thoroughly mixed together in an almost random fashion. This will not only keep an informant from becoming bored, but it relieves any anxiety created by the test-like-effect of structural and contrast questions. Take a question like ''Can you tell me all the different kinds of cars?'' Most of us would immediately feel overwhelmed if asked this question. However, by asking, ''What are *some* of the different kinds of cars?'' and by interspersing answers with descriptive questions about the cars one has owned, the cars owned by friends, and the cars one would like to own, the task becomes easier. The concurrent principle is a guide to making interviews as much like friendly conversations as possible.

Explanation Principle

Structural questions often require an explanation. Although ordinary conversation is sprinkled with structural questions in one form or another (What kind of car did you buy? What kinds of cars have you thought about buying?), they are not as common as descriptive questions. In a sense, the ethnographer moves further away from the friendly conversation when introducing structural questions. Unless informants understand this, a structural question may take them off guard and limit their response. Consider two examples drawn from a study of ballet culture; each example uses the same structural question, but one does not include an explanation.[2]

1. What are all the different kinds of exercises you do in ballet class?
2. We've been talking about your ballet classes and you've mentioned some of the different exercises you do in class. Now, I want to ask you a slightly different kind of question. I'm interested in getting a list of *all* the different kinds of exercises done in class or at least all the ones you have done since you started taking ballet. This might take a little time, but I'd like to know all the different types, what you would call them.

The second example will assist informants to respond far more than the first one. Sometimes an ethnographer can go further and explain the purpose of gathering a long list of included terms. Consider the following example from a study of Collier's Encyclopedia salespeople:[3]

ETHNOGRAPHER: I've learned from other salespeople that certain phrases or sayings are used pretty often, like "Hooray for Colliers!" Would you use that phrase?
INFORMANT: Oh, yes, all the time.
ETHNOGRAPHER: Well, if I'm going to understand the meaning of phrases like this, what they mean to you and other salespeople, I need to go into this whole area in depth. First, I'd like to know all the different phrases that are used frequently when you're with other salespeople. After we get a list of all the different ones we can go back over them and find out how each kind is different from the others. O.K., let's begin. Can you tell me some different phrases I would hear from Colliers salespeople when they are together?
INFORMANT: Well, there is "Hooray for Colliers," "Rock 'em and sock 'em," "Fantastic," "I'm enthused," and "Are we oysters or are we eagles?"

Native-language explanations are especially important when asking structural questions (see Step Two). The ethnographer merely prefaces the structural questions with a reminder like "I'm interested in the way you and other ballet dancers refer to exercises, what you would call them in class."

Or, in asking about exercises, one might include the word *name*. "What are the names you would use for all the different kinds of exercises?" Informants need continual reminders that the ethnographer wants to understand their ordinary language.

Explaining the nature of structural questions will often take the form of examples. For instance, the ethnographer can take some familiar domain, possibly one shared with the informant, and use that as an example to make clear the nature of a structural question. In a study of a large midwestern costume shop, a structural question could be introduced in the following way:[4]

I'm interested in all the different kinds of masquerade wear (folk term for costumes) that you rent to customers. Now, if I asked you, are there different kinds of trees, you could probably think of some, like pine tree, an oak, and a birch. Either of us could list a lot of trees. But you have learned to recognize many different kinds of masquerade wear, and I've never heard of most of them. In fact, I'd probably call them all *costumes*. Can you list as many different kinds of masquerade wear as you can think of?

Another type of example, one used almost all the time, repeats the included terms already discovered. I make it a rule never to ask a structural question without repeating at least some of the included terms (if I know them) for the informant. This serves to make clear what I want to know and it jogs the memory of the informant. Here are two typical structural questions which include this repetition of included terms:

1. I'm interested in knowing all the different ways the deaf use to communicate. You mentioned *ASL, signed English, pantomiming, speaking, Qued Speech,* and *writing.* Can you think of any other ways the deaf use to communicate?
2. We've talked about your classroom and all the things you do there during school. Now, I'd like to ask you a different kind of question about all the parts of the room, so I can get them clear. You said there was the *doorway,* where you come in; and there's the *blackboard,* that's a part of the room. And the *reading center,* and the *bulletin board.* Can you think of any other parts of the classroom?

By listing several known included terms in this manner, most informants immediately recall additional terms. One such example speaks more clearly than several explanations.

Repetition Principle

Structural questions must be repeated many times to elicit all the included terms of a folk domain. Take the example of kinds of flops. This large domain was explored by the question "What are all the different kinds of flops?" Never once did an informant volunteer all the more than one hundred different types in answer to this single question. For one thing, most informants did not believe I could possibly want to know all the types. More important, they couldn't recall them all. By repeating the question many times during an interview ("Can you think of any other flops?") and during many different interviews, I was able to assist informants to remember the entire list.

In his study of plants (folk botany) among the Haunoo in the Phillippines, Harold Conklin found that informants knew nearly 1400 types of plants. To elicit all the names in this folk domain required great ingenuity to think of ways to vary the question and to repeat it under many different circumstances (Conklin 1954).

One reason for asking structural questions concurrently with descriptive questions is to reduce the boredom and tediousness that come with constant repetition. The goal in all this repetition is to exhaustively elicit the folk terms in a domain, to discover all the included terms known to informants. Only then can the ethnographer proceed to find the differences and similarities among the domain members.

Context principle

When asking structural questions, provide the informant with contextual information. This places the informant in the setting where the domain is relevant. For example, a brief structural question like "Can you think of any other kinds of flops?" was effective for someone whom I had previously asked numerous structural questions about flops. However, it was not effective for a new informant. When a structural question of this sort is first introduced, the following kind of contextual information is required.

ETHNOGRAPHER: I've learned from other tramps that one thing tramps do when they travel is make a flop. Is that right? Is making a flop something common among tramps?

INFORMANT: Yes, they're always lookin' for a flop, especially when you're on the road.

ETHNOGRAPHER: I suppose that as you travel from one town to another you have come across a lot of different kinds of flops?

INFORMANT: Sure have. One time in Chattanooga, I made a flop in a mortar box, in an old filling station. And some guys make a flop in a hotel lobby or the toilet of an old hotel.

ETHNOGRAPHER: Well, I'm interested in finding out about all the different kinds of flops that tramps make use of. Not only the ones you have used, but those used by tramps you have talked to. Do tramps ever talk about the flops they make?

INFORMANT: Yes, they talk about that a lot, 'cause making a flop is one of the most important things to a tramp. You often see a guy on the skid and you know he's either trying to make a jug or trying to make a flop. He might be panhandling or something but he's trying to make a flop.

ETHNOGRAPHER: O.K., now let's go back to my earlier question and I'd like to write down as many kinds of flops as you can tell me about. What are all the different kinds of flops that you know about? I realize there may be a lot and if you can't think of them all now, that is O.K. We can come back to it later, but why don't you start with the ones you can think of?

Consider another example which recreates the contexts in which an informant would normally use the information desired.

ETHNOGRAPHER: Colliers salespeople often work together and you attend a lot of meetings with other salespeople, right?

INFORMANT: Oh, yes. We're together almost every day, either on the road or in training classes or meetings.

ETHNOGRAPHER: Well, from what others have said and from what you have told me, when salespeople are together, they often use short phrases, things that might get people ready to sell or keep them going even when times are tough. Like "Hooray Colliers!"

INFORMANT: (Laughs) Sure, you hear things like that all the time.

ETHNOGRAPHER: Well, if I went out selling with a group and we were all together in the car, say just arriving at a place where we would sell, what kinds of sayings or phrases that people repeat a lot would I hear? If you can't think of them all, that's fine, we can come back to it later, but why don't you tell me the ones you can think of.

Adding contextual information expands a structural question. It aids greatly in recall and will avoid the problem of making an informant feel he is being tested with a series of short questions. The series of structural questions generated from a domain analysis are not the same as a questionnaire that lists a series of questions. They are not even the same as a set of questions one might prepare for an interview guide, questions to be asked one after the other. Rather, structural questions must be seen as tools, each to be adapted to particular informants, each used over and over to exhaustively explore a folk domain. Providing contextual information is merely one way to better adapt an extremely useful tool to the interview situation.

Cultural Framework Principle

The ethnographer must phrase structural questions in cultural as well as personal terms.[5] In a previous example the question was asked in both ways:

Personal: What are all the different kinds of flops that *you* know about?
Cultural: I'm interested in finding out about all the different kinds of flops that *tramps* make use of.

It is often easier for an informant to begin responding to questions about his or her own personal experience. "What are the kinds of masquerade wear that you have rented to customers?" "What are all the kinds of drinks you have served at Brady's Bar?" But before exhausting the information known to an informant, it is important to rephrase questions in cultural terms. "What are all the drinks served at Brady's?" "What are all the kinds of masquerade wear a person could possibly rent at the store?" Sometimes an informant needs to be reminded that they know about the experiences of others: "You have heard from other waitresses about the hassles they have, I'm sure. I'd like to know, not only the ones you know about from personal experience, but all the ways that waitresses might get hassled, all the ways you can recall from what others have told you or what you have seen."

As we now discuss the different kinds of structural questions, keep in mind that their exact form will change as you follow the concurrent principle, the explanation principle, the repetition principle, the context principle, and the cultural framework principle.

KINDS OF STRUCTURAL QUESTIONS

There are five major types of structural questions and several subtypes (Figure 7.1). Although some serve different functions, most represent alternative ways to verify the existence of a folk domain or to elicit folk terms included in a folk domain. With some informants I have used all five types of questions; with others, a particular structural question works better than others. The ethnographer must be sensitive to individual responses to each type of question, using those best suited to each informant.

1. Verification Questions

Verification questions ask an informant to confirm or disconfirm hypotheses about a folk domain. They provide the informant with information and a request for a yes or no answer. Let's say I have hypothesized that a *hotel*

FIGURE 7.1 Kinds of Structural Questions

1. Verification Questions
   1.1. Domain Verification Questions
   1.2. Included Term Verification Questions
   1.3. Semantic Relationship Verification Questions
   1.4. Native-Language Verification Questions
2. Cover Term Questions
3. Included Term Questions
4. Substitution Frame Questions
5. Card Sorting Structural Questions

lobby and an *alley* are both kinds of flops. I can confirm or disconfirm this hypothesis by asking, "Is a hotel lobby a kind of flop? Is an alley a kind of flop?" In addition to asking verification questions about terms discovered during domain analysis, the ethnographer also seeks to verify those elicited directly from informants. If an informant gives a long list of items in response to a question during one interview, it is important to begin the next interview with a verification question. For example, one might say, "During our last talk you told me many of the different kinds of masquerade wear. I'd like to go over the ones you told me, just to quickly see if I have them all correct. You would say that *animals* are one kind of masquerade wear? *Clown things? Eastern costumes? Thirties-type stock? Tiger suit? Gorilla suit? Superman?*" After each question informants should respond yes or no to indicate whether the terms belong to the domain.

1.1 Domain Verification Questions.   This type of question seeks to verify the existence of a domain for which the ethnographer has hypothesized a cover term. It takes the following form: "Are there different kinds of Y's?" (Y is a cover term.)

In her study of midwest junior high school teachers, Gregory (1976) hypothesized the cover term *kinds of groups*. Her informant confirmed this hypothesis by an affirmative answer to the verification question: "Are there different kinds of groups here at Midwest Junior High?" It is also possible to confirm domains by examining interview data or other field notes. If informants make direct reference to the existence of different kinds of groups, one can move on to other kinds of structural questions. For example, from participant observation Starr knew that people recognized different ethnic groups in Lebanon (1978). He merely started asking, "What kinds of groups are there in Lebanon?" People responded to this query with folk terms like *Moslems, Alawi, Kurds, Japanese,* and *foreigners*. This confirmed the folk domain and also led to included terms.

1.2. Included Term Verification Questions.   This type of question seeks to verify whether one or more terms are included in a domain. It takes the form "Is X a kind of flop?" or "Is X a way to hassle waitresses?" One could verify the ethnic groups from the last example by asking, "Are Moslems a kind of group in Lebanon?" This type of structural question assumes that both a cover term and one or more included terms are known to the ethnographer.

1.3. Semantic Relationship Verification Questions.   The ethnographer may have hypothesized a domain on the basis of some universal semantic relationship which informants find awkward. For this reason it is often necessary to test the appropriateness of the way a semantic relation is expressed. For example, although *kinds of groups* might be the best way to express the relationship for people at Midwest Junior High, this can be tested. You could ask, "How would most teachers say it, that administrators are a kind of group? Or that administrators are one group?" You can ask directly in many cases: "Would tramps ever say, 'a hotel lobby is a kind of flop?' " Some semantic relationships require testing more than others. For example, in studying a school classroom one might hypothesize that there are different parts of a classroom. "Would you say, 'different *parts of a class*?' " This might lead to the response, "No, there are different *places in a class.*" I might search for several possible semantic relations which would express a domain, then ask, "Would it be better to say that a bulletin board is part of the classroom or a place in the classroom?" Sometimes an informant will say, "Either one is OK," suggesting two closely related domains or two ways to express the same relationship. By emphasizing the semantic relationship, the ethnographer can quickly gain the help of an informant to identify the most appropriate phrase.

1.4. Native-Language Verification Questions. No matter how long one has interviewed an informant, the tendency to translate never disappears. For this reason it is necessary to continually verify whether a particular term is a *folk term* rather than a *translation* created for the benefit of the ethnographer. Native-language verification questions take the form "Is this a term you would use?" or "Would most tramps usually say _____ when talking with other tramps?" Consider the following example of how a native-language verification question might be used to discover if the phrase *places to sleep* is a translation of a native folk term:

ETHNOGRAPHER: Tramps have a lot of different places they can make a flop, is that right?"
INFORMANT: Yes. You can sleep in a box car or at the Sally or in a flophouse.
ETHNOGRAPHER: Are there any other places?
INFORMANT: Yes, you can sleep in a hotel lobby, a window well, there must be dozens of other places to sleep.
ETHNOGRAPHER: What would you call all these places?
INFORMANT: Well, they're just all places to sleep?
ETHNOGRAPHER: Would tramps ever call them *flops*?
INFORMANT: Oh yes! That's the term we would always use. I'm trying to make a flop, or I had a good flop last night.

It may seem an unimportant distinction made between *places to sleep* and *a flop*. However, our assumption is that people code and store information about their experience by using highly salient folk terms. Certainly one attribute of *flop* is that it is a place to sleep, but that is not synonymous with *flop*. If you ask, "What are all the places a tramp can sleep?" you will not elicit all the terms in a folk domain about flops. Even if the two terms were synonymous, it is our assumption that recall will be much more exhaustive by using folk terms most familiar to the informant. Native-language verification questions about domains will be interspersed throughout every interview, for they allow the ethnographer to check on the tendency of most informants to translate.

2. Cover Term Questions

This type of structural question is the one most frequently used. It can be asked whenever you have a cover term. Here is a list of examples:

Kinds of bulls	Are there different kinds of bulls?
Kinds of groups	Are there different kinds of groups at Midwest Junior High?
Ways to get tips	Are there different ways to get tips?
Steps in making a sale	What are all the different steps in making a sale of encyclopedias?

When your informant answers such questions affirmatively, it is easy to continue asking, "Could you tell me what some of them are?" or "Can you think of any others?" If your informant answers in the negative, it may indicate that you do not have a cover term or that it is an area outside your informants' knowledge.

3. Included Term Questions

Every folk domain has two or more included terms. Sometimes these surface before you have discovered the cover term for the domain (if it exists). For example, a clerk at the costume shop might say, "I rented so many things today—Peter Pan, Robin Hood, Raggedy Andy, Little Lord Fauntleroy, and a bunch of others." You could then ask the following questions:

ETHNOGRAPHER: Are Peter Pan, Robin Hood, Raggedy Andy, and Little Lord Fauntleroy all the same kind of thing?
INFORMANT: Yes, they're all kinds of miscellaneous character costumes.
ETHNOGRAPHER: Are there any other kinds of miscellaneous character costumes?

Included term questions are often awkward to ask. If you only have one term, they may confuse your informant: "Is rainy weather a reason for something? Is panhandling a way to something?" For this reason, it is probably best to reserve these questions for times when you have collected several terms, which by their use you are sure belong in the same domain.

129

4. Substitution Frame Questions

Substitution frames are a way to ask structural questions. They are constructed from a normal statement used by an informant. One term is removed from the sentence and an informant is asked to *substitute* other meaningful terms. Here is a sample substitution frame:

1. Original statement: You find bulls in the bucket.
2. Substitution frame: You find ——— in the bucket.
3. Substitution frame question: Can you think of any other terms that might go in that sentence?
4. Responses: (a) You find *drunks* in the bucket.
   (b) You find *turnkeys* in the bucket.
   (c) You find *trusties* in the bucket.

Obviously, these three kinds of people could have been discovered by asking a cover term question: What are all the different kinds of people in the bucket. However, under some conditions, substitution frames are more effective. Because they do not alter the original utterance, they may be easier for informants to use. At one point in my research with tramps I became interested in knowing about relationships between bulls and tramps. I began with a single informant sentence: "Sometimes a bull will hit a tramp for no reason at all." This led to two substitution frames. (1) Sometimes a bull will ——— a tramp for no reason at all, and (2) Sometimes a bull will hit a tramp ———————. The first frame elicited things like, *take shoes to, bust, pinch, break a bottle over,* etc. The second frame elicited things like *because he's down on you, because he thinks you're going to fight, because he's had a hard day.*

When using substitution frames the same sentence has numerous possibilities, but it is best to make the sentences short and simple, with a single term removed for substitution. One of the best strategies for asking substitution frame questions is to write the original sentence out on a piece of paper. Then, write it again just below the first one, but insert a blank for the words you have removed. This visual representation makes it easy for an informant to fill in the blank with appropriate terms.

5. Card Sorting Structural Questions[6]

Structural questions almost always elicit a list of folk terms. A particular list may begin quite small but often it grows, making it difficult for informants. Writing terms on cards helps to elicit, verify, and discuss a domain. For example, I wrote all the different kinds of tramps on cards. Then I placed these cards in front of an informant and asked, "Are these all kinds of tramps?" This verification question was made easier by the use of cards.

Card sorting can occur in several ways. After I had collected a list of many different things that bulls could do to tramps, I wrote the terms on cards. Then I gave the pack of cards to an informant (nearly fifty cards) and asked, "Which of these would a *turnkey* (one kind of bull) do?" "Which of these would a *ragpicker* (another kind of bull) do?" If you have collected a number of terms that appear to go in the same domain, writing them on cards and asking informants to sort out the ones which are all the same kind of thing quickly leads to finding the boundary of a folk domain.

I have found it useful to write cover terms on a card of one color, included terms on cards of another color. As new included terms are discovered during an interview, they can be written on a separate card and placed beneath the cover term. This gives informants a visual sense of the relationships among the folk terms you are investigating and enables them to cooperate more fully.

Structural questions all function to explore the organization of an informant's cultural knowledge. They lead the ethnographer to discover and verify the presence of folk domains, cover terms for these domains, and the included terms. By using structural questions, the ethnographer does not need to impose analytic categories to organize the data from interviews or participant observation. Ethnography is more than finding out what people know; it also involves discovering how people have organized that knowledge.

Tasks

7.1 Prepare, in writing, structural questions of each type for several domains. Prepare explanations for these questions.

7.2 Conduct an ethnographic interview using structural questions to verify terms already collected and to collect terms for new domains. (Alternate with descriptive questions.)

7.3 Prepare a list of all verified domains with cover terms and included terms.

OBJECTIVES
1. To select a tentative focus for in-depth analysis.
2. To understand folk taxonomies and how they organize domains.
3. To learn how to do a taxonomic analysis.
4. To construct a folk taxonomy for one or more domains by
   following the steps for doing taxonomic analysis.

By following the steps in the Developmental Research Sequence you have now identified many different domains in
the cultural scene you selected for study. Through four
ethnographic interviews, in which you have asked both descriptive and structural questions, you have elicited a growing body of cultural information. In combination with domain analysis, these questions have begun to unravel the
meaning system of the cultural scene in its own terms. You
have probably also become keenly aware of the fact that to
study all the relationships among all the folk terms in this
cultural scene represents an enormous task. A complete and
exhaustive ethnography, even for a rather limited cultural
scene, would take years of intensive research. All ethnographers, whether studying the way of life in an Eskimo
village or a Bushman band, or investigating a limited cultural
scene in a large city, must limit their investigation in some
way. Some aspects of the culture will have to be studied
more exhaustively than others. In this chapter I want to
discuss how to limit the scope of ethnography and then
move on to the next step in making an in-depth analysis of
meaning for a few selected domains.

SELECTING A TENTATIVE FOCUS

We can gain a better perspective on the nature of ethnographic research through a simple analogy. Imagine for a
moment that a cultural scene is like a ship with a crew,
supplies, a cargo, and a destination. Working together the
crew carries out routine tasks, keeps the ship on course,
adapts to storms or other hazards at sea, and engages in
many other daily activities. The crew has acquired a large
repertoire of knowledge about their ship, the members of
the crew, how to navigate, what to do in storms, how to
perform the various tasks to be done, and how to fill up the

hours of free time. In short, the crew shares a way of life aboard the ship; their lives make sense because they have learned a common system of cultural symbols.

Now, imagine that instead of having all these symbols and their relationships in their minds, the crew actually stored them in boxes, bins, cabinets, trunks, lockers, and other containers scattered everywhere about the ship. As an ethnographer, you board the ship with the goal of finding out what the crew knows; you want to discover all the symbols and their relationships, which crew members use to organize their behavior and interpret their experiences. By listening and asking ethnographic questions you discover that all the symbols (folk terms and others) are stored in the various containers. You find out that all the boxes and bins containing these symbols are *named.* That one is *kinds of storms,* this one is *ways to pass time on watch,* and another is called *parts of the ship.* A small container in each cabin is named *steps in making a bed,* and a large, important container on the bridge is called *ways to navigate.*

Through a careful domain analysis you begin to identify these boxes of symbols (their domians of knowledge). Then you formulate structural questions and these lead to discovering more boxes of symbols and also lists of the symbols included in each container. You haven't identified all the containers or all the contents, but you do know many of the most important ones.

At this point you face a choice regarding further research. You can either carry out a *surface analysis* of as many domains as possible or you can conduct an *in-depth analysis* of a limited number of domains. If you decide to do a surface analysis, you would start describing all these containers of symbols based on general descriptions of each. You would ask questions to find out the relationships among the various boxes, bins, cabinets, and lockers. For example, you would want to know about the various parts of the ship, and, with a few descriptive and structural questions, your informants could identify them and give you some surface clues to their meaning. "The captain works in the bridge; we eat in the galley; the engine room is down below; the crew have their own cabins where they sleep," etc. In making a surface analysis of the cultural meaning system, you would undoubtedly identify some cultural themes and gain many insights into the way of life aboard ship. You could write an ethnographic description that would be a *translation,* one that showed outsiders the cultural meanings (as far as you had pursued them) known to members of the crew.

On the other hand, if you decided to do an *in-depth analysis* of the cultural meaning system, you would have to stay on board the ship for many years or decide on a more limited focus for your research. In either case, you would realize that, having identified many or all of the boxes and bins of symbols (the domains), you had only scratched the surface of the culture. Each container has many different folk terms in it, and these terms are all arranged in a myriad of complex relationships. Your task would be to *unpack the meaning* stored in each of the containers. By a careful procedure you would take one box at a time and try to find out all the symbols inside it and all the relationships among those symbols. This would require that you ask new questions of informants, that you watch informants take all the items from each container, and that you observe how they use these symbols in different situations ("Don't ask for meaning, ask for use.").

Ethnographers have long debated the advantages of the in-depth and surface strategies.[1] Those who advocate the in-depth strategy argue that cultural meaning is complex; if we only skim the surface we will never know how informants understand things. It is better, they say, to study a single domain intensively and without distorting the insider's point of view, than to study many domains superficially.

Those who advocate studying the surface of cultural meanings argue that we need to see a culture or cultural scene in *holistic* terms. It is the relationships among domains that are important; then later, if time allows, we can come back and examine each domain in exhaustive detail. But, because time and resources are limited, most ethnographers agree that an exhaustive study of an entire culture will never be accomplished.

In actual practice, most ethnographers adopt a compromise: they study a few, selected domains in depth, while still attempting to gain a surface understanding of a culture or cultural scene as a whole. In order to accomplish this we must adopt strategies for both in-depth analysis and for a more holistic, surface analysis. Actually, in following the steps in the Developmental Research Sequence, you have been doing both kinds of analysis. In the last four steps the emphasis has been on identifying as many containers on board ship as possible. In this step and the next two, we will discuss strategies for studying the contents of a single container—identifying all the symbols in a domain, finding subsets of symbols, and then discovering all the complex relationships among the symbols in these subsets. Finally, in the last two steps we will return to a broader perspective of finding the relationships among domains to gain a holistic picture of the culture. This sequence of research activities, in terms of a surface and in-depth analysis, is shown in the diagram in Figure 8.1.

It is important for every ethnographer to keep a balance between these two strategies or styles of research. During interviews one should ask questions about many different containers on board ship; at the same time, part of each interview should focus increasingly on unpacking the meaning in one or two containers. Interviews must range *widely* over many topics; they must also go *deeply* into particular topics. This still leaves one question unanswered: how does one select a focus for in-depth analysis? Out of all the domains you have identified, which ones should you select for taxonomic analysis and componential analysis? Whatever domains are selected, the choice of focus must be *tentative*. New domains that are more interesting or

FIGURE 8.1. Focus in Ethnographic Research

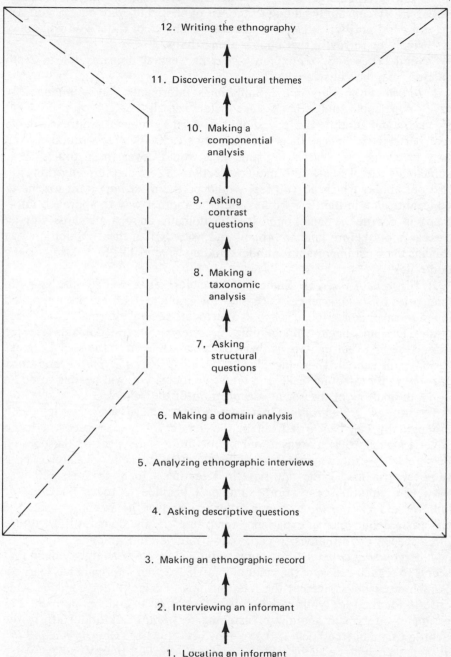

The D.R.S. steps begin with a wide focus, then with Step 7 begin to narrow for intensive investigation of a few selected domains. The dotted lines inside the box represent this change in focus; they suggest that both a narrow and wide focus occur simultaneously, but with more emphasis on one or the other at various stages of research.

important often emerge along the way and lead to a shift in the focus of research. By constantly adding to the list of all identified domains, you will be in a good position either to make a wise choice of those you will study intensively or to revise that choice along the way.

Several criteria for tentatively selecting several domains for in-depth analysis may be considered.

1. *Informant's suggestions.* Sometimes informants will spontaneously say, "You should study what it's like inside that jail," or "If you really want to understand Brady's Bar you should study the problems waitresses have with bartenders." These suggestions do not specify the precise domains, but they give clues to several domains that would cover these topics. It is sometimes useful to ask informants directly: "There are so many things to find out about; which do you feel would be the most important for me to concentrate on in the time we have left?" Another way to approach informants is to write the names of most of the domains on separate cards. Spread the cards out before your informant and ask, "Of all these, which do you think is the most important for understanding what its like to be an air-traffic controller?"

2. *Theoretical interest.* Some folk domains relate well to the analytic categories of social science. Let's say, for example, that you are interested in the social organization of schools. You locate several informants in a third-grade class and begin ethnographic interviews. Several domains emerge during the first four interviews that you see are related to the social organization of the school. These include *kinds of kids, kinds of teachers,* and *kinds of groups.* By selecting these as a tentative focus, you will be able to do an in-depth analysis of the social organization of the school.

3. *Strategic ethnography.* In Chapter One I discussed ways in which ethnography can be carried out in the service of human needs. I listed several major problem areas in our own culture and suggested these could help guide the ethnographer in selecting a cultural scene for research. These same criteria may guide you now in selecting a focus for research in a particular cultural scene. For example, I decided to focus on *kinds of inmates* and *parts of the bucket* in order to discover the extent to which the jail was a dehumanizing experience for tramps. Some domains in a culture offer special opportunities to carry out strategic ethnography.

4. *Organizing domains.* Sometimes you will discover a large domain that seems to organize most of the cultural knowledge your informant has learned. Somehow, it pulls together the relationships of many other domains. One criteria for focusing your research is to select an organizing domain. For example, after many months of listening to tramps talk about life in the Seattle City Jail (the bucket), I saw that one domain, *stages in making the bucket,* seemed to tie all the other information together. It provided me with a dynamic perspective of all the experiences tramps went through as they progressed from the first encounter with a bull on the street, through their

sentencing, back into jail to do time, and finally to their release when they go back to skid row until their next arrest. This domain then became the focus of my research and it helped organize the final writing of the ethnography.

One final thing to keep in mind in selecting several domains for in-depth analysis is your research goals. If you are a beginning ethnographer and your goal is primarily to learn to study cultural meaning from the informant's point of view, almost any domain can become the basis for in-depth analysis. In this case, you might select one you find interesting or one that your informant appears to want to talk about. If you select a domain and find that your informant has only limited knowledge of it, shift to a new one for your research focus. Whatever domains are selected, your next step is to begin a taxonomic analysis of these domains.

FOLK TAXONOMIES[2]

Like a domain, a folk taxonomy is a set of categories organized on the basis of a single semantic relationship. All of us have learned scores of folk taxonomies and use them every day. I stop at a drugstore to buy a magazine, and without thinking I make use of my folk taxonomy, *kinds of magazines.* Let's say I want to purchase the latest issue of *Time.* The magazine rack is full to overflowing with dozens of different magazines. As I scan their covers I notice that some are *sports magazines,* others are *comic books* (a kind of magazine), and still others are *girlie magazines* with partially clothed females on the covers. I spot *U.S. News and World Report* and begin to look in that vicinity for other *news magazines,* since I classify *Time* in that group. In the same way you might use your folk taxonomies for kinds of cards, furniture, clothes, and dozens of other things. All involve large sets of categories organized on the basis of a single semantic relationship.

A taxonomy differs from a domain in only one respect: it shows the relationships among *all* the folk terms in a domain. A taxonomy reveals subsets of folk terms and the way these subsets are related to the domain as a whole. We can see this difference in the following example of a domain:

WAYS TO MAKE A JUG

bumming
making a frisco circle
panhandling
making a run
making the V.A.
cutting in on a jug

The relationships among included terms in this domain are not shown. A taxonomy reveals such relationship as shown in the following chart.

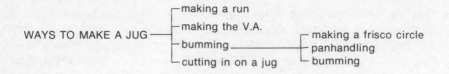

These folk terms are all ways to do something; in this case, ways to acquire an alcoholic beverage or "jug." But some terms in this domain are more inclusive, more general than others. Thus, we see that bumming (a general form of begging) includes three more specific kinds of begging (panhandling, making a frisco circle, and another form of bumming).[3]

Consider another example of a taxonomy, this time from an ethnography of an actual boat used for tuna fishing. The crews on these ships, described by the anthropologist Robert Orbach (1977), are referred to as tuna fishermen or *seinermen*. They use a fishing method known as *seining*. An important part of their cultural knowledge is the tunaboat itself. Each crew member must know how to locate himself on a boat, know what behavior is appropriate for different parts of the boat, and know how to travel from one part of the boat to another. Spatial knowledge like this makes up a part of every culture in the world. Orbach describes this cultural domain, identifying nearly thirty different spaces or *parts of a tunaboat*. From his description it is possible to identify many relationships among the included terms. We can construct a taxonomy to show the way this domain is internally organized (Figure 8.2).

This taxonomy is not exhaustive, but it does show that certain parts of the boat are included in other parts. It reveals that the meaning of *deck,* for example, is much more complex and elaborate than the meaning of *mast*. The concept *deck* includes more than twenty more specific locations; *mast* includes only two.

This taxonomy reveals an important feature of all folk taxonomies: they have different *levels*. This one has five different levels from the cover term, *parts of a tunaboat,* to the most specific terms included in the three types of decks. Some taxonomies have only two levels; when this is the case, there is little difference between the domain and the taxonomy which shows its structure. For example, *kinds of ethnographic analysis* is a domain from the culture of ethnographers which I have been discussing in this book. It includes four folk terms introduced in Step Five: *domain analysis, taxonomic analysis, componential analysis,* and *theme analysis*. The structure of this domain can be represented with a very simple taxonomy.

People seldom talk about their folk taxonomies in a systematic or exhaustive manner. We must infer this organization from what people say and do. We can also use structural questions to elicit taxonomies. During routine social interaction we only get a partial view of this kind of structure. However, we use it constantly to interpret what people say and to communi-

FIGURE 8.2. Taxonomy of Parts of a Tunaboat

PARTS OF A TUNABOAT			
SHAFT ALLEY			
MAIN ENGINE ROOM			
MAST	Crow's nest		
	Platform		
DECK	UP TOP (upper deck)	Speedboat deck	
		Bridge	The stack
			Skipper's cabin
		Netpile	Seine net
			Skiff
	ON DECK (middle deck)	Main working deck	Main winch
			Deck hatch
			Shark slide
			Brailing booms
		Main deckhouse	Cabins
			Galley
		The bow	Anchor winches
			Rail-mounted winch
	BELOW (lower deck)	Well deck	
		Upper engine room	

KINDS OF
ETHNOGRAPHIC ANALYSIS

Domain Analysis	Taxonomic Analysis	Componential Analysis	Theme Analysis

cate meaning. The following example shows how such a structure is used, even though it remains tacitly below the surface. It also shows how a folk taxonomy is partially revealed during an episode, and how misunderstandings can arise due to lack of taxonomic knowledge.

On the night of April 30, 1975, someone broke into my garage and stole three bicycles. The next morning, when I discovered the theft, I called the St. Paul Police Department and two officers appeared at my door within the hour. I answered their questions and they informed me there was little hope of ever retrieving the stolen bicycles. After they left, I called my insurance agent and was relieved to discover that the bicycles were covered by insurance.

"It will take a few weeks to process the claim," the agent said. So I settled back to wait.

On the tenth of May, I received a letter from the insurance company asking for information on the original price of each bicycle and also the case number on the theft as recorded by the St. Paul Police Department. I assumed they wanted to verify whether the theft had actually occurred. I dialed 726-1234 to call the police department for the case number.

"Police department," said a voice on the other end of the line.

"Hello," I said, "I'd like to check the case number of a robbery that I reported on May 1."

"Sorry, but you'll have to call 726-1000." I hung up the phone, assuming I had called the wrong part of the department, probably the one for reporting emergencies. I dialed the new number, the phone rang twice and someone else in the police department answered.

"Hello, I'd like to check on the case number of a robbery that I reported on May 1."

"Just a minute. I'll give you that unit." I waited, listening to the clicks and buzzes of a changing connection; then another phone began to ring.

"Hello, this is robbery," a voice answered with appropriate male gruffness.

"Hello. I'd like to check the case number of a robbery that I reported on May 1."

"Your address?"

"1980 Goodrich," I said and waited.

"Let's see," the voice said, obviously stalling for time. "There were three robberies on May 1." He paused and I could imagine someone going through a card file looking for my record.

"Goodrich!" he said suddenly, pleased to have found it. "That was where they took your wallet with a gun."

"No," I said, feeling a bit impatient.

"Did they break in and steal something?" he asked.

"Yes," I said, now feeling annoyed. "They broke into my garage and stole three bicycles."

"Did they use a gun?" he asked.

"No!" I answered. "It was during the night. I was asleep. They broke into my garage. I don't know if they had a gun or not, but if they did, I wasn't there to see it!"

"Then there wasn't any face-to-face encounter? You weren't personally involved?" he asked.

"No," I said, wondering why he was so interested in all these details that I had already reported on the morning after the robbery.

"Oh!" he exclaimed, as if he had solved the problem. "You got the wrong place. You see, you kinda got the wrong terminology. Robbery is when they use a gun. You want burglary. You're in the right church but the wrong pew! I'll transfer you."

Again I waited. As the phone clicked and buzzed, I wondered where all these units in the police department were. My invisible guide told the switchboard operator to transfer the call to burglary; the phone rang again in some other office or at some other desk.

"Hello," a woman's voice said.

"Hello, I want to check on the case number of a *burglary*," I said confidently emphasizing the word; I at least had the right terminology. "I reported it on May 1."

"Your address?" she asked before I had a chance to explain anything about the burglary.

"1980 Goodrich Avenue." Another long pause.

"You're sure it was on May 1?" she finally asked.

"Yes, I'm positive."

"You sure you reported this burglary to the police?"

"Yes," I said, somewhat exasperated. "Two policemen came to my house, they wrote everything down." At the same instant another possibility crossed my mind. Maybe those two policemen had never reported it after leaving my house. Three new ten-speed bicycles worth nearly $500 began to look more remote than ever.

"What did they steal?" the woman asked next, after a long pause.
"Bicycles!" I almost shouted into the phone, fighting to control my voice.
"Three of them. They broke into my garage while we were all asleep!"
"Oh! Bicycles!" she exclaimed, all the confusion gone from her voice.
"That would go to juvenile." Once again I waited, listened to the now
familiar clicks and buzzes; "Transfer this to juvenile," she told the switch-
board operator and I listened while another phone began to ring.

"I had three bicycles stolen on May 1," I said wearily when someone
answered. "I need the case number for my insurance. I live at 1980 Goodrich
Avenue."

"Just a minute," said the voice. I settled down for another delay and
wondered what new inquisition lay in store for me about the details of the
bicycle theft or robbery or burglary or whatever it was.

"That case number is 2718564," said the voice in less than fifteen seconds.
Surprised, I grabbed my pencil and wrote down the number, thanked him,
then hung up the phone exhausted. I had finally managed to follow the folk
taxonomy of the police department to my destination. I was still only
vaguely aware of how the police classified events and records, but I had
found out what I needed to know. Apparently this "church" had at least
three "pews"—*burglary* (a property theft), *robbery* (using a weapon to steal
from a person), and *juvenile* (which recorded thefts common to juveniles). It
seemed like a strange way to divide up the world. If I had understood this
culture I could have begun with a simple question: "What part of the police
department has records of bicycles stolen from a garage when no one was
present?"

Sometime later, I asked several structural questions of two informants
from the St. Paul Police Department. In moments I discovered the *parts of
the police department*, and saw the entire taxonomy that represented this
domain (Figure 8.3). Members of the police department know this taxonomy
well; they use it routinely to carry out everyday tasks. At the same time they
are often unaware that outsiders lack any knowledge of this domain. In order
to understand the cuture of this police department it was necessary to go
beyond routine conversations and elicit all the folk terms and their relationships.

TAXONOMIC ANALYSIS

In Step Five, ethnographic analysis was defined as *a search for the parts
of a culture, the relationships among the parts, and their relationships to the
whole.* Combined with ethnographic interviewing, ethnographic analysis
leads to the discovery of a particular cultural meaning system. The first kind
of analysis (domain analysis, Step Six) enabled you to isolate the fundamental units of cultural knowledge, the domains into which informants organized
what they know. Then, by using structural questions (Step Seven), you

FIGURE 8.3. Taxonomy of Parts of the Police Department

PARTS OF THE POLICE DEPARTMENT	PATROL		
	ADMINISTRATIVE		Police artist
			Volunteer services
			Crime lab
			Public relations
			Captains' center
			Records and identification
			Communications
			Operations
			Personnel
			Training
			Inspection
	INVESTIGATIVE (Detective)	CRIMES AGAINST PEOPLE	Auto theft
			Juvenile
			Burglary
			Traffic and accident
		CRIMES AGAINST PROPERTY	Sex crimes
			Homicide
			Robbery
		NARCOTICS	
		VICE	
	CHIEF		
	INTERNAL AFFAIRS		

verified the domains and elicited the folk terms which were included in those domains. Now, with taxonomic analysis, we will shift our attention to the internal structure of domains. In the rest of this chapter I want to discuss specific procedures for identifying subsets within a domain and the relationships between these subsets. The experienced ethnographer often combines domain analysis and taxonomic analysis into a single process. But, in order to learn to do them, it is best to treat each separately.

Step One: Select a Domain for Taxonomic Analysis. Begin with a domain for which you have the most information. You will undoubtedly discover additional included terms as you make a componential analysis, but it is best to select a domain for which you have collected most of the included terms. After I learned that my informants spent much of their lives in the Seattle City Jail, I began to inquire about that specific *bucket*. Informants had intimate knowledge of its spatial arrangement (parts of the bucket), processing procedures (steps in making the bucket), temporal dimensions of life in jail (kinds of time), and many other domains. One of the first domains I encountered involved the social structure of the jail. I heard informants refer to the fact that they had been inmates before arriving at the alcoholism treatment center, that other inmates wanted to come to the center, and that if sent back to jail they would probably become inmates again. Some men even maintained that instead of being patients at the center, they were actually inmates. I decided to investigate this domain.

I reviewed my field notes and began asking structural questions about the different *kinds of inmates in the bucket.* The following lists represents some of the folk terms I collected:

lockup	drunk	lawn man
trusty	barber	harbor patrol man
ranger	bull's barber	seventh-floor man
mopper	bull cook	head trusty
pastry man	sweeper	elevator man
bullet man	odlin's man	inmate's barber

Taxonomic analysis always begins with a domain such as this, even though the list may be incomplete.

Step Two: Identify the appropriate substitution frame for analysis. At this point in the analysis we have identified only the relationship between the cover term (kinds of inmates) and a single set of included terms (the specific inmates). In order to divide up this set of inmates and discover how these included terms are organized into subsets, we must use a substitution frame. Such a frame must be based on the primary relationship of this domain. It is important to keep in mind that a domain and the taxonomy associated with it are always based on a single semantic relationship. Beginning ethnographers tend to introduce closely related but different semantic relationships into their analysis, and this creates many problems.

Let's look at our example again and identify the appropriate substitution frame.

1. Domain: kinds of inmates
2. Semantic relationship: __A drunk__ (is a kind of) __inmate__.
3. Underlying semantic relationship: __X__ (is a kind of) __Y__
4. Substitution frame: _____ (is a kind of) _____

This substitution frame will now become the main tool for all the analysis to follow. For this reason, it is important to work out such a frame carefully for the domain you will analyze.

Step Three: Search for possible subsets among the included terms. This search begins with the substitution frame. Check to see if any of the included terms fit the blank spaces of this relationship. Sometimes it helps to say the relationship aloud to get a sense of whether the fit is appropriate. An inspection of the preceding list reveals the following possibilities:

___bulls' barber___ (is a kind of) __barber__
___inmate's barber___ (is a kind of) __barber__
___head trusty___ (is a kind of) __trusty__

We can add to this list by reviewing field notes and past interviews. For example, consider the following statement: "I made *trusty* the last time I was in for drunk; worked as a *ranger* for more than sixty days." From such a statement we can make a tentative inference that

___ranger___ (is a kind of) __trusty__

Beginning ethnographers often feel that the only way to identify the relationships among included terms in a domain is to ask informants structural questions. They tend to overlook the fact that reviewing all earlier interviews and field notes often yields clues to these relationships. In the process one discovers new terms and verifies their relationships. A thorough search might easily reveal the following relationships for the domain under consideration:

(1) Drunks
(2) Trusties
    (2.1) Kitchen men

                2.1.1 pastry man
                2.1.2 elevator man
            (2.2) Seventh-floor man
                2.2.1 mopper
                2.2.2 sweeper
                2.2.3 head trusty
            (2.3) Barber
                2.3.1 bulls' barber
                2.3.2 inmate's barber
        (3) Lockups
        (4) Odlin's man
        (4) Bull cook
        (5) Harbor patrol Man
        (6) Laundry man

By the end of this search you should have gone as far as you can without consulting an informant. You have exhausted your ethnographic record; you cannot find any new terms and you cannot identify any new relationships among these terms.

Step Four: Search for larger, more inclusive domains that might include as a subset the one you are analyzing. Imagine that you are visiting California as an ethnographer from the treeless tundra of the arctic. Unfamiliar with the plants in California you begin asking informants to identify them. Pointing to a large plant, your informant says, "That's an evergreen." Immediately you formulate an appropriate structural question, "What are all the different kinds of evergreens?" To which your informant replies with a long list of folk terms like *pine, cedar, redwood, jack pine, white pine, norway pine, giant redwood,* and *douglas fir.* Following the steps for doing a taxonomic analysis you begin to identify subsets such as *pines* and *redwoods.* Now you need to search for larger domains that might include *kinds of evergreens.* You might do this by asking an included term question: "Is an evergreen a kind of something?" Or perhaps your informant casually mentions that a "giant redwood is a unique *tree.*" By one means or another you will have discovered that *evergreens* is only one part of the larger domain *trees,* which is only one part of a still larger domain *plants.*

One can begin to search for larger, more inclusive domains by reviewing field notes and interview data and also by trying to recall unrecorded data. In thinking about a more inclusive domain for *kinds of inmates in the bucket,* I immediately recalled that there were *bulls* who guarded and processed inmates. I also knew that at least one *civilian* worked in the jail, the *doctor* who visited the jail hospital. In my field notes were terms like *court liaison officer* and *nurse,* both persons identified as being *in the bucket* by one or another informant.

Later I asked hypothetical descriptive questions to encourage my informants to talk about all the other people in the jail. A typical exchange went
like this:

ETHNOGRAPHER: I've never been inside the Seattle City Jail. I suppose if I went in
and walked around, I would see lots of people, right?
INFORMANT: Sure. You'd see people all over the place.
ETHNOGRAPHER: Could you sort of lead me on a tour of the jail, from the time you get
off the elevator on the first floor, and tell me all the people I might see?
INFORMANT: O.K. As you get off the elevator on the seventh floor you'd be locked
out by the steel bars, but you could see the *booking-desk bull* and he could press a
button to let you in. Then, there would probably be at least one *turnkey* and maybe
some other *bulls* bringing in some *drunks*, taking *lockups* to court, or lining up the
kickouts of the day. You'd probably see a *runner*, maybe one of the *seventh floor
men*. Then if you went into the jail hospital you would see the *pill pusher* and the
nurse.

Our analysis has taken us from the domain *kinds of inmates,* to the more
inclusive one, *kinds of people in the bucket.* Because you are now working
with a larger taxonomy, it may be necessary to review field notes for new
terms. Or, you may decide to conduct your taxonomic analysis on only one
part of the larger taxonomy, leaving the rest until a later date. As soon as you
have exhausted your sources of information in field notes, you are ready to
construct a tentative taxonomy of the domain.

Step Five: Construct a tentative taxonomy. A taxonomy can be represented in several ways: a box diagram, a set of lines and nodes, or an
outline. Figure 8.4 shows these three methods of representation. The first
two (lines and nodes and box) provide a clear picture of the semantic
relationships among all the folk terms. Here is a tentative taxonomy in
outline form of the *kinds of people in the bucket.*

I. Bulls
   A. Booking-desk bull
   B. Turnkey
   C. Court liaison officer
II. Civilians
   A. Pill pusher
   B. Nurse
III. Inmates
   A. Kickouts
   B. Drunks
   C. Trusties
      1. Laundryman
      2. Harbor patrol

FIGURE 8.4. Types of Taxanomic Diagrams

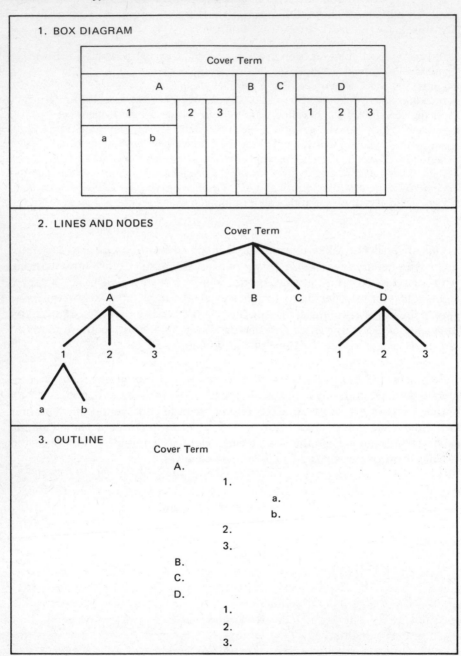

1. BOX DIAGRAM

2. LINES AND NODES

3. OUTLINE

3. Bull cook
4. Odlin's man
5. Runner
6. Kitchen men
    a. Pastry man
    b. Elevator man
7. Seventh-floor man
    a. Mopper
    b. Sweeper
    c. Head trusty
8. Ranger
    a. Bullet man
    b. Lawn man
9. Barber
    a. Bull's barber
    b. Inmate's barber

Step Six: Formulate structural questions to verify taxonomic relationships and elicit new terms. Using the same semantic relationship, it is a simple matter to prepare structural questions (see Step Seven). Several examples of such questions for the domain *kinds of people in the bucket* follow:

1. What are all the different kinds of bulls? (civilians, inmates, drunks, kickouts, trusties, etc.)
2. Is a booking-desk bull a kind of bull?
3. Is a pastry man a kind of kitchen man? Are there other kinds of kitchen men?
4. Are there any other kinds of people in the bucket?

When asking structural questions about a large taxonomy, it is often facilitated by asking card sorting structural questions. Informants can then sort the cards into sets based on all being the same kind of person. Again, informants must be reminded that you are only looking for terms that fit the semantic relationship for the particular taxonomy you are analyzing.

Step Seven: Conduct additional structural interviews. The analysis and tentative taxonomy must now be checked with informants. You have prepared a number of structural questions for this purpose; more can be developed during the interview itself. Rather than show informants the tentative taxonomy or a diagram of any kind, it is usually best to ask them to instruct you on how they *use* their folk terms. For example, I might ask, "Is it appropriate to say, 'A trusty is a kind of inmate?' " or "Would most tramps say, 'A bull cook is a kind of trusty?' "

149

You are now at a stage in the research where alternating periods of interviewing and analysis become more necessary than ever. In a few minutes you can collect so much new information about a taxonomy that it will take a period of analysis to sort it out and prepare to ask the appropriate questions. You can begin to alternate structural questions about a taxonomy with asking for *examples* of the folk terms in that taxonomy. I might ask, "Can you give me an example of what a bull cook would do?" or "Can you remember any experiences you had when you were a runner?" Slowly, through analysis and questions, you will begin to finalize your analysis of one or more taxonomies.

Step Eight: Construct a completed taxonomy. At some point it becomes necessary to stop collecting data and analyzing a taxonomy and instead accepting it as relatively complete. It is well to recognize that taxonomies always *approximate* the way informants have organized their cultural knowledge. They are not exact replicas of that knowledge. More important, you can continue your search for meaning with a componential analysis even if you have not discovered all the terms or all the relationships in a taxonomy. As stated earlier, ethnography is both science and art. We seek to discover how informants conceptualize their world; at the same time we recognize that every ethnographer solves problems in ways that go beyond the data or on the basis of insufficient data.

Let me give an example of the choices. When I began to read about taxonomic analysis and see the clear taxonomies other ethnographers had collected, I thought it would be possible to find the same kind of thing. The fact that the ethnographer must decide how to arrange some folk terms was never discussed in many works. In Figure 8.5 I have presented a taxonomy of *kinds of people in the bucket,* and in Figure 8.6 I have expanded one part of this taxonomy (kinds of trusties) in a fairly complete form. However, during my interviews many informants referred to two kinds of trusties not on this diagram: *inside trusties* and *outside trusties.* Were these terms that should appear in this taxonomy? I had difficulty deciding how to treat them; at first I included them as kinds of trusties, then it seemed that they were descriptive of the *locations* of certain trusties in the jail system. And this did not exhaust the locations, since there were numerous places outside and inside the jail where trusties could be found. I decided to leave these two terms out of this taxonomy (Figure 8.6) and discuss this information as two important attributes of spatial location. As we shall see in a later chapter, the information itself was important, the exact location in my analysis was not. In every taxonomic analysis there are problems which suggest alternative solutions, and informants alone can not always clear up these problems. No discovery procedures can unambiguously solve every problem; the ethnographer must take an active role in creating the final description of a culture.

Another brief example of this role used in another taxonomy may be

FIGURE 8.5. Taxonomy of Kinds of People in the Bucket

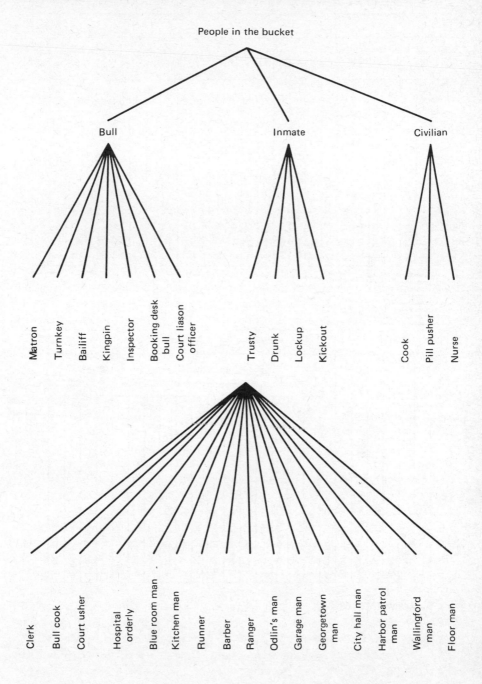

FIGURE 8.6.   Taxonomy of Kinds of Trustees

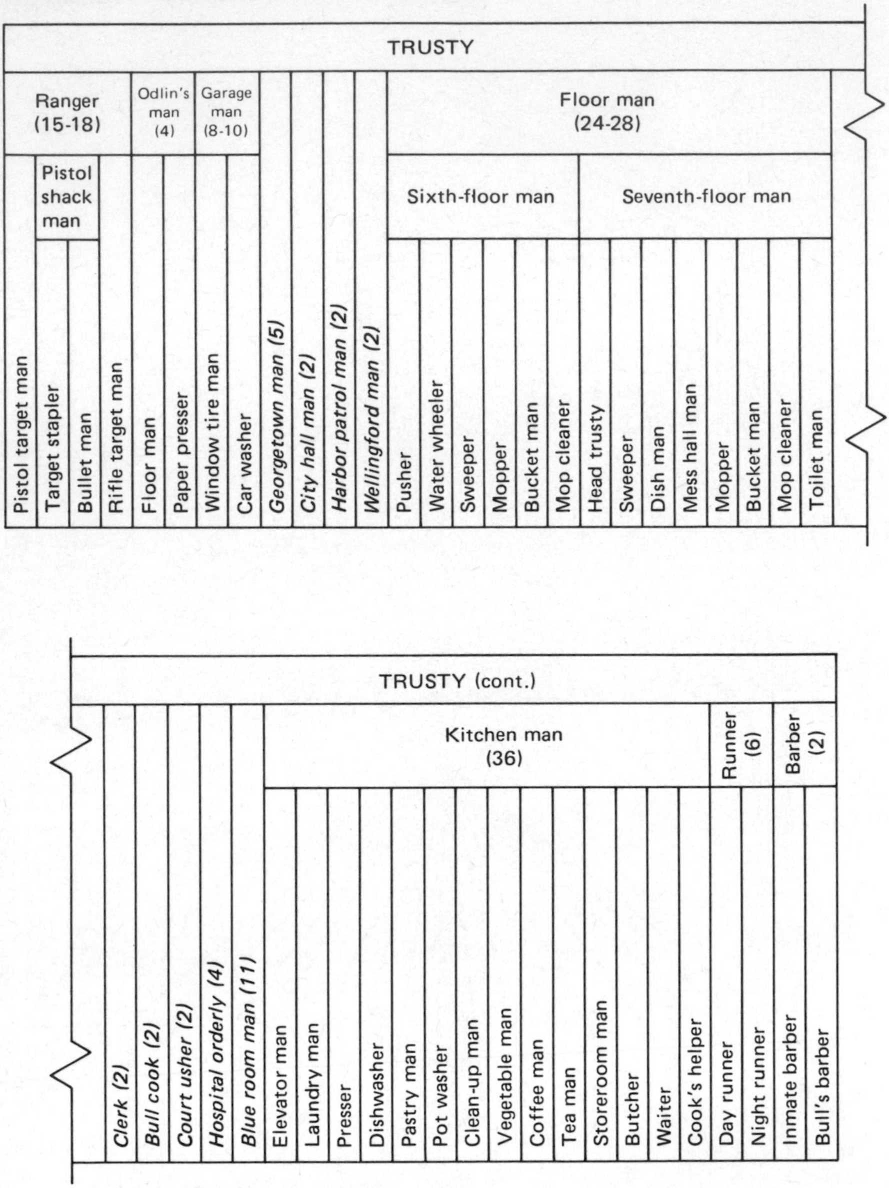

From Spradley: 1970: 88–89.

FIGURE 8.7. Taxonomy of Ways to Make a Jug

WAYS TO MAKE A JUG			
	Making the Blood Bank		
	Bumming	Panhandling (stemming)	
		Making a frisco circle	
		Bumming	
	Stealing	Boosting	
		Rolling	Rolling
			Jackrolling
		Beating	
		Clipping	
	Peddling		
	Taking a rake-off		
	Pooling		
	Cutting in on a jug		
	Borrowing		
	Buying		
	Making your own	Making pruno	
		Making rasin jack	
		Making sweet lucy	
		Making home brew	
		Squeezing heat	
		Squeezing shoe polish	
		Straining shellac	
		Mixing bay rum	
		Mixing solax	
		Mixing shaving lotion	
		Mixing ruby dub	
		Mixing gasoline	
	Meeting a live one		
	Hustling a queer		
	Hustling a board		
	Making a run		
	Spot jobbing		
	Making the mission		
	Making the V.A.		
	Junking		

instructive. At the beginning of this chapter I showed a small part of the taxonomy, *ways to make a jug*. The completed taxonomy is shown in Figure 8.7. One strategy for making a jug is to *make your own* and tramps have learned many recipes for mixing substances or making alcoholic beverages from scratch. Under *making your own*, I have included twelve different folk terms; in fact, there are only *four* different ways to make your own— *making, straining, mixing,* and *squeezing*. I decided to include the specific things made because they were few in number and I could not tell whether isolating only the verb forms (making, squeezing, mixing, straining) would have been meaningful in tramps' culture. They *always* used the verb form, along with one or more nouns, to indicate how to make your own. But what if there were five hundred different substances you could make, squeeze, mix, or strain? Would they all go in this taxonomy? Probably not. I included them here because it seemed the best place to represent an important part of tramp's cultural knowledge. In all your taxonomic analyses you will have to make similar decisions about how to represent your data.

In this chapter we have examined procedures for discovering the internal structure of a domain. Taxonomic analysis leads to finding subsets and the relationships among these subsets. In the next chapter we will examine ways to make a componential analysis to find out how symbols are related within these subsets. Our goal throughout our analysis remains the same: to grasp the cultural meanings by tracing all the relationships among the symbols of a culture.

Tasks

8.1 Conduct a taxonomic analysis on one or more domains following the steps presented in this chapter.

8.2 Conduct an ethnographic interview using both descriptive and structural questions.

8.3 Prepare a completed taxonomic diagram of one or more domains.

OBJECTIVES
1. To understand the major discovery principles in the study of cultural meaning.
2. To learn the ways to discover contrasts among cultural symbols.
3. To formulate and use contrast questions.

In the last few chapters we have moved from analyzing the broad surface of many domains in a cultural scene to an in-depth analysis of one or more domains. By now you should have completed a folk taxonomy and you no doubt have several other folk taxonomies in various stages of analysis. It is important to view folk taxonomies from the perspective of the relational theory of meaning presented in Step Five: they represent the *meaning* of symbols by showing their relationships to other symbols in a domain. However, the degree of meaning revealed in a folk taxonomy is minimal because it only reveals a *single* relationship among a set of folk terms. Imagine that a person only knew that the term *foreign sports car* was a member of the taxonomy, *kinds of cars.* It would only convey one bit of information. The folk taxonomy would not provide a single clue to the status an owner might derive from such a car; nor would it tell such important information as horsepower, interior design, manufacturer's defects, or E.P.A. mileage rating. And a taxonomy of cars would not say anything about how a sports car was related to activities like racing, courting, working, or shopping. Because our goal is to understand cultural meaning, we must go well beyond constructing taxonomies of cultural domains. In this chapter we will review several strategies for discovering meaning and then show how constant questions can lead to finding many additional relationships among folk terms.

DISCOVERY PRINCIPLES IN THE STUDY OF MEANING

One of the most basic capacities of human beings is the ability to discover meaning. Children in every society discover the meaning of verbal and nonverbal symbols with great ease. Although they sometimes receive explicit instruction, children learn most of their culture's meanings without it. People can move from one society or social setting to another where people are using different symbols. Without realizing it they become participant observers and interviewers; before much time passes, they have acquired the meanings of the new cultural scene. The tacit meanings take longer to learn, and we all recognize that the "old timers" in any scene have a rich stock of knowledge that others do not have.

Ethnography is an explicit methodology designed for finding out both the explicit and tacit knowledge familiar to the most experienced members of a culture. The methodology of ethnography can reduce the learning time by many years. Furthermore, because much of our cultural knowledge is tacit, outside awareness, the ethnographer ends up having far more *explicit* knowledge than informants. The ethnographer will not have the skill required to use that knowledge to generate behavior as the natives do, but the ethnographer will be able to talk about and communicate the knowledge in a way the natives cannot. Underlying the various methods of ethnography we have been discussing in this book are a number of discovery principles. I want to review some already discussed or implied, and introduce the principles of contrast, for it will lead to the next type of ethnographic question and the next type of ethnographic analysis.

The Relational Principle

This discovery principle was introduced in Step Five. It states: *the meaning of a symbol can be discovered by finding out how it is related to all other symbols*. Ultimately, all ethnography is designed to identify cultural symbols and discover their relations within a complex system of symbols. In an earlier chapter we saw that all folk definitions arise from the way folk terms are linked by semantic relationships. Two empirical findings lend support to this discovery principle: that all cultures create meaning from relatively few semantic relationships, and that certain semantic relationships are universal.

The Use Principle

This principle states that *the meaning of a symbol can be discovered by asking how it is used rather than asking what it means*. If we ask for meaning, we will only discover the explicit meanings, the ones that people can talk about. If we ask for use, we will tap that great reservoir of tacit meanings which exists in every culture. This principle is also based on the relational theory of meaning discussed earlier. One reason ethnographers almost always combine participant observation with interviewing is to observe how folk terms are used in ordinary settings. Indeed, at this point in your research you may find that visiting the setting in which your informant carries out daily activities will reveal usages that have not been discussed in interviews.

The Similarity Principle

This principle states that *the meaning of a symbol can be discovered by finding out how it is similar to other symbols*. Let's go back to the world of tramps for an example. My informants used two folk terms that held almost no similarity to me: *graveyard* and *bathtub*. "You can make a flop in a graveyard and you can flop in a bathtub." Later, asking structural questions I discovered that both graveyard and bathtub were considered *flops*, along with many other folk terms. What I had discovered was that tramps saw a very important similarity between these two symbols. And, by discovering this similarity, I had taken a step into the meanings of their culture.

Although not stated previously, this discovery principle underlies both domain analysis and taxonomic analysis. When we look for members of a domain (the included terms), we are really looking for symbols that share some feature of meaning, symbols that are similar in some way. When we go further to study the internal structure of a domain, to construct a taxonomy of the way a domain is organized, we are still seeking similarities among symbols. For example, the *deck hatch, shark slide, mast,* and *bridge* are all similar—they are parts of a *tunaboat* (Figure 8.2). But from the taxonomy of this domain we can see that *deck hatch* and *shark slide* have a closer similarity not shared with the other folk terms: they are both parts of the *main working deck*.

One of the most important skills required by ethnography is the ability to *see similarities* among symbols in the way informants see them. Every ethnographer should practice looking for similarities. One should place folk terms side by side and ask, "Is there any way these appear similar?" We can inspect domains in the same way, looking for all possible similarities. The decision as to whether symbols are really similar in some way must be made by our informants or inferred from the way they behave towards these symbols. But coming up with possible similarities gives the ethnographer hypotheses to test.

Although we have focused on similarities in both domain and taxonomic analysis, similarity always implies contrast. Every domain has a boundary; when we discover that some folk terms belong inside that boundary because of similarity, we also discover others belong outside because of differences. Similarity and contrast are two sides to the same coin. Up to now our emphasis has been on the similarity principle; in the rest of this chapter and the next we will turn to discovery procedures based on the principle of contrast.

The Contrast Principle[1]

This principle states that *the meaning of a symbol can be discovered by finding out how it is different from other symbols*. This principle is based on

157

the fact that the meaning of any folk term depends on what it does not mean. Whenever we use language we call attention to what things *are;* but we also call attention to what they *are not.* To say, "I'm holding a book," identifies an object in my hand. It also implies that I am not holding a tree, a magazine, a wallet, a house, or anything else that we could communicate about. To say, "A boy is riding the bicycle," implies that it is not a girl, not a woman, not a chimpanzee, and not anything else. Whenever we talk we convey meaning by these implicit contrasts.

For practical purposes of field work it is useful to distinguish two kinds of semantic contrast: *unrestricted* and *restricted.*[2] Unrestricted contrast refers to the fact that a particular folk term contrasts with all other folk terms in the language. *Boy,* for example, contrasts with *girl, chimpanzee, house, Augustus Caesar, hydrogen bomb,* and any other folk term that can be used in a referential way. These are all unrestricted contrasts or differences. Some, such as between *hydrogen bomb* and *boy,* are so great that we can hardly find any similarity between them. This degree of difference operates constantly in all languages, but it is so great that it holds little use in our search for meaning.

For ethnographic purposes, folk terms in *restricted contrast* contain a gold mine of cultural meaning. Restricted contrast means that a folk term belongs to a set of terms which are both alike and different. The contrast is *restricted* to a limited amount of semantic information. It is easy to recognize, for example, that although *boy, girl, woman, man, adult,* and *young man* are all different, they all share important similarities. They share the semantic information of being human beings at different stages of development and of different sex. In a very important way, the meaning of *boy* depends on the fact that it is in restricted contrast with *girl, woman, adult,* and *young man.* When someone says, "A boy is riding a bicycle," it is implied (to those inside the culture) that a *not-girl,* a *not-woman,* a *not-man,* and a *not-young man* is riding the bicycle. All of us learn the symbols of our culture in sets that are in restricted contrast. When we hear the term *boy,* for example, we fill in the implied contrasts and derive the meaning of boy without thinking.

Contrast sets always operate in the background of human communication.[3] At the tacit level of awareness, these groups of symbols enable us to interpret instantly the meanings of our culture. Consider the following exchange:

"Boy, it's a hot day, Grandpa," said John.

"Oh, Johnny, when you're a man like me, instead of a boy, you'll not think it's hot. It's not too hot for me to go out with the boys tonight."

Although the word *boy* appears three different times in this exchange, it has three different symbolic meanings that no reader can miss. How do we interpret these meanings? In part, by making immediate reference to the contrast sets each usage of the word *boy* belongs to. Each contrast set implies a structural question, as we can see by examining these three uses of *boy*.

1. What are some other exclamations you might use when saying it's very hot? Gee, wow, man, whew, etc.
2. What are some other stages in a person's life besides boy and man? Baby, child, little boy, big boy, adult, old man, etc.
3. What are some other ways you would refer to your friends besides *the boys?* Friends, colleagues, old geezers, our group, etc.

The differences in meaning then depend on membership in different contrast sets.

The ethnographer who is a stranger to a culture faces a formidable task: to find the appropriate contrast sets for interpreting the meaning of symbols. Consider an example from the culture of tramps. An informant points to another man and says, "John is a *mission stiff.*" He goes on to explain that a mission stiff is someone who hangs around skid row missions, perhaps sleeps there frequently, and may even work at the mission. My informant fully appreciates the meaning of mission stiff because he implicitly contrasts it with a set of terms with which *mission stiff* is in restricted contrast. As an outsider I do not know the contrast set this term belongs to. Although my informant tells me something of its meaning, his explanation barely scratches the surface. In order to uncover the meaning of this symbol I must first find out how it is *different from* the other terms in some contrast set. *Mission stiff,* it turns out, is one kind of tramp and belongs to a contrast set of more than fifteen other kinds of tramps. Before I can fully grasp my informant's meaning of *mission stiff,* I must find out the differences between this kind of tramp and all the others. I must take the contrast principle seriously and find out how *mission stiff* is different from *bindle stiff, airedale, home guard tramp,* and all the other kinds of tramps.

Let's consider the principle of contrast in one other example. I interviewed a kindergarten student about the culture of her school. She described typical days and various activities that took place in class. She used symbols like *rig-a-jigs, train,* and *science table.* My first task in discovering their meaning was to locate the contrast set to which they belonged. It turned out that to my informant they were all kinds of *work,* a contrast set of nearly twenty folk terms. Now I could proceed to search for the ways in which all these kinds of work were different. My informant easily responded to my questions to tell me that *rig-a-jigs* was work usually done by girls; both *train* and *science table* were usually done by boys. Furthermore, you sat down to do *rig-a-jigs* but stood up with the other two kinds of work. Slowly, through searching out these differences, I began to grasp what each kind of work meant to my informant.

Each domain of a culture consists of folk terms in restricted contrast. Each subset of terms within a domain (the parts of a taxonomy) consists of a contrast set. One of the reasons that domain analysis and taxonomic analysis are so important is that they yield numerous sets of terms in restricted contrast; these sets can now be used to search for the kinds of differences that reveal symbolic meaning.

There are two major ways to search for differences among folk terms in restricted contrast. First, you can review all field notes looking for informants' statements which suggest differences. For example, in one interview a tramp informant began to discuss mission stiffs, saying they seldom rode freight trains like certain other tramps, but instead they traveled from one place to another by public transportation. Also, they didn't travel from one job to another but from one mission to another. Implied in these comments were several differences with other tramps which shed light on the meaning of *mission stiff*. It is important to look at all past interviews. These interviews contain a rich mine of information about semantic contrasts which define folk terms.

The second way to search for differences among folk terms is to ask contrast questions. These are the third major type of ethnographic question presented in this book. Each type of contrast question is designed to elicit differences among the folk terms in a contrast set. As you will see in using them, contrast questions are powerful tools for discovering many tacit relationships among the folk terms you have collected from informants. In the remainder of this chapter I want to identify the different kinds of contrast questions.

CONTRAST QUESTIONS

There are seven different types of contrast questions (Figure 9.1). With literate informants, folk terms written on cards and placed in front of the informant facilitate the question-and-answer process. I almost always use cards when asking any kind of contrast question. In the examples which follow I will make many references to the use of cards. One of their greatest values lies in the fact that they enable the informant to sit and think about

FIGURE 9.1   Kinds of Contrast Questions

1. Contrast verification questions
2. Directed contrast questions
3. Dyadic contrast questions
4. Triadic contrast questions
5. Contrast set sorting questions
6. Twenty Questions game
7. Rating questions

differences while keeping in mind many different folk terms. Cards can be grouped quickly into twos and threes on the basis of contrasting characteristics, then regrouped again. With nonliterate informants pictures drawn on cards or actual photographs serve the same purpose. However, some informants feel intimidated by cards, equating the contrast questions with some form of testing. For this reason it is best to introduce cards slowly, explain their use clearly, and perhaps ask contrast questions without cards to begin with.

In asking contrast questions the same principles apply that I discussed in Step Seven for asking structural questions. You may want to review the discussion of these principles, which I only restate here:

1. Concurrent principle: Ask contrast questions concurrently with both descriptive questions and structural questions.
2. Explanation principle: Contrast questions often require an explanation.
3. Repetition principle: Contrast questions must be repeated with the same terms to elicit all the differences.
4. Context principle: When asking contrast questions, provide the informant with contextual information.
5. Cultural framework principle: Phrase contrast questions in cultural as well as personal terms.

1. Contrast Verification Questions

This type of question can only be formulated after discovering some difference between two folk terms. Then this difference is presented to an informant with a request to confirm or disconfirm the difference. Let's say you have spent many hours interviewing the vice-president of a corporation that produces food. In reviewing your field notes in search of contrasts for the contrast set *types of decisions,* you come across the following statement:

Well, I have to make a lot of different decisions. In fact, that's my job, making decisions. For example, I had to make a staffing decision this week, so I had to check with the executive committee. And this afternoon I need to make four or five packaging decisions on those breakfast cereals. I don't need to meet with the executive committee on that but I'll probably ask advice from several staff people.

In another interview you elicited more than sixteen kinds of decisions that your informant has to make and so *staffing decision* and *packaging decision* are familiar terms to you. But now you notice a contrast: one requires checking with the executive committee; the other does not. On the basis of this you formulate a contrast verification question:

I'm interested in the differences among all the kinds of decisions you have to make in the course of your work. In looking over some of our earlier conversations I came across some differences that I'd like to double check with you. Would you say that a staffing decision has to be checked with the executive committee, but that a packaging decision does not?

Contrast verification questions can frequently confirm differences and similarities among a large group of folk terms. In studying the meaning of *flop* with tramp informants I worked with a large stack of cards. I had established numerous differences through interviews and going over field notes but needed to verfiy these with other informants. One important difference that emerged was whether you could lie down in a particular flop or whether you had to sit up and sleep. I would present an informant with two stacks of cards on which the names of various flops occurred. I had tentatively established that one stack were all flops where you could lie down and sleep, the other stack were flops where you would have to sit up. "Can you tell me if all these flops are places you can lie down?" I would ask, pointing to the first pile.

My informant would quickly look through the cards, perhaps setting one or another card aside with a comment like, "There you have to sit up" or "I don't know about this one." Then I would point to the other stack of cards and say, "Can you tell me if all these flops are places you must sit up?"

Another way to ask contrast verification questions has to do with multiple contrasts. In studying *mission flops* I discovered that one important difference had to do with the number of nights a person could *consecutively* sleep there. Three differences emerged: (1) one night a month, (2) three nights a month, and (3) every night of the year. I went through all the specific mission flops (such as the Sally, Bread of Life Mission, Holy Cross Mission, etc.) and identified the number of nights for each the best I could. If I wasn't sure I would simply place a card in one of the three stacks randomly, knowing that my informant would correct me if it was wrong. Then, during an interview, I would set three stacks of cards before an informant and say something like

All of these are mission flops, but here are places you can flop one night a month (pointing to the first stack). This second group are missions you can flop at three nights a month, and the last one are places you can flop every night of the year. Could you look through and see if I have them right?

In asking verification questions, as well as each of the other types, new contrasts always emerge. Halfway through a stack like *mission flops* where you can only flop one night a month an informant may say, "Not only can you only flop there one night a month, but you have to take a nosedive if you want a flop." This immediately leads me to ask the next type of contrast question, one that is combined will all the other types.[4]

2. Directed Contrast Questions

A directed contrast question begins with a known characteristic of one folk term in a contrast set and asks if any other terms contrast on that characteristic. Take the previous example. If an informant casually points out that a *nosedive* is required in a particular mission flop, without even knowing anything about *nosedives,* I can ask a directed contrast question like the following:

Could you look through all the other mission flops and tell me which ones require you to take a *nosedive* in order to get a flop and which ones do not?

And so my informant looks through each of the cards and sorts them into flops requiring a *nosedive* and those which do not. Near the end, another casual comment occurs: "Well, this one, the Pacific Garden in Chicago, they don't require a nosedive but you got to take an earbanging." Immediately I would move on to another directed contrast question, this time without using the cards:

Oh, so in some mission flops you have to take an earbanging? Let me read off this list of mission flops and could you tell me for each one whether you have to take an earbanging? How about Holy Cross? Bread of Life? Sally? etc.

Much later I discover that a *nosedive* involves going to the front of the mission chapel after a service and praying, perhaps expressing sorrow for one's condition and at least pretending to turn over a new leaf. To take an *earbanging* means that you must sit through a religious sermon or you will not be able to sleep at the mission that night.

Directed contrast questions can also arise from one's field notes. Let's say that while reviewing my notes I come across the following statement about *couples,* one kind of customer at Brady's Bar: "Couples almost always sit in the upper section at the back." This immediately raises a question in my mind: "Are other customers the same or different from couples?" So, during the next interview I ask a question like the following:

One time earlier you mentioned that couples always sit in the back of the upper section. Do real regulars sit there also? Do loners? Do drunks? etc.

And my informant will almost always tell me where these people usually sit, how they contrast with the customary behavior of couples.

Keep in mind the fundamental rule in using all contrast questions: *ask for contrasts among members of the same contrast set.* In each of the previous examples the folk terms were always drawn from the same contrast set. Some were domains: *kinds of decision, kinds of flops, kinds of customers.*

One contrast set (*mission flops*) was a large category in the taxonomy *kinds of flops*.

3. Dyadic Contrast Questions

This type of contrast question, as well as all the remaining ones, differ in an important way from the first two. The ethnographer asks the question *without having any differences to suggest to the informant*. You merely ask informants to identify any difference they can see between folk terms. Informants are then free to reveal contrasts that are meaningful to them, some that the investigator would not think of. This strategy leads to discovering contrasts known and used by informants rather than imposing contrasts thought relevant by the ethnographer. At every point in the ethnographic process our goal is to describe the culture *in its own terms*. Looking back over this process we can identify at least the following points where the ethnographer must choose to discover informant's terms or impose the analytic categories of social science.

1. Formulating questions in native terms or outsider terms.
2. Identifying domains in native terms or using imposed categories from social science.
3. Identifying the taxonomic structure of domains in native terms or imposing an alien structure from social science to organize the domain.
4. Identifying contrasts in native terms or seeking those of interest to an outsider.

Dyadic contrast questions present informants with two folk terms and ask, "Can you tell me any differences between these terms?" For example, here is a typical exchange between an ethnographer and informant that uses a dyadic contrast question:

ETHNOGRAPHER: Bulls seem to be pretty important to most tramps, would you agree?

INFORMANT: Hell yes! Why, every tramp is on the lookout for bulls most of the time.

ETHNOGRAPHER: I've been trying to find out all the different kinds of bulls that tramps usually recognize. Here are the ones I've found so far (spreads more than a dozen cards in front of the informant with each type written on a different card).

INFORMANT: Yeah, I know all those. One you don't have here is *ragpicker,* they're a kind of bull. (Ethnographer quickly writes this folk term on a new card.)

ETHNOGRAPHER: Now, I'm interested in the differences among all these kinds of bulls. Lets begin with these two: *ragpicker* and *turnkey*. (Ethnographer picks up all the remaining cards, leaving the two in front of the informant.) Can you tell me any differences between a ragpicker and turnkey?

INFORMANT: Sure, a ragpicker is dressed like a tramp and a turnkey always wears a uniform.

Dyadic contrast questions such as this will elicit contrasts between all the other folk terms in the contrast set *kinds of bulls*. I would prepare a list of all the kinds, then work my way through every possible combined *pair* with questions like the following:

1. Do you see any difference between ragpicker and flyboy?
2. Do you see any differences between a flyboy and a turnkey?
3. What are the differences between a flyboy and a beat bull?
4. What are the differences between a beat bull and ragpicker?

Some of these questions ask for a single difference, others ask for multiple differences. Somethimes I will repeat a question after my informant has responded with contrasts. For example:

ETHNOGRAPHER: Do you see any difference between a ragpicker and a flyboy?

INFORMANT: Sure, a flyboy is riding a motorcycle and a ragpicker is always walking.

ETHNOGRAPHER: Can you think of any other differences between a flyboy and a ragpicker?

INFORMANT: Sure, a ragpicker will try to trap you by getting you to beg from them. Like they'll come up and say, "How much you holdin' on a jug?" When you say, "Thirty cents," they'll hold out some change, like they're offering it to you. Then you take some, cause they're offering it and you're trying to make a jug, and then they show you their badge and bust ass. Now a flyboy will never do that. He might pinch you for drunk and call a paddy wagon, but he won't trap you.

ETHNOGRAPHER: Can you think of any other differences between a flyboy and a ragpicker?

INFORMANT: Well, a ragpicker dresses in tramp's clothes and a flyboy wears a uniform.

4. Triadic Contrast Questions[4]

This type of question presents an informant with three folk terms and asks, "Which two of these are alike and which one is different from the others?" This procedure makes explicit recognition of the fact that differences always imply similarities. This is one of the most effective types of contrast questions.

With some informants, triadic contrast questions will require an explanation or even an example. Here is a typical explanation and question I would use when beginning with this type of contrast question.

ETHNOGRAPHER: You have told me about nearly all the different kinds of drinks that you serve in Brady's Bar. Now, I'd like to ask you a different kind of question, one that has to do with the differences among drinks.

INFORMANT: O.K. I'll try to answer the best I know how.

ETHNOGRAPHER: Let me start with an example of the kind of question I want to ask.

If I were to show you these three books and ask you, "Which two are alike and which one is different," you would probably say something like this. "These two are alike, they are both paperbacks; this one is different because it isn't a paperback." Or take another example. If I asked you about three people who work at Brady's Bar, Joe, Molly, and Sharon, and I asked which two were alike and which one was different, you could say, "Molly and Sharon are alike, they are both female, and Joe is male." Now, I want to ask you about kinds of drinks in this way. Is that clear?

INFORMANT: Well, sort of, but I'm not sure.

ETHNOGRAPHER: O.K. It will become clear as we go along. Here are three kinds of drinks, a *gin and tonic,* a *scotch and soda,* and a *Brandy Seven.* Now, can you tell me which two of those are alike and which one is different?

INFORMANT: Sure, a gin and tonic and a scotch and soda are both *fizzy* and a Brandy Seven is *bubbly.*

With both triadic contrast questions and dyadic contrast questions the ethnographer can follow up each response with a directed contrast question. For example, the last example resulted in two contrasts that waitresses use to distinguish drinks: some are fizzy and some are bubbly. It turns out that this information is extremely important to a waitress. Brady's Bar is dark and noisy; when bartenders mix drinks they do not point to each drink as they pass it to the waitress and say, "This is a Brandy Seven and this is a scotch and soda." The waitress must learn the cues for distinguishing drinks at the bar and again when she reaches the customer's table. If she gives customers the wrong drinks she will have to retrace her steps; it will upset the bartender; and the customer will probably not tip her. One cue for distinguishing drinks is whether they are *bubbly* or *fizzy.* Now with this information I could ask the following directed contrast question: "Now, let's go down this list of all the other drinks and as I read them off, can you tell me which ones are bubbly and which ones are fizzy?" A typical response almost always leads to more contrasts:

ETHNOGRAPHER: Rusty Nail.

INFORMANT: Bubbly.

ETHNOGRAPHER: Vodka Gimlet.

INFORMANT: That's not bubbly or fizzy.

ETHNOGRAPHER: What is it?

INFORMANT: Well, its cloudy. That's how I would tell it from the other drinks on my tray.

ETHNOGRAPHER: Gin Gimlet.

INFORMANT: That's cloudy too.

ETHNOGRAPHER: Calvert's and Water.

INFORMANT: That's clear.

And so I would work through the entire list of drinks until I could tell the cue for each one, whether bubbly, fizzy, cloudy, clear, or whatever. The directed contrast question has enabled me to discover other drinks that were fizzy or bubbly; it also led to the discovery of new contrasts.

Sometimes triadic contrast questions (as well as some other contrast questions) will elicit what I call the *test question response*. This response is so frequent and so detrimental to ethnographic research that every ethnographer must be alerted to its possibility. Let me give an example of the test question response. I began studying skid row men out of an interest in alcoholism. I wanted to find out why these men drank as they did. But soon I realized that drinking was not the most important thing to informants. They were far more concerned with making a flop, strategies for coping with the police, staying out of jail, and traveling. Then I came across the term *tramp*, the major identity category used by these men when out of jail. I began investigating this folk term, eliciting all the different kinds of tramps. When I asked the first contrast questions, many informants answered with the *test question response*. Here is a typical encounter.

ETHNOGRAPHER: Here are three kinds of tramps, a bindle stiff, an airdale, and a home guard tramp. Which two of these are alike and which one is different?
INFORMANT: What do you mean alike or different?

These informants sometimes asked this question in other ways, like "What kind of difference do you want?" or "Different in what way?" All these responses were asking me to give them some information that I wanted to know about these three kinds of tramps.

The great hazard of the test question response is that the ethnographer may actually respond with information. Because I was interested in drinking behavior, I was tempted to say, "Well, which of these tramps drink the most and which drinks less?" or "Which do you think have the most serious drinking problem, and which one has the less serious drinking problem?" It also crossed my mind to ask for differences about the marital status and educational background of these tramps. But all of these questions would have given informants contrasts primarily relevant to an outsider. In a very subtle way, these questions would have imposed my interests onto the folk terms used by tramps. Informants would have tried to give their opinions in response to each of these questions.

In responding to the *test question response* the ethnographer should place the responsibility for making contrasts in the hands of the informant. Here are some ways I usually respond to questions about what contrasts or differences I am interested in:

1. Well, I mean alike or different in any way that you can think of.
2. I'd like to know any differences that you think are important to most tramps.
3. I'm sure there are many ways that these three kinds of tramps are

different, but I'm interested in the ways that tramps see these differences. Can you think of two that are alike and one that is different in some way that is important to you?''

Informants almost always relax and begin to give contrasts freely and eagerly when they are given a response such as these. They have been reassured that the contrast question is not a test, that the ethnographer still wants to know the culture from their point of view, that they are the experts and ethnographer is the learner. Whenever informants offer a test question response, I take it as an opportunity to reaffirm the fact that I want them to teach me the meaning of their symbols. When used in this way, the test question response from informants can enhance the work of ethnography.

5. Contrast Set Sorting Questions

This type of question makes use of all the terms in a contrast set at the same time. The ethnographer writes each folk term on a card ahead of time. The cards are then presented to the informant with a simple instruction: ''Would you sort these into two or more piles in terms of how they are alike or different?'' Here is an example of a contrast set sorting question with a four-year-old informant about the work done in kindergarten.

ETHNOGRAPHER: Last time we talked you told me about a lot of different kinds of work you do at school. Do you do work everyday?

INFORMANT: Oh yes, like today we did big blocks and clay most of the morning.

ETHNOGRAPHER: Well, here are some cards. I have pasted or drawn pictures on each one that represents each kind of work you do. This one is for *tinker toys*, this crayon is for *coloring*, and so on. Can you recognize all these kinds of work?

INFORMANT: (going through all the cards) Oh, yes. That's *farm*, and that's *train*, etc.

ETHNOGRAPHER: Now, I'd like to play a little game together. I want you to place these cards in different piles. But first you have to think about the cards and put the same ones together in one pile that are alike, and then others in another pile that are alike, and other ones in still another pile. You can make only two piles or as many piles as you want. OK?

INFORMANT: Sure, that's easy. (She begins sorting the cards into piles, stopping occasionally to move a card from one pile to another.) OK, I'm done.

ETHNOGRAPHER: Now, can you tell me why you put these cards in this pile? (Points to the first pile.)

INFORMANT: Sure, all these kinds of work are ones that both boys and girls do, but mostly the boys do them. And this second pile is ones that both boys and girls do but mostly girls do them. This last pile is one that only girls do, that's *paper dolls*.

I would then place all the cards together in a single pile and ask the same question over again: ''Can you place these in two or more piles in terms of some way that the cards are alike and different?'' After the first two or three times, it is sufficient to say merely, "OK, that's great, now let's do it again, only put them in different piles this time." Sometimes it will take more than ten different sorting exercises to exhaust the contrasts that an informant knows or can recall.

Frequently an informant will give a test question response such as: "What kind of piles do you want me to make?" And as with the triadic sorting question, the ethnographer merely states that any way the informant thinks is important or any way that the informant can think of is appropriate.

6. Twenty Questions Game

Perhaps you have played the game of "Twenty Questions," in which one person thinks of an object and others try to guess that object by asking twenty questions. If the object cannot be discovered in twenty questions the person who thought of the object wins. Sometimes this game is referred to as "Animal, Vegetable, Mineral," because some rules require that the object thought of be labeled as an animal, vegetable, or mineral for a beginning clue. The main rule underlying this game is that the questioners must only ask questions that can be answered yes or no.

In adapting the Twenty Questions game to ethnography, instead of saying animal, vegetable, or mineral (which are simply large domains in our cultural knowledge), the ethnographer selects a single contrast set and picks one folk term from that. The informant is told which contrast set the folk term comes from, but not the folk term itself. The task placed before the informant is to ask yes and no questions of the ethnographer until the informant can guess which term the ethnographer is thinking of.

This game reveals the hidden contrasts that underly a contrast set. In the course of playing the game the ethnographer discovers the appropriate questions that informants would ask about all the folk terms in the set. As you can see from the following example, the ethnographer must still ask some questions during the course of the game. This example comes from an actual game played with an elderly tramp who had spent many years in the Seattle City Jail. I placed before him sixteen folk terms, all of which referred to the different kinds of trusties in the jail. These are the terms:

ranger	odlin's man	garage man
georgetown man	city hall man	harbor patrol man
wallingford man	floor man	clerk
bull cook	court usher	hospital orderly
blue room man	kitchen man	runner
barber		

The questions and answers went something like this:

169

ETHNOGRAPHER: I'd like you to ask me questions to see if you can guess which of these terms I'm thinking of. You can only ask questions that I can answer yes or no. You can't simply point to a card and say, "Is it this one?"

INFORMANT: OK. Are you thinking of an outside trusty?

ETHNOGRAPHER: Well, before I can answer that, will you tell me which trusties are outside trusties?

INFORMANT: Sure, these (he picks up all the terms which are outside trusties and shows them to me).

ETHNOGRAPHER: (While writing down which terms are outside trusties.) No, it isn't an outside trusty, can you ask me another question?

INFORMANT: Is it a trusty who works on the first floor of the jail?

ETHNOGRAPHER: Well, before I can answer that, you will have to tell me which ones work on the first floor of the jail.

INFORMANT: Well, its only the kitchen men. All the others work someplace else.

ETHNOGRAPHER: No, the one I'm thinking of doesn't work on the first floor of the jail. Can you ask me another question?

INFORMANT: Does the one you're thinking of work mostly with bulls or also with inmates and civilians?

ETHNOGRAPHER: Before I can answer that, you will have to tell me which ones work mostly with bulls.

INFORMANT: The ranger, odlin's man, garage man, georgetown man, harbor patrol man, wallingford man, blue room man, and clerk.

ETHNOGRAPHER: Yes, he works mostly with bulls.

INFORMANT: Well, then it must be the blue room man or the clerk.

ETHNOGRAPHER: How do you know?

INFORMANT: Because you said it wasn't an outside man, and they are the only ones who work mostly with bulls and are not outside men.

ETHNOGRAPHER: O.K., it's one of those two, but can you ask me a question to find out?

INFORMANT: Does the one you're thinking of work mostly with food?

ETHNOGRAPHER: Which ones work mostly with food?

INFORMANT: Of these two, only the Blue room man.

ETHNOGRAPHER: Yes, the one I'm thinking of works mostly with food.

INFORMANT: Then it has to be the blue room man.

ETHNOGRAPHER: Right. Now, let's start again. I'm thinking of a different trusty. Can you ask me questions, this time different questions, to see if you can guess?

This game works especially well with young informants but can be used with those of any age. After a few times through most informants will begin to generate many different questions, thus revealing the underlying contrasts they use to code a set of folk terms such as this.

7. Rating Questions

Rating questions seek to discover the values placed on sets of symbols. They ask informants to make contrasts on the basis of which folk terms are best, easiest, most difficult, worst, most interesting, most desirable, most undesirable, or any other rating criteria. Many times a rating question must be asked in the form of a directed contrast question which gives the informant one contrast, then asks for others.

All the other contrast questions, will, on occasion, yield evaluations and ratings. However, due to the importance of finding out the values that people attach to the symbols of a culture, I have identified this as a distinct question. After eliciting many different contrasts from my kindergarten informant about the types of work, I introduced a rating question such as, "Which type of work do you like the best?" or "Which types of work would you like to do first, which ones next, and which ones last?"

The ethnographer must be alert to folk terms that refer to rating scales. Tramps would refer to one or another trusty job as "shitty," "soft job," and "worse than lockup." These terms then became the basis for asking them to rate all the trusty jobs. Informants can often create their own scales. Thus, instead of merely saying that some trusty jobs are "soft jobs" and others are not, they would place them in rank order from the least soft to the most soft. Sometimes each job would appear in a separate category or degree of "softness," and sometimes several would appear together as the same degree of softness. When this set of contrasts was compared with ratings about the degree of difficulty of the job, many new insights about the culture emerged.

I began this step by identifying four *discovery principles* used in the study of cultural meaning systems. One of these, the contrast principle, was discussed in detail. It states that the meaning of a symbol can be discovered by finding out how it contrasts with other symbols. I presented seven different types of contrast questions, each designed to elicit differences among folk terms which belong to the same contrast set. These questions can also be used with nonverbal symbols to discover differences. For example, an ethnographer could present an informant with items of clothing, tools, paintings, or any other artifact to elicit contrasts with the seven questions.

At the same time, I want to stress that it is possible to discover many of the contrasts implicit in a culture without ever asking a single question. Through participant observation with tramps, I am certain one could eventually find out all the differences among kinds of flops or kinds of trusties. However, this would take a very long time and require that the ethnographer visit more than one hundred types of flops. But contrasts can also be discovered from interview data without asking contrast questions. By searching for statements made about a set of symbols in restricted contrast it is possible to distinguish them. The contrast questions are tools which enable the ethnographer to discover contrasts, both tacit and explicit, with great ease. However, the same tool is not always useful with every informant; neither is it necessary to use all these tools to discover contrasts. I have presented a range of questions so that you can draw on those that work best with each particular informant. I have known some ethnographers, for example, who found it best not to use any contrast questions in a direct, formal manner. Throughout their descriptive interviews they would casually ask for differences, but never call attention to what they were doing.

The various differences which emerge from contrast questions and from reviewing field notes have been called by various names, including dimensions of contrast, attributes, and components of meaning. This last term has given rise to a method of analysis called *componential analysis* that we will discuss in the next step. Componential analysis will enable you to take all the contrasts you have discovered, organize them in a systematic fashion, identify missing contrasts, and represent the components of meaning for any contrast set.

TASKS

9.1 Review your field notes and search for contrasts that distinquish folk terms in one or more contrast sets you have already identified.

9.2 Formulate contrast questions of each type presented in this step for one or more contrast sets.

9.3 Conduct an interview in which you use descriptive, structural, and contrast questions.

OBJECTIVES
1. To understand the role of componential analysis in the study of cultural meaning systems.
2. To identify the steps in making a componential analysis.
3. To carry out a systematic componential analysis on one or more contrast sets.
4. To use contrast questions to verify and complete a componential analysis.

Let us review briefly where the Developmental Research Sequence has brought us. First, our goal in ethnography is to discover and describe the cultural meaning system that people are using to organize their behavior and interpret experience. Meaning always involves the use of symbols. Although symbols can be created from anything in human experience, in this book we have focused on linguistic symbols: those created from vocal sounds or physical movements (such as the sign language of the deaf). Linguistic symbols form the core of the meaning system of every culture, and with these we can communicate about all other symbols in a culture. Ethnographic interviews are one means for gathering a sample of linguistic symbols.

Second, we saw that symbolic meaning arises from the way symbols are related to one another. Ethnography is the study of cultural meaning *systems*; it is the search for all the relationships among symbols, in this case, the folk terms used by your informant. If we could trace all the relationships that any symbol has in this system, we would have fully defined that symbol.

The D.R.S. Method began by locating an informant and conducting interviews using descriptive questions. Initially, the main purpose was to collect a sample of linguistic symbols: the folk terms and their relationships. This, of course, is an ongoing process, one you will continue until the last interview. In order to find how these folk terms were organized, you began with a domain analysis. This involved the systematic search for the cover terms and included terms that make up the categories of cultural knowledge your informant knows. In making a domain analysis, you used the semantic relationships which structure domains. This enabled you to locate, verify, and elicit more folk terms in a number of domains. By repeating the steps for making a domain analysis (and using structural questions), you identified a long list of domains. This gave you an overview of the cultural scene and some idea as to how the surface structure of that scene was organized. You have probably continued to add to this list of domains and will continue it until you have finished writing the ethnographic description.

You then shifted from the surface structure to begin an in-depth analysis of selected domains. Using the technique of taxonomic analysis, you discovered new relationships among folk terms which also revealed the internal structure of domains. Then, in the last chapter, you shifted from looking for similarities among folk terms (their inclusion in domains and taxonomies) and began to focus on differences. Using the discovery principle of contrast, you were able to discover numerous contrasts for a number of contrast sets. You are now ready to organize this information and more systematically identify the components of meaning for folk terms. This will be accomplished through making a componential analysis.

COMPONENTIAL ANALYSIS[1]

Componential analysis is the systematic search for the attributes (components of meaning) associated with cultural symbols. Whenever an ethnographer discovers contrasts among the members of a category, these contrasts are best thought of as the attributes or components of meaning for any term. For example, a *ranger* and a *runner* are both kinds of trusties. Until recently, our emphasis has been on their similarity: they are both related by being included in the set, *kinds of trusties*. But each of these folk terms has acquired meanings for tramps that are not revealed by this similarity. When contrasted, we discover that a ranger is a trusty who leaves the jail each day and travels to the pistol range; a runner, on the other hand remains within the jail until released. Each fact (leaves the jail, remains in the jail) is a component of meaning for the respective folk terms. When a tramp says to someone, "I made *ranger* last time I was in the bucket," this folk term carries the component of meaning that he left the jail each day to travel to the pistol range. We say that ranger has the *attribute* of leaving the jail.

We can define an attribute as any element of information that is regularly associated with a symbol.[2] Take a folk term like *pine tree* from our own culture. If we identify this term as a member of the domain *tree,* we have one bit of information. However, *pine tree* has a great deal of other things associated with it: it is a plant, a living object, an evergreen tree; it goes through stages of development; it produces pine cones; it can be used for lumber; it sometimes drips pitch; it has needles instead of leaves; its needles are usually green; it sheds needles from the inner branches in the fall. We could go on and on. Furthermore, it is possible to associate any kind of information conceivable with the folk term *pine tree*. We can imagine a society that adds these attributes: pine trees are homes for supernatural beings; pine trees require complex rituals to remove these beings; pine tree sap has curative powers; the needles of pine trees should be worn by all brides around their wrists and ankles. All this information represents the attributes of the symbol *pine tree*.

Attributes are always related to folk terms by additional semantic relationships. In placing a folk term within a particular domain, and again in finding its place within a particular taxonomy, you isolated a *single* semantic relationship. In making a componential analysis, you will focus on *multiple* relationships between a folk term and other symbols. Even when we ask structural questions, most informants volunteer additional relationships, additional information (or attributes) about the folk terms we are studying. Let's say you formulate a structural question: What are all the different kinds of trees? An informant will probably never respond simply by listing all the kinds of trees. A typical informant will say something like the following:

Well, there are lots of different kinds. There are oaks, you know, the ones that have acorns. And birches. And cedars, douglas fir, maple; those are really pretty in the fall, their leaves turn bright red and then gold. Let's see, a sycamore is a kind of tree and so is a pine tree. They have lots of green needles and at Christmas we always make wreaths from pine cones.

Up until now you may have wondered how to handle all this extra information, things that simply couldn't go into a taxonomy because they involved other semantic relationships. A componential analysis will lead to specific ways to represent all this extra information. In Figure 10.1 I have shown a single folk term with some of its *attributes* in a diagram that shows how each attribute is related to the term by a semantic relationship.

There are two ways that anthropologists have carried out componential analysis of folk terms. The first approach has limited itself to discovering those attributes that are conceptualized by informants. This kind of componential analysis seeks to discover the *psychological reality* of the informant's world, and is the approach taken throughout this book.[3]

However, some investigators have sought the formal or logical differences among members of a contrast set. In doing so, they have made free use of their own concepts without being concerned whether their analysis reflected the attributes salient to those who knew the culture. This type of analysis has sought to discover the *structural reality* which did not necessarily coincide with the informant's perceptions.[4]

Although most of the componential analyses using the structural reality approach have been done with kinship terms, we can illustrate with almost any domain. Take, for example, the domain of *work* mentioned earlier for a kindergarten classroom. By observing children working and by thinking about what their activities involve, it is possible to *assign* attributes to

FIGURE 10.1 Some Attributes and Semantic Relationships of Trusty

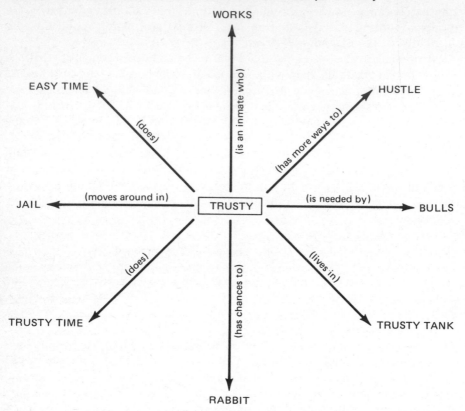

various activities. A social psychologist, for instance, might assign the following attributes to these terms:

rig-a-jigs: involves primarily manual dexterity skills
farm: involves primarily social skills
science table: involves primarily analytic skills

My informant, on the other hand, never recognized such attributes but instead identified ones like "done mostly by girls," "you have to pick up a mess afterwards," and "you have to sit down to do it." Componential analysis, like all other forms of analysis, can always make use of information *unknown* to informants to distinguish a set of terms. Our goal is to map as accurately as possible the psychological reality of our informant's cultural knowledge.

By asking contrast questions you have already elicited numerous attributes for many different folk terms. It is useful to represent graphically the most important attributes for any set of folk terms. This can be done with a *paradigm.*[5] A paradigm is a schematic representation of the attributes which distinguish the members of a contrast set. Whereas a taxonomy shows only a single relationship among a set of terms, a paradigm shows multiple semantic relationships. Let's look first at an empty paradigm in order to identify the basic elements; then we can place a small contrast set within it.

CONTRAST SET	DIMENSIONS OF CONTRAST		
	1	2	3
Folk term A	Attribute A-1	Attribute A-2	Attribute A-3
Folk term B	Attribute B-1	Attribute B-2	Attribute B-3
Folk term C	Attribute C-1	Attribute C-2	Attribute C-3

The first column contains the members of a contrast set, the folk terms that go together by reason of a single semantic relationship. If we take a single folk term, the row of spaces opposite that term contain the attributes for that particular term. In this empty paradigm, each term has spaces for three attributes. If we shift our attention from a single folk term and consider the entire set, the first column of attributes becomes a *dimension of contrast*. This is any dimension of meaning where some or all of the terms contrast. For example, the different kinds of *work* in the kindergarten class mentioned earlier differ for the dimension of contrast: that is, the sex of pupil who usually does the work. There are several different *values* on this dimension of contrast: (a) usually done by boys, (b) usually done by girls, and (c) always done by girls. Many times it is useful to focus our attention on a dimension of contrast, irrespective of the folk terms in the contrast set; at those times we will refer to the different contrasts as *values*. When we shift back to talking about the folk terms, these values are referred to as *attributes*.

The dimensions of contrast are given numbers in this empty paradigm, but in an actual case will be named or referred to by a descriptive phrase. Sometimes a dimension of contrast will come directly from something an informant says; at other times it must be inferred from what has been said. For example, my kindergarten informant never said, "These are all different because of the sex of the pupil who usually does the work." What she did say was, "Boys usually do that, girls usually do that, and only girls do that." From these statements, I simply made the generalization that they all referred to the sex of who was doing a particular kind of work. The name of a dimension of contrast is always more general than any of the specific values for that dimension of contrast.

In Figure 10.2 I have shown a small paradigm that partially defines the contrast set *kinds of inmates* from my study of the Seattle City Jail. This paradigm shows five folk terms (members of the contrast set): *trusty, drunk, lockup, kickout, rabbit*. All share a feature of meaning: they are all identities conferred on tramps by the jail system. Actually, as we shall see, a *rabbit* is

FIGURE 10.2 Paradigm for Kinds of Inmates[6]

CONTRAST SET	DIMENSIONS OF CONTRAST					
	Works	Doing Time	Living Location	Difficulty of Time	Ability to Hustle	Type of Hustling*
Drunk	No	Does drunk time	Drunk tank	Dead time = hard time	Limited	1,2,3,7
Lockup	No	Does lockup time	Lockup cells	Usually does hard time	Limited	1,2,3,5,6, 7,8,9,10
Trusty	Yes	Does trusty time	Trusty tank/ outside	Usually does easy time	Unlimited	All: 1-11
Kickout	No	Is doing short time	N/A**	Is doing easy time	Limited	2,3,7,10,11
Rabbit	No	Isn't doing time	Outside the jail	N/A	N/A	N/A

* Inmates recognize eleven kinds of hustling that can be carried out in jail to gain needed goods and services. These are 1. conning, 2. peddling, 3. kissing ass, 4. making a run, 5. taking a rake-off, 6. playing cards, 7. bumming, 8. running a game, 9. making a pay-off, 10. beating, 11. making a phone call. (See Spradley 1970: 225-251, for a detailed analysis of this domain.)
** N/A indicates a dimension of contrast is not applicable.

one who has run away from the jail and so at any moment may not actually be inside of the jail. Indeed, many *trusties* will spend much of their time outside the jail, but in a very different capacity than the *rabbit*. From this paradigm we can see that at least six different dimensions of contrast define the various kinds of inmates: whether they work, what kind of time they do, where they live, whether their time will be "hard" or "easy," whether they can "hustle" for things they want, and which hustling strategies they can use. For any particular term, we can now identify six attributes of the meaning of that term. We can also see the ways in which these folk terms are different. This paradigm, then, shows numerous semantic relationships for the terms which belong to the category *kinds of inmates*. It does not exhaust the distinctions that tramps make; neither does it fully define any single term. But it does give some of the most important information in summary form and allows us to examine quickly the differences among inmates.

This paradigm represents one small part of the cognitive map known to tramps. It enables them to *anticipate* future situations, plan for them, and make decisions of various sorts. They will know, for example, that certain kinds of inmates will do "hard time" and others will do "easy time." A person's cultural knowledge is made up of hundreds of such "maps," all interrelated into a complex system of cultural meanings.

STEPS IN MAKING A COMPONENTIAL ANALYSIS

A componential analysis includes the entire process of searching for contrasts, sorting them out, grouping some together as dimensions of contrast, and entering all this information onto a paradigm. It also includes verifying this information with informants and filling in any missing information. Although this may appear complex, you have already done most of the work involved. It will simplify the process by indicating a series of steps from start to finish.

Step One: Select a contrast set for analysis. In order to illustrate these steps, I will examine another contrast set from the domain *people in the bucket*. By now you have at least some idea about the meaning of the term *trusty*. However, what I have presented thus far is only in contrast to other inmates. In order to fully understand this folk term, we would need to contrast it with all other terms in the entire domain. Most important, we would need to find out the meaning of all the folk terms *included* in *trusty*. As an example of the steps in making a componential analysis, the contrast set *kinds of trusties* will help illuminate the meaning of *trusty*. Although there are more than sixty different kinds of trusties, I will only analyze the first level in the taxonomy which includes the following terms:

ranger	odlin's man	garage man
georgetown man	city hall man	harbor patrol man
wallingford man	floor man	clerk
bull cook	court usher	hospital orderly
blue room man	kitchen man	runner
barber		

Step Two: Inventory all contrasts previously discovered. Many contrasts will probably come directly from interviews in which you asked contrast questions. Others will be discovered in interviews not specifically centered on contrasts. Any statements about any member of the contrast set can be used. These can be inventoried and written down on a separate sheet of paper, thus compiling a list of contrasts. Here are some from my field notes to give you an idea of what the contrasts for this analysis looked like.

A hospital orderly is different from the blue room man and the georgetown man because he works with the nurse, he's under her jurisdiction.

A ranger is different from a blue room man 'cause the ranger is outside.

A harbor patrol man cleans up boats, but the garage man cleans up cars.

The clerk works with other inmates, he assigns them to things; the blue room man deals mostly with the bulls.

The runner sees most of what's going on; he goes all over the jail.

The harbor patrol has more freedom than either the ranger or the odlin's man cause he don't have to be in at a certain time.

179

City hall and garage men have to come back into the jail two times each day; the ranger goes out once and comes back.

From interviewing numerous informants I had collected many more statements about contrasts, but these are sufficient to show the type of information you must inventory.

Step Three: Prepare a paradigm worksheet. A paradigm worksheet consists of an empty paradigm in which you enter the folk terms in the left-hand column labeled "contrast set." The worksheet should have attribute spaces large enough for you to write a number of words and short phrases. As you begin your analysis you will want to enter more information on the paradigm than will appear when it is completed. On a large worksheet you can make notes to yourself and show links between this paradigm and other domains.

Step Four: Identify dimensions of contrast which have binary values. A dimension of contrast is an idea or concept that has at least two parts. For example, the concept *has leaves* is a dimension of contrast that is related to trees. It has two values or parts: (1) Yes, a tree does have leaves, (2) No, a tree does not have leaves. This dimension of contrast has two (binary) values. In the previous example of a paradigm (Figure 10.2), the first dimension of contrast had to do with the concept *work*. It implied a question, "Does this kind of inmate work?" As this paradigm is constructed, there are only two possible answers, so this dimension of contrast is binary. One inmate works; all the others do not.

Here are some examples of contrast statements that I have used to generate dimensions of contrast with binary values:

1. A hospital orderly is different from the blue room man and the georgetown man because he works with the nurse. *Works with nurse:* yes, no.
2. A harbor patrol man cleans up boats. *Cleans up boats:* yes, no.
3. City hall and garage men have to come back into the jail two times each day; the ranger goes out once and comes back. *Jail departure and return:* once daily, twice daily.

As you generate dimensions of contrast, be sure to enter the values of folk terms on your paradigm worksheet. For example, when identifying the dimension of contrast *jail departure and return,* I would immediately enter *twice daily* in the attribute spaces opposite *city hall man* and *garage man;* I would enter *once daily* in the attribute space opposite *ranger.* All other values for the other terms on this dimension of contrast would be unknown until further research was carried out. In Figure 10.3 I have identified a number of dimensions of contrast and filled in known values on a paradigm worksheet.

FIGURE 10.3 Paradigm Worksheet: Kinds of Trusties

CONTRAST SET	Works with boats	Works with cars	Works outside the jail	Must always eat jail food	Confined to a restricted area in jail	Only short timers are assigned	Provides service to the court
			DIMENSIONS OF CONTRAST				
Ranger	No	No	Yes	Yes	No	Yes	
Odlin's man	No		Yes	Yes		Yes	
Garage man	No	Yes	Yes	Yes	No		
Georgetown man	No		Yes	Yes	No		
City hall man	No		Yes	Yes	No		
Harbor patrol man	Yes	No	Yes	No	No		
Wallingford man	No		Yes	No	No		
Floor man	No	No	No	Yes	Yes		
Clerk	No	No	No	Yes	Yes		
Bull cook	No	No	No	Yes	Yes		
Court usher	No	No	No	Yes			Yes
Hospital orderly	No	No	No	Yes			No
Blue room man	No	No	No	Yes	Yes	No	
Kitchen man	No	No	No	Yes			
Runner	No		No	Yes	No		
Barber	No	No	No	Yes	No		

Step Five: Combine closely related dimensions of contrast into ones that have multiple values. The major reason for beginning with dimensions of contrast which have binary values (as the ones in Figure 10.3) is their simplicity. Most of these can be formulated as questions that are answered yes or no. Almost always, two dimensions of contrast which have binary values will, on inspection, prove to be closely related. For example, consider the first two dimensions of contrast in Figure 10.3. Harbor patrol men work with boats, and this led to a dimension of contrast *working with boats.* My data indicated that no other trusties worked with boats; I entered yes and no in all the appropriate attribute spaces. The second dimension of contrast is similar: *works with cars.* Again, I entered as many yes and no attributes as I had information on. Now, it is possible to combine these two dimensions of contrast into a slightly more general one: *What do they work with?* At first, it appeared that there would be three values: (1) boats, (2) cars, and (3) neither. However, this combining operation raised another question: What do other trusties work with? I was now ready to go back to my informants and ask them. Eventually I discovered six categories of things they worked with: vehicles (cars and motorcycles), boats, guns, buildings, food, and people.

Step Six: Prepare contrast questions to elicit missing attributes and new dimensions of contrast. One of the great values of a paradigm worksheet is that it will quickly reveal the kinds of information needed from informants. It offers a check sheet that will guide you in preparing contrast questions or specific questions like, "Does a clerk provide service to the court?"

Step Seven: Conduct an interview to elicit needed data. As a result of combining dimensions of contrast you will undoubtedly find many gaps in the data. Furthermore, you will find that dimensions of contrast sometimes suggest entirely new domains. For example, if an informant states, "Odlin's men have it nice because they can take a rake-off and do other kinds of hustling," it suggests a new domain: *kinds of hustling.* And so you could, in the next interview, ask a structural question to see if there are many folk terms in this domain, which originally appeared to you as a dimension of contrast.

Step Eight: Prepare a completed paradigm. From your interview data you will probably be able to complete the paradigm you had partially analyzed before the interview. Sometimes a single contrast set is best analyzed with two or more paradigms. For example, in addition to the information provided in Figure 10.4 (the completed paradigm for kinds of trusties), I elicited information on the visual characteristics of trusties. The police department requires the various kinds of trusties to wear distinctive uniforms, and these visual characteristics could become the basis for a separate paradigm. Or, it would be possible to do an extensive analysis of the differences among trusties for various hustling strategies. This might well become the basis for another paradigm.

Sometimes, as in the completed paradigm on *kinds of trusties,* it is necessary to use numbers in each attribute space, rather than writing out a verbal description of the attribute. In this analysis (Figure 10.4) the attributes related to confinement were so detailed and specific that a paradigm that included such written material would have become unwieldy.

In this chapter I have presented the steps in making a componential analysis. In the study of any particular cultural scene, you must decide which domains to examine in this kind of detail. Some ethnographers seek to make a componential analysis of as many domains as possible; others limit this detailed investigation to one or more central domains, describing other aspects of a cultural scene in more general terms. We have now completed a discussion of in-depth analysis of domains and in the next step we will move back to the surface of a cultural scene to try and construct a more holistic view.

FIGURE 10.4 Completed Paradigm: Kinds of Trusties

TRUSTY	DIMENSIONS OF CONTRAST				
	1.0	2.0	3.0	4.0	5.0
Ranger	1.2	2.2		4.1	5.1
Odlin's man	1.2	2.4		4.2	5.1
Garage man	1.2	2.3		4.3	5.1
Georgetown man	1.2	2.2		4.2	5.1
City hall man	1.2	2.3		4.2	5.2
Harbor patrol man	1.2	2.1		4.4	5.1
Wallingford man	1.2	2.1		4.2	5.1
Floor man	1.1		3.3	4.2	5.4
Clerk	1.1		3.3	4.6	5.1
Bull cook	1.1		3.3	4.2	5.3
Court usher	1.1		3.3	4.6	5.5
Hospital orderly	1.1		3.3	4.6	5.6
Blue room man	1.1		3.3	4.5	5.1
Kitchen man	1.1		3.1	4.5	5.6
Runner	1.1		3.2	4.6	5.4
Barber	1.1		3.3	4.6	5.4

DIMENSIONS OF CONTRAST

1.0 Restricted Mobility
    1.1 Inside
    1.2 Outside
2.0 Freedom
    2.1 Live outside the jail in another part of town. Eat at restaurants, are free to go to stores and movies, and may have visitors throughout the week.
    2.2 Leave the jail each morning and return in the late afternoon. Must eat a lunch prepared in jail. Some opportunity to go to stores but items must be smuggled back into jail.
    2.3 Leave the jail in morning, return at noon to eat lunch, and then go back out until late in the afternoon.
    2.4 Leave jail in morning, return at noon to eat lunch, then go back out until late afternoon, but the place of work is in the same building as the jail.
3.0 Confinement
    3.1 Leave 6th and 7th floors of public safety building and travel by elevator to the jail kitchen on first floor. Upon return at the end of the work day will often be examined for contraband.
    3.2 Remain within the bucket itself (6th and 7th floors) but have freedom to move throughout these two floors.
    3.3 Must work in a restricted area on a single floor.
4.0 Work Focus
    4.1 Guns
    4.2 Buildings
    4.3 Wheeled vehicles (cars and motorcycles)
    4.4 Boats
    4.5 Food
    4.6 People

5.0 Direct Service (provided to others)
    5.1 Bulls
    5.2 Bulls and civilians
    5.3 Bulls and trusties
    5.4 Bulls and inmates
    5.5 Court
    5.6 Bulls, inmates, and civilians

From Spradley (1970:292-293).

Tasks

10.1 **Make a componential analysis of one or more contrast sets following the steps presented in this chapter.**

10.2 **Conduct an ethnographic interview to gather the necessary data to complete your componential analysis.**

OBJECTIVES
1. To understand the nature of themes in cultural meaning systems.
2. To identify strategies for making a theme analysis.
3. To carry out a theme analysis on the cultural scene being studied.

The ethnographer must keep in mind that research proceeds on two levels at the same time. Like a cartographer engaged in mapping a land surface, the ethnographer both examines small details of culture and at the same time seeks to chart the broader features of the cultural landscape. An adequate cultural description will include an in-depth analysis of selected domains; it will also include an overview of the cultural scene and statements that convey a sense of the whole.

Some ethnographers convey a sense of the whole culture or cultural scene by what I call the *inventory approach*. They identify all the different domains in a culture, perhaps dividing them into categories like *kinship, material culture,* and *social relationships*. Although a simple listing of all domains is a necessary part of ethnography, it is not sufficient. I believe it is important to go beyond such an inventory to discover the conceptual themes that members of a society use to connect these domains. In this chapter we will examine the nature of cultural themes and how they can be used to give us a holistic view of a culture or cultural scene.

CULTURAL THEMES

The concept of cultural theme was first introduced into anthropology by Morris Opler who used it to describe general features of Apache culture. Opler proposed that we could better understand the general pattern of a culture by identifying recurrent themes. He defined a theme as "a postulate or position, declared or implied, and usually controlling behavior or stimulating activity, which is tacitly approved or openly promoted in a society" (1945:198). An example of a postulate that he found expressed in many areas of Apache culture is the following: Men are physically, mentally, and morally superior to women. Opler found this tacit premise expressed itself in such things as the belief that women caused family fights, that they were more easily tempted sexually, and that they never assumed leadership roles in Apache society.

The concept of theme has its roots in the general idea that cultures are more than bits and pieces of custom. Rather, every culture is a complex pattern. In her book, *Patterns of Culture,* Ruth Benedict was the first to apply this idea to entire cultures. She examined the details of Kwakiutl, Pueblo, and Dobuan cultures in search of general themes that organized these ways of life into dynamic wholes. For example, she saw the dominant pattern of Kwakiutl culture as one that emphasized the value of ecstasy, frenzy, and breaking the boundaries of ordinary existence. This theme emerged again and again in dances, rituals, myths, and daily life; Benedict called it Dionysian. Although her analysis has been questioned, Benedict's important contribution was her insight into the nature of cultural patterning. Every culture, and every cultural scene, is more than a jumble of parts. It consists of a system of meaning that is integrated into some kind of larger pattern. Many other anthropologists have sought to capture this larger pattern with such concepts as values, value-orientations, core values, core symbols, premises, ethos, eidos, world view, and cognitive orientation.[1]

For purposes of ethnographic research I will define cultural theme as any *cognitive principle, tacit or explicit, recurrent in a number of domains and serving as a relationship among subsystems of cultural meaning.*[2]

Cognitive Principle

Cultural themes are elements in the cognitive maps which make up a culture. Themes are larger units of thought. They consist of a number of symbols linked into meaningful relationships. A cognitive principle will usually take the form of an assertion such as "men are superior to women," or "you can't beat a drunk charge." A cognitive principle is something that people believe, accept as true and valid; it is a common assumption about the nature of their experience.

The assertions that make up what people know differ in respect to their *generality.* One assertion common among tramps is that "you can't trust a rubber tramp." This is a rather specific assertion, limited in its application to a single member of a single domain. Other assertions apply to a much larger realm of experience. For example, when a tramp says, "you can't beat a drunk charge," he makes an assertion about a universal experience among tramps (getting busted for drunk), an assertion that would occur in many contexts (in and out of jail), and one that is related to many domains (ways to beat a drunk charge, kinds of time, stages in making the bucket, etc.).

Themes are assertions that have a high degree of generality. They apply to numerous situations. They recur in two or more domains. One way that themes can be detected is by examining the dimensions of contrast from several domains. Among tramps a recurring dimension of contrast has to do with the concept of *risk*. When contrasting all the different *kinds of flops*, tramps continually make reference to the risk of sleeping in one or another place. When a tramp says, "Sleeping under a bridge is a good flop; *its a call job*," he means that the risk is low. A bull probably will not spot you there, someone must call to tell them you are there. Again, in contrasting the different *ways to hustle* in jail, the amount of risk involved with each type emerges as a dimension of contrast. Likewise, in contrasting all the *ways to beat* a drunk charge, the degree of risk assigned to each one is an important dimension of contrast. When a single idea recurs in more than one domain such as this, it suggests the possibility of a cultural theme.

Let's take another example, this time from the culture of cocktail waitresses at Brady's Bar. Several domains were examined for contrasts, including *places in the bar, kinds of employees, kinds of drinks,* and *kinds of customers*. One dimension of contrast that emerged from making a componential analysis for each of these domains had to do with *sex*. Waitresses distinguished different places in the bar in terms of male space and female space; they distinguished kinds of employees primarily by their gender; they distinguished drinks on the basis of male and female; customers also were divided up by male and female attributes. As we inspected these various domains, it became clear that an important aspect of meaning was maleness and femaleness. A general principle or cultural theme emerged: *life in this bar should clearly demarcate male and female realms*. Once we discovered this theme, we began looking for other specific instances of this general principle. It turned out that even very small domains like *ways to tip* and *ways to pay for drinks* clearly expressed this cultural theme.

It is important to recognize that cultural themes need not apply to every symbolic system of a culture. Some themes recur within a restricted context or only link two or three domains. Most ethnographers consider that the search for a single, all-encompassing theme, as Ruth Benedict attempted to do, is futile. It is more likely that a culture or a particular cultural scene will be integrated around a set of major themes and minor themes. In beginning to search for themes, the ethnographer must identify all that appear, no matter how broad their general application.

Tacit or Explicit

Cultural themes sometimes appear as folk sayings, mottos, proverbs, or recurrent expressions. The Mae Enga, for example, who live in the highlands of New Guinea recognize several themes related to pigs. Pigs are highly valued, they symbolize status, they are exchanged in important rituals, and they frequently live in the houses with people. A common expression among the Mae Enga sums up this cultural theme: "Pigs are our hearts!"[3] Tramps will readily state, "You can't beat a drunk charge." One ethnographer studied a Japanese bank which had the official motto, "Harmony and Strength.''[4] This motto summed up a recurrent theme in the social structure and ritual activities of bank employees. Sometimes such explicit expressions of a theme do not contain the full principle; they do however provide clues which enable the ethnographer to formulate the cultural theme.

But most cultural themes remain at the *tacit* level of knowledge. People do not express them easily, even though they know the cultural principle and use it to organize their behavior and interpret experience. Themes come to be taken for granted; they slip into that area of knowledge where people are not quite aware or seldom find the need to express what they know. This means that the ethnographer will have to make inferences about the principles that exist. Agar, in his study of heroine addicts, identified themes and also emphasized that they are frequently tacit. He analyzed numerous domains involving events in the lives of heroine users.

Throughout the different events, then, there is a recurrent concern with 'knowing the other.' The principle involved might be characterized as: Assume that everyone is a potential danger unless you have strong evidence to the contrary. [This principle] was never articulated by any of the junkies who worked in the study, though it might have been by a reflective junkie philosopher talking about the life (Agar 1976:3–4).

In my own research with tramps many of the themes remained tacit. Several themes emerged from the study of courtroom behavior and interviewing court officials. I was perplexed by the fact that the judges gave suspended sentences to those who had families, jobs, and other resources. Any man who had twenty dollars could bail out on a drunk charge and never appear in court at all. I talked to the judge about these practices at length and he assured me that he released tramps with families, jobs, or other resources because he felt they had a better chance of stopping their drinking. Whatever the reasons, it became clear that some tacit themes ran through the sentencing practices in the court. I formulated these on the basis of many inferences from what the judge said, from observations in the court, and from interviews with tramps. I stated these tacit themes as rules to be followed when dealing with men charged with public drunkenness (Spradley 1971a:351–358):

RULE ONE: When guilty of public drunkenness, a man deserves greater punishment if he is poor.
RULE TWO: When guilty of public drunkenness, a man deserves greater punishment if he has a bad reputation.
RULE THREE: When guilty of public drunkenness, a man deserves greater punishment if he does not have a steady job.

These themes actually form part of the overlap in cultures between judges

188

and tramps. In neither cultural scene are these themes entirely explicit; indeed, they are often denied by judges, but they still reflect the working tacit knowledge used to sentence public drunks.

Themes as Relationships

Themes not only recur again and again throughout different parts of a culture, they also *connect* different subsystems of a culture. They serve as a general semantic relationship among domains. As we shall see when we discuss theme analysis, one way to discover domains is to look for the relationships among them.

In studying Brady's Bar, several domains came to our attention early in the research: *ways to ask for a drink, hassles,* and *kinds of customers.* We quickly discovered that the female cocktail waitresses considered most of their hassles to come from female customers. Indeed, much to our surprise, we found that they dreaded waiting on female customers and constantly berated them when talking together. After eliciting the terms in these domains and doing some intensive analysis, we began seeking relationships among the domains. A major theme emerged, one tacitly known to waitresses and customers, but never expressed. This theme is related to the emphasis upon male and female differences in the bar. It can be stated in the following assertion: *female customers consider the purchase of drinks as an economic transaction; male customers consider it as an opportunity to assert their masculinity.* This theme began to link other domains together and made clear why waitresses often enjoyed the way males ordered drinks but not the way females did. When the men ordered they teased, complimented, and joked with the waitresses, calling attention to their own masculinity and to the intrinsic femininity of the waitresses. After such a transaction, the waitresses gained more than an order for drinks or a tip after serving; they received a kind of sexual affirmation, something that the simple economic exchange with female customers never offered.[5]

In an earlier chapter I suggested that ethnographic analysis consisted of a search for (a) the parts of a culture, (b) the relationship among those parts, and (c) the relationship of the parts to the whole. In studying folk terms, domains, and taxonomies, you have been searching for parts and their relationships. The search for themes involves identifying another part of every culture, those cognitive principles that appear again and again. But the search for themes is also a means for discovering the relationships among domains and the relationships of all the various parts to the whole cultural scene. In the remainder of this chapter I want to present a number of strategies for conducting a theme analysis.

STRATEGIES FOR MAKING A THEME ANALYSIS

The techniques for making a theme analysis are less well developed than those used in other types of analysis presented in this book. What follows is a list of strategies I have gleaned from my own research, the work of other ethnographers, and suggestions from students. This area of cultural analysis invites the most experimentation on the part of the ethnographer.

Immersion

This first strategy is the time-honored one used by most ethnographers. By cutting oneself off from other interests and concerns, by listening to informants hours on end, by participating in the cultural scene, and by allowing one's mental life to be taken over by the new culture, themes often emerge. Sometimes immersion, broken by brief periods of withdrawal, generates insights into the themes of a culture. D'Andrade has called attention to this strategy as well as to the need for understanding how insights come to an ethnographer totally immersed in another society (1976:179).

At present, the most frequently used (and perhaps most effective) technique for the study of cultural belief systems is for the individual ethnographer to immerse himself in the culture as deeply as possible and, by some series of private, unstated, and sometimes unconscious operations, to integrate large amounts of information into an organized and coherent set of propositions. To make these operations explicit, public, and replicable, or to develop a means of testing the accuracy of these operations, is likely to be a difficult and lengthy task. Nevertheless, it is a necessary task if the study of culture is to continue as a science (quoted in Agar 1976).

The ethnographer who has not gone to live in another society for a year or two can still make use of this strategy. For example, if you have been conducting interviews each week over a period of several months, you can take a day or two to spend entirely on reviewing the data collected. Or several days can be set aside to review the interviews, visit with additional informants, go to the setting where your informant is, and begin writing during the evenings. After several intensive days, new relationships will emerge that a superficial acquaintance with a cultural scene can never give. The next strategy is one designed to bring about an intensive immersion in your data. If at all possible, it is a good idea to take enough time to carry out the next strategy without intervening time spent on other activities.

Make a Cultural Inventory

By this point in the research your ethnographic record has grown to considerable size. You have undoubtedly made many interpretive and analytic entries in your field notes. You may have a number of interviews on tape which need to be transcribed. Even a few weeks can lead to a loss in the easy familiarity you had with early interview data and insights. It is time to make a careful, written inventory of all the data you have collected. This will serve to review what you do have, point to gaps in the data, and help bring about a deeper immersion so necessary to discovering cultural themes. Here are a number of specific ways to inventory your data. You can probably add others to the list.

1. Make a list of cultural domains. If you have continued to add to the list prepared during Steps Five and Six, this may be a relatively simple task. However, it is well worth the time to *reread all ethnographic interviews* to search for any domains you may have overlooked. Without realizing it, as you have progressed through the tasks in the D.R.S. Method, your skills have improved. You will find it much easier to identify domains you would have easily missed at an earlier stage.

One approach to making a list of cultural domains is to list the cover term at the top of a three-by-five card in large print. Then, below this, in smaller print, list the included terms. If you have domains with a large number of included terms, you may want to merely list the included terms at the first level. Your goal here is to make an inventory of the domains, not identify every single term. In the upper right-hand corner of each card indicate the degree to which each domain has been analyzed. You will probably have domains at all the following stages:

1. Completely analyzed (taxonomy, paradigm)
2. Complete taxonomy, partial paradigm
3. Incomplete taxonomy and partial paradigm
4. Cover term and all included terms but no taxonomy or paradigm
5. Cover term only (or with a few included terms)

As you make your list, you may see relationships among domains even though you haven't started to search for them. In fact, this may occur at any time during the process of making a cultural inventory. Keep your mind open to seeing new relationships and quickly make a note of any that you think of. Do not try to evaluate or check on them now but simply record them.

2. Make a list of possible unidentified domains. By now your familiarity with the cultural scene has increased to the point where you can imagine possible domains your informant has never discussed. For example, I spent many hours interviewing tramps about the stages in making the bucket. I wanted to know each step in the process from arrest through incarceration to release from jail. And I wanted to know the folk terms they used to encode this information. I also studied their terms for the different kinds of tramps. Now, it occurred to me that there might be a domain *stages in becoming a tramp.* In studying cocktail waitresses, we collected many terms for *hassles* and for *kinds of customers*. Many hassles came from the various customers. It occurred to me that waitresses would have a variety of feelings in the course of their work and dealing with these hassles. Indeed, some were expressed in interviews. A new domain, one we never investigated, might be *kinds of feelings* that waitresses have during the course of an evening.

In generating a list of possible unidentified domains, it is useful to examine the domains from other cultures, such as the list given at the end of Step Six for the culture of encyclopedia salespeople. One can also formulate some very general structural questions as an aid to thinking up possible unidentified domains. Here is a sample:

1. Are there any other kinds of objects?
2. Are there any other kinds of events?
3. Are there any other kinds of acts?
4. Are there any other kinds of actors?
5. Are there any other kinds of activities?
6. Are there any other kinds of goals?
7. Are there any other ways to achieve things?
8. Are there any other ways to avoid things?
9. Are there any other ways to do things?
10. Are there any other places for things?
11. Are there any other causes of behavior?
12. Are there any other effects of behavior?
13. Are there any other reasons for doing things?
14. Are there any other places for doing things?
15. Are there any other things that are used for something?
16. Are there any other stages in tasks?
17. Are there any other stages in activities?
18. Are there any other stages in events?
19. Are there any other objects that have parts?
20. Are there any other places that have parts?

As you compile your list of possible, unidentified domains, allow yourself to entertain ideas about relationships between these unidentified domains and the ones you have analyzed. Enter any tentative ideas about themes into your notes immediately; later you can test, evaluate, and clarify them.

3. Collect sketch maps. Go through your field notes and make a copy of all sketch maps made by your informants. By asking task-related descriptive questions, you will probably have collected different kinds of maps. In addition, you can draw sketch maps yourself from verbal descriptions. For example, I had a detailed map of the inside of Brady's Bar that pulled together a great deal of information. I also had a description of the route to work for many of the waitresses and could construct a sketch map from that description.

Informants often provide the ethnographer with sketch maps of activities or events as well as places. A ceremony that goes through stages can be placed on a chart indicating the major sequence of activities. A network of friends, a genealogy of relatives, routes taken from one place to another, insides of rooms, and spatial arrangements in stores, factories, schools, and towns all lend themselves to diagrams and sketch maps.

Before going on to the next inventory task, make a short list of additional sketch maps you could obtain from informants. Note the ones that would help you in completing your ethnography so you can collect them during the next interview.

4. Make a list of examples. An example is a verbal description of a concrete experience. It can come from interviews or from your own observations. An example always gives *details,* specific facts of the situation. An ethnography consists of much more than folk terms and taxonomies. Folk terms and taxonomies represent the skeletons of a culture's structure; examples put flesh on these skeletons. In your final written ethnography you will need to illustrate the folk terms and their meaning. That means you will need examples. If your informant has been a good storyteller, your field notes are probably crammed with examples. However, you can't assume you have examples until a careful inventory has been made.

To make a list of examples, take the cards on which you listed domains and record the pages in your field notes which contain examples. By quickly skimming through your field notes you will be able to make an estimate of gaps in your data. If you are short on examples for domains that will form a major part of your written ethnography, you can collect them in the next interview.

In preparation for writing, some ethnographers abstract examples for various topics onto cards. For example, I had identified eleven *ways to hustle* when in jail. I did a careful componential analysis of these folk terms and decided to write an ethnographic description. I started searching for examples and recorded each one on a separate card with the folk term entered at the top. When I began to write the paper, I could easily sort through the cards and find the appropriate example. This speeded up my writing as well as gave me an exact inventory of how many examples I had collected.

5. Inventory miscellaneous data. In addition to interviews you will undoubtedly have additional data. These include your journal, ideas that have gone into your analysis and interpretation of field notes, and anything else you have collected. In studying a first-grade classroom, you may have collected lesson plans, student worksheets, and memos sent home with pupils. During a study of air traffic controllers you might have found an article in the newspaper about local conflicts between the controllers and the airline companies. Don't overlook pictures, magazines, or artifacts related to the cultural scene you are studying. Make a list of all miscellaneous data so that by the end of your inventory you have an index to the cultural material collected. This index tells you what you have done and also gives clues to new avenues of research.

The process of making a cultural inventory lays the foundation for discovering cultural scenes. The hours spent on this will allow you to move quickly to using other strategies.

Make a Componential Analysis of Folk Domains

After making an inventory, you have the basis for doing a componential analysis using all the cover terms as a contrast set. This macrodomain can be referred to as *things informants know*. For example, in my own research on a small factory which makes tannery equipment, I reviewed many hours of interviews and came up with the following list of domains:

1. Kinds of people
2. Kinds of jobs
3. Kinds of machines
4. Kinds of hardware
5. Kinds of tools
6. Kinds of wood
7. Kinds of tanneries
8. Kinds of drums
9. Kinds of jobs
10. Kinds of accidents
11. Steps in making a lunch run
12. Steps in making a drum
13. Steps in making a vat
14. Steps in making a paddle wheel
15. Steps in getting hired
16. Steps in getting fired
17. Reasons for taking time off
18. Reasons for working at the Valley
19. Reasons for quitting
20. Reasons for assigning jobs
21. Reasons for fucking off
22. Parts of the Valley
23. Parts of the day
24. Times of the day
25. Times of the week
26. Times of the year
27. Ways to talk
28. Ways to fuck off
29. Ways to prevent accidents
30. Ways to get fired
31. Ways to work
32. Ways the boss gets down on you
33. Places to deliver
34. Places to pick up
35. Places to go after work
36. Things to talk about
37. Things you eat
38. Things you do after work
39. Things you can't do at work
40. Things people do
41. Things people make

This list of domains represents hundreds of included folk terms, some of which I had identified; others were still undiscovered at the time I made this list. A large paradigm worksheet would list all these domains down the left hand column and a search for contrasts would begin.

Cultural themes serve as *relationships* among domains. By making comparisons and contrasts among domains such as this, the ethnographer can begin to find some relationships. Because themes are often *tacit,* it is often difficult to find explicit contrasts in your field notes which distinguish entire domains. I think it is best to begin asking yourself contrast questions. For example, the following question could be put to an informant or to the ethnographer:

You know a lot about what goes on at the Valley (the name of the factory). You and other employees know the following three things: kinds of people, steps in making a lunch run, and steps in making a drum. Which two are alike and which one is different?

On the basis of my own familiarity with this culture I can see the following contrast which I think my informant would see:

Knowing about *kinds of people* and *steps in making a lunch run* are things you pick up without anyone telling you; *steps in making a drum* is very complex and someone has to teach you that.

This suggests that one relationship among domains might be that some are learned by formal instruction and others by informal learning.

Once you have made as many contrasts as possible, you will want to ask your informant for contrasts. I begin by writing each domain on a separate card and spreading all the cards in front of my informant. Then I would explain what I wanted to know:

In the last few months I've been trying to find out everything that you and others at the Valley know. I'm interested in finding out everything that an old-timer would know as a result of working at the Valley. Now, I've written down on cards all I can think of after going over all the interviews. If I were going to understand what it is like to work at the Valley, I would have to know about all the different *kinds of people*, all the *kinds of jobs*, all the *kinds of machines*, etc. (I would then review each card, ending with the following question). Can you think of anything else I would have to know if I were going to know everything an old-timer had learned?

In almost every case, an informant will now recall additional areas of cultural knowledge. These can be written on cards. Then I would ask contrast questions and seek out similarities and differences among these domains of cultural knowledge.

With one informant from the Valley I asked this question:

Out of all these things that people who work at the Valley know, which do you think would be the most important for me to find out about if I'm going to really understand what it is like to work there?

My informant's immediate response was: "things people talk about." This was a domain I had not previously investigated so I quickly elicited the following folk terms: *getting layed, bar fights, drugs, stuff they used to do, stories, families, money, next weekend, the past weekend, cars, hunting,* and *vans.* It would be possible to continue finding out which other domains my informant considered important and then seek the reasons for the ranking of domains.

Search for Similarities among Dimensions of Contrast

Another strategy for discovering cultural themes is to examine the dimensions of contrast for all the domains you have analyzed in detail. The dimensions of contrast represent a somewhat more general concept than the individual attributes associated with a folk term. Themes are more general still, but dimensions of contrast can sometimes serve as a bridge between the most specific terms and their attributes and the themes that relate subsystems of cultural knowledge.

I mentioned earlier how the dimensions of contrast that had to do with *risks* in the culture of tramps suggested possible themes about the insecurity of their daily lives. Let me give another example of dimensions of contrast. As I began to make a componential analysis of the different folk terms included in *tramp,* I thought contrasts such as amount of drinking or age might be important. Instead, the dimensions of contrast almost all had to do with *mobility.* My informants distinguished among all the different kinds of tramps in terms of (1) their degree of mobility, (2) their mode of travel, (3) the type of home base they had when traveling, and (4) the survival strategies employed when on the road (see Spradley 1970:65–96 for an extended discussion of this domain). When I examined the dimensions of contrast that tramps used to distinguish kinds of trusties (see Figure 10.5), a similarity appeared. The different kinds of trusties were contrasted in terms of their mobility in and out of jail, down to very small degrees. Outside trusties had the most mobility, but even here some had less and were required to return to the jail each night or at noon and again at night. Those trusties who worked inside the jail were distinguished in terms of the degree of freedom to move around inside the jail. I concluded that something I called "mobility" was very much a part of the identities of my informants, both as tramps and as inmates in the jail. I then began to look for other evidence of mobility and how it might be important in the lives of tramps. It turned out that mobility was directly related to drinking behavior. When a tramp travels he leads a somewhat isolated life. Arriving in a new town in need of human companionship, a spot job, or other resources, he heads for skid row and the bars. Bars are classified into more than a dozen different kinds in terms of the resources they provide. Bars, to a tramp, are like churches, social clubs, employment agencies, and the welfare office, all rolled into one. But bars are also places for drinking and they reinforce the symbolic value of drinking to tramps. Without going into more detail, I soon discovered that the courts, missions, and even the alcoholism treatment center reinforced the tramp's desire to travel. The theme of mobility emerged as one of the most important in the entire culture of what I came to all "urban nomads." I discovered this theme originally by comparing the dimensions of contrast between two domains.

Identify Organizing Domains

Some domains in a cultural scene dynamically organize a great deal of information. This is particularly true of those based on the semantic relationship X is a stage of Y. One of the most useful strategies for discovering cultural themes is to select an organizing domain for intensive analysis. In her study of directory assistance operators Ehrman (1977) selected two domains to organize most of the data collected. One was *stages in a typical day* and the other was *stages in a directory assistance call*. Although a typical call lasted only a few seconds, the calls could be broken down into thirteen basic stages, repeated over and over throughout the day.

One of the best kinds of organizing domains are events or a series of related events. Agar, in his ethnography of heroine users, has shown the power of analyzing events and their interrelations (1973). In studying the culture of the Seattle City Jail from the perspective of inmates, I selected the domain *stages in making the bucket* as the major organizing domain. I placed this domain as a central focus of the ethnography; then, as I described each stage in detail, I easily connected other domains to this one. For example, at each stage in the process, informants talked about smaller events encoded by verbs for action or activities. Organizing domains were discussed in Step Eight, and at that point you may have selected one for investigation. If so, you can now examine it in relation to others to discover cultural themes.

Make a Schematic Diagram of the Cultural Scene

Another strategy for discovering cultural themes is to try and visualize relationships among domains. Figure 11.1 is a schematic diagram of the *places* tramps find themselves as they go through the *stages in making the bucket*. It also includes information about the events that occur during this process. Although it doesn't begin to represent the entire cultural scene, even this partial diagram suggests many relationships and themes in this culture.

One can begin making schematic diagrams by selecting a limited number of domains and themes. For example, in Figure 11.2 I have shown some of

FIGURE 11.1. Stages in Making the Bucket

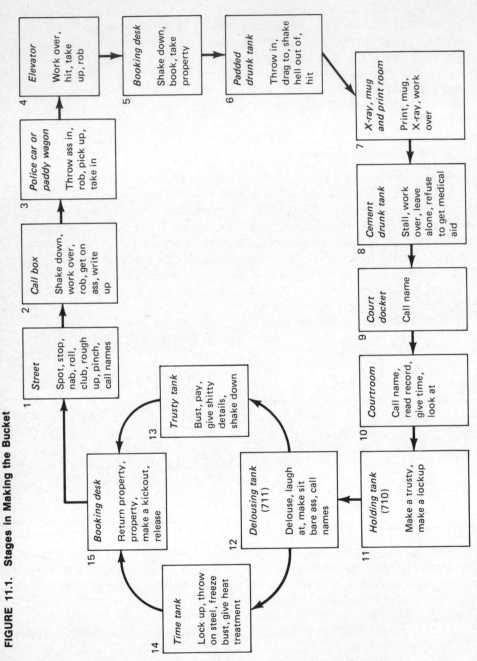

From Spradley 1970: 138.

FIGURE 11.2. Mobility and Drinking

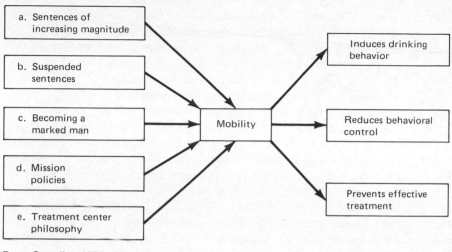

From Spradley 1973: 29.

the relationships that occur between the theme of mobility in tramp culture and various aspects of their lives. The final diagram you create is not nearly as important as the process of visualizing the parts of a cultural scene and their relationships. This thinking process is one of the best strategies for discovering cultural themes. Some of the diagrams you create may find their way into your final ethnographic description, helping to make the relationships clear to those who read the report.

In addition to making diagrams of limited aspects of the cultural scene and larger ones that attempt to encompass the entire scene, it is useful to go beyond the scene you are studying. A simple square or circle in the center of a sheet of paper can represent the entire cultural scene you have been studying. Then, with various sorts of lines to show the relationships, additional symbols can be used to represent other scenes within the wider culture or even within other cultures. For example, the culture of tramps is connected to at least the following: their families, judges, the police department, the welfare office, the liquor stores, the religious missions, the junk yard dealers, the railroads and their employees, farmers, social scientists, and many more. By creating a diagram of all these possible other scenes that connect to the world of tramps, I could see areas for future research and gain insights into the culture of tramps itself.

Search for Universal Themes

In the same way that there appear to be universal semantic relationships, there appear to be some universal cultural themes, the larger relationships among domains. The ethnographer who has a familiarity with universal themes may use them as a basis for scrutinizing the data at hand. The following list is a tentative, partial inventory of some universal or nearly universal themes that ethnographers have identified. Many more could be discovered by going through ethnographic studies and the literature of the social sciences. This list is merely intended to be suggestive of possible themes that might be found in the scene you are studying.

1. Social conflict. In every social situation conflicts arise among people; these conflicts often become worked into cultural themes in ways that organize cultural meaning systems. A useful strategy in studying any society is to look for conflicts among people. Tramps have conflicts with the police and this conflict shows up in most of the domains in the culture. It is clearly related to the *risks* that they take in the course of daily life.

2. Cultural contradictions. Cultural knowledge is never consistent in every detail. Most cultures contain contradictory assertions, beliefs, and ideas. Robert Lynd, in his classic analysis of American culture, proposed twenty fundamental values or themes, most of which stood in opposition to others (1939). For example, one stated, "Honesty is the best policy, but, business is business and a businessman would be a fool if he did not cover his hand." One cultural contradiction that occurs in many cultural scenes has to do with the official "image" that people seek to project of themselves, and the "insider's view" of what really goes on. Cultural contradictions often are resolved by *mediating themes.* Every ethnographer is well advised to search for inherent contradictions that people have learned to live with and then ask, "How can they live with them?" This may lead to discovering important themes.

3. Informal techniques of social control. A major problem in every society is controlling behavior. Every society must get people to conform to the values and norms that make social life possible. Although formal means of control, such as police force or incarceration, occur, these are not the major techniques employed. In every society and every social situation, people have learned informal techniques that effectively control what others do. Gossip and informal social rewards are two means which function as mechanisms of control. By examining the various domains to find relationships to this need for social control, you may well discover important cultural themes. In Brady's Bar, for example, waitresses will seek to control customers' behavior. Sometimes a waitress will go so far as to kick or verbally abuse a male customer, but most of the time more subtle, informal strategies are used. In an excellent study of tipping in another bar, Carlson has shown how waitresses control the tipping behavior of customers with subtle reminders such as leaving the change on the tray and then holding the tray at eye level. If the customer reaches for it, he will appear awkward and the waitress can quickly lower the tray and say, "Oh, I thought that was a tip" (Carlson 1977).

4. Managing impersonal social relationships. In many urban settings, impersonal social relationships make up a major part of all human contact. In almost any urban cultural scene people have developed strategies for dealing with people they do not know. This theme may recur in various domains of the cultural scene. In an excellent discussion of this nearly universal theme, Lyn Lofland (1973) has shown how it operates in many urban scenes.

5. Acquiring and maintaining status. Every society has a variety of status and prestige symbols; people often strive to achieve and maintain these symbols. We quickly think of money or athletic skill, but these are not the only status symbols. In every cultural scene there are status symbols, many of which are more subtle. Appearing "cool" under pressure may give one status; expressing a high degree of religious devotion confers status in some scenes. Cultural domains often reflect the status system of a culture and can become the basis for one or more major cultural themes.

6. Solving problems. Culture is a tool for solving problems. Ethnographers usually seek to discover what problems a person's cultural knowledge is designed to solve. For example, much of what tramps know appears to be aimed at solving a limited set of problems: making a flop, acquiring clothes, getting enough to eat, beating a drunk charge, escaping loneliness, finding excitement, and making it (acquiring resources such as money or alcoholic beverages). One can relate many of the domains in the culture of tramps by showing how each is related to the problems tramps are trying to solve. This same approach can be used in the study of almost any cultural scene.

In looking for universal cultural themes, a rich source lies in novels.[6] Themes in novels often reflect universal cultural themes, and by examining them carefully one can find clues to themes in the cultural scene being studied. For example, Joanne Greenberg has written an excellent novel about deaf people in the United States called *In This Sign*. A number of themes run through this novel, such as "sign language is a symbol of membership in the deaf community" and "sign language is a stigma among hearing people." Anyone doing ethnographic research among the deaf would find this novel a rich source of possible cultural themes that relate many domains.

Write a Summary Overview of the Cultural Scene

This strategy for discovering cultural themes will help to pull together the major outlines of the scene you are studying. In several brief pages, write an overview of the cultural scene for someone who knows nothing about what you are studying. Include as many of the major domains as you can, as well as any cultural themes you have identified. The goal of this overview is to condense everything you know down to the bare essentials. In the process of writing this kind of summary, you will be forced to turn from the hundreds of specific details and deal primarily with the larger parts of the culture; this, in turn, will focus your attention on the relationships among the parts of the culture and lead to discovering cultural themes.

Make Comparisons with Similar Cultural Scenes

A fruitful strategy for discovering themes is to make limited comparisons with other cultural scenes. This can be done by mentally reviewing other scenes of which you have some knowledge, visiting other social situations to make an on-the-spot comparison, or actually conducting an interview with informants who have knowledge of other scenes. As Glaser and Strauss point out in their book, *The Discovery of Grounded Theory* (1967), it is useful to make limited comparisons with similar social situations. For example, an ethnographer studying the culture of McDonald's fast-food restaurants might visit other fast-food restaurants and other kinds of restaurants, looking for striking contrasts.

In studying cocktail waitresses, we compared them with other kinds of waitresses and with women who work in other occupations, such as nurses and secretaries. We went even further to make comparisons with other cultures. For example, we began to look for comparisons that might shed light on the relationship between bartenders and waitresses, finding that this relationship had many similarities with the widespread "joking relationship" in non-Western societies. As we examined these joking relationships from the ethnographic literature, we discovered themes that were applicable to what occured between waitresses and bartenders (Spradley and Mann 1975:87–100).

In this chapter we have examined the concept of cultural theme and presented some strategies for discovering cultural themes. Every ethnographer will be able to develop additional ways to gain insights into the cultural themes which make up part of the tacit knowledge informants have learned. Each of the strategies discussed here will best be viewed as tentative guides to discovering cultural themes, not as a series of steps that inevitably lead to themes. Immersion in a particular culture still remains one of the most proven methods of finding themes. One way to gain a greater immersion into the ideas and meanings of a culture is to begin writing a description of that culture. Many ethnographers delay writing in the hope that they will discover new themes or complete their analysis in a more detailed manner. But writing the ethnographic description is best seen as part of the process of ethnographic discovery. As you write, new insights and ideas for research will occur. Indeed, you may find that writing will send you back for more ethnographic interviews to fill in gaps in the data and test new hypotheses about cultural themes. In the next chapter we will discuss some ways to go about writing the final ethnographic report.

Tasks

11.1 Make a cultural inventory using the procedures set forth in this chapter.

11.2 Identify as many cultural themes as you can by means of the strategies presented in this chapter and any others you find useful.

11.3 State all the cultural themes as brief assertions.

WRITING AN ETHNOGRAPHY

OBJECTIVES
1. To understand the nature of ethnographic writing as part of the translation process.
2. To identify different levels of ethnographic writing.
3. To identify the steps in writing an ethnography.
4. To write an ethnography.

Every ethnographer probably begins the task of writing a cultural description with the feeling it is too early to start. Doing ethnography always leads to a profound awareness that a particular cultural meaning system is almost inexhaustibly rich. You know a great deal about your informant's culture, but you also realize how much more there is to know. It is well to recognize that what you write, indeed that every ethnographic description, is partial, incomplete, and will stand in need of revision. Most ethnographers would do well to set aside their feelings that writing is premature and begin the task sooner rather than later. In the process of writing one discovers a hidden store of knowledge gained during the research process.

As most professional writers will affirm, the only way to learn to write is *to write*. In the same way that learning to swim cannot occur during classroom lectures on swimming, discussion of principles and strategies to follow in writing do not take us very far in learning to write. It is best to observe other swimmers, get in the water yourself and paddle around, and then have an experienced swimmer point out ways to improve your breathing and stroke.[1]

One of the best ways to learn to write an ethnography is to read other ethnographies. Select those which communicate to you the meaning of another culture. Seek out ethnographies written in a way that brings that culture to life, making you feel you understand the people and their way of life. If you read well-written ethnographies during the process of writing, your own writing will improve without conscious effort.

Every ethnographer can identify books and articles that are well-written cultural descriptions. In the past eight years, my colleague David McCurdy and I have scoured the professional literature in search of brief examples of ethnographic writing of the highest calibre. Our standard has been to identify writing that translates the meanings of an alien culture so well that someone unfamiliar with ethnography grasps these meanings. These selections of ethnographic writing have been collected in three successive editions of *Conformity and Conflict: Readings in Cultural Anthropology* (1971, 1974, 1977). For sheer readability, two of the best, longer ethnographies are Elliot Liebow's urban ethnography, *Talley's Corner* (1967), and Colin Turnbull's study of the Pygmies, *The Forest People* (1962).

In this chapter I want to examine briefly the nature of ethnographic writing as part of the translation process. Then I want to discuss the principles of the D.R.S. Method as applied to writing an ethnography. In the process I will give some specific suggestions on writing, but always keep in mind that *the way to learn to write an ethnography is to write an ethnography.*

THE TRANSLATION PROCESS[2]

Translation includes the entire process of discovering the meanings of one culture and communicating these meanings to people in another culture. The ethnographer, like the translator, has a dual task. On the one hand you must enter the cultural scene you hope to understand. You must get inside the language and thinking of your informants. You must make their symbols and meanings your own. The more fully you apprehend and digest the cultural meaning system learned by informants, the more effective your final translation. One of the main reasons for presenting the intensive analysis strategies gleaned from ethnographic semantics is that these strategies are powerful tools in learning another language and culture. They lead to a kind of mental saturation in the thinking patterns of your informants. But this intensive investigation into another culture is only half the task of translation.

The second task of ethnographic translation is to *communicate* the cultural meanings you have discovered to readers who are unfamiliar with that culture or cultural scene. This means that every ethnographer must develop the skills of communicating in written form. It requires us to take into consideration our audience as well as our informants. In a real sense, a truly effective translation requires an intimate knowledge of two cultures: the one described and the one tacitly held by the audience who will read the description.

Many highly skilled ethnographers fail to finish the work of ethnographic translation. They give months of time to the intensive study of another culture, analyzing in great detail the meanings encoded in that culture. Then, without taking time to learn the skills of written communication, without understanding their audience, without even feeling the importance of communicating in a way that brings the culture to life, they write an ethnography. Their audience becomes a very small group of other ethnographers, who, by virtue of their interest in the culture, are willing to wade through the vague and general discussions, examine the taxonomies, paradigms, and other tables or charts, and glean an understanding of the people and their way of life. The ethnographic literature is plagued by half-tranlations that cannot be used as guides to another way of life.

In discussing the steps in writing an ethnographic description I will make numerous suggestions for creating a full translation, one that communicates the cultural meanings you have discovered. However, one fundamental cause of inadequate cultural translations lies in the ethnographer's failure to understand and use different levels of writing. During the writing of any ethnographic description, the ethnographer must keep these various levels in mind and consciously use them to increase the communicative power of the translation.

Levels of Ethnographic Writing[3]

Every ethnographer deals with the most specific, concrete human events as well as the most general. In our field notes we identify an infant with a specific name, held by a specific mother, nursing at that mother's breast, at a specific time and in a specific place. In those same field notes we will make observations about human love, nurturance, and the universal relationship of mothers and children. In the final written ethnography, the range of levels is enormous. More than anything else, the way these levels are used will determine the communicative value of an ethnographic translation.

Kenneth Read, in his beautifully written ethnography of the Gahuku peoples of highland New Guinea, *The High Valley* (1965), suggests the underlying cause of partial translations in ethnography:

Why, then, is so much anthropological writing so antiseptic, so devoid of anything that brings a people to life? There they are, pinned like butterflies in a glass case, with the difference however, that we often cannot tell what color these specimens are, and we are never shown them in flight, never see them soar or die except in generalities. The reason for this lies in the aims of anthropology, whose concern with the particular is incidental to an understanding of the general (1965:ix).

In anthropology, as in all social sciences, *the concern with the particular is incidental to an understanding of the general.* But when this principle is transported wholesale into doing ethnography, it creates a travesty of the translation process. When an ethnographer studies another culture, the only place to begin is with the particular, concrete, specific events of everyday life. Then, through the research process described in this book, the ethnographer moves to more and more general statements about the culture. With the discovery of more general folk categories and cultural themes, the ethnographer begins to make comparisons with other cultures and even more general statements about the culture studied. And all too frequently, it is primarily this kind of analysis and understanding that finds its way into the ethnographic description.

In writing an ethnography as a translation, *the concern with the general is incidental to an understanding of the particular.* In order for a reader to see the lives of the people we study as they see themselves, we must *show them through particulars,* not merely talk about them in generalities.

There are at least six different levels that can be identified in ethnographic writing as we move from the general to the particular. Let's examine each of these different kinds of translation statements.

Level One: Universal Statements. These include all statements about human beings, their behavior, culture, or environmental situation. They are all-encompassing statements. The beginning ethnographer often feels in-compentent to make any universal statements. However, all of us know things that occur universally and can include them in our ethnographies. Most cultural descriptions include such universal statements. A study of air traffic controllers, for example, might assert that, "In all societies, people manage the movement of their bodies through space in such a way that they do not constantly collide with other human beings." Such a statement is relevant to controlling the movement of vehicles in which humans move about as well. A study of clerks who record burglaries in the police department might assert the following universal statement, "In all human societies, some people keep records of one sort or another about their affairs."

For each level of abstraction that appears in ethnographic writing, I want to give an example from *The Cocktail Waitress: Woman's Work in a Man's World* (Spradley and Mann 1975). This example will clarify the nature of the various levels by showing their expression in a single work. The following universal statement is one among several:

Every society takes the biological differences between female and male to create a special kind of reality: feminine and masculine identities (1975:145).

In the context of a specific bar in a specific city, we made an assertion about a universal feature of human experience.

Level Two: Cross-Cultural Descriptive Statements. The second level of abstraction includes statements about two or more societies. It consists of assertions that are true for some societies, but not necessarily true for all societies. Consider the following statement from *The Cocktail Waitress:*

When anthropologists began studying small, non-Western societies they found that people participated in a single web of life. . . . When we turn to complex societies such as our own, the number of cultural perspectives for any situation increases radically (1975:8,9).

This statement says something about two very large classes of human societies—the small, non-Western ones and the complex ones. Such a descriptive statement helps to convey an understanding of even the most specific place such as Brady's Bar. Cross-cultural descriptive statements help place a cultural scene in the broader picture of human cultures, something every ethnographer is concerned about doing. These kinds of statements say to the reader, "This cultural scene is not merely one little interesting group of people; it is a part of the human species in a particular way. It is like many other cultural scenes, but it is also different from many others." By means of contrast you have conveyed an important dimension of the culture.

Level Three: General Statements about a Society or Cultural Group. This kind of statement appears to be specific, but in fact remains quite general. "The Kwakiutl live in villages along coastal bays" is a general statement about a cultural group. "The Pygmies live in the forest and play musical instruments" is another general statement. We can make such statements about complex societies also: "American culture is based on the value of materialism." Or we can make such statements about recurrent cultural scenes or groups of people who have learned similar cultural scenes: "Air traffic controllers work under great stress;" "Police departments must gather, classify, and record a great deal of important information."

In our study of Brady's Bar, we included statements at this level. They did not refer only to Brady's Bar, but to all the institutions of which Brady's was one example:

Bars, in general, are places of employment for hundreds of thousands of women, almost always as cocktail waitresses. Their role in bars tends to be an extension of their role at home—serving the needs of men. . . . Like most institutions of American society, men hold sway at the center of social importance (1975:145).

Level Four: General Statements about a Specific Cultural Scene. When we move down one level of abstraction, we note many statements about a particular culture or cultural scene. Most ethnographies are filled with statements at this level: "The Fort Rupert Kwakiutl engage in seine fishing," "The air traffic controllers at the Minneapolis International Airport work one of three shifts."

Ethnographic interviews provide many such statements. An informant might say, "The waitresses at Brady's get hassled by customers" or "Tramps aren't really tramps unless they make the bucket." These are descriptive statements about a particular group. But even though they refer to a specific scene or group, they are still general in nature. Moreover, even when expressed by an informant and used in ethnography as a quotation from an informant, they represent an abstraction. Every culture is filled with these low-level abstractions, and they must find their way into any ethnographic description. Here is an example from Brady's Bar:

At one level, Brady's Bar is primarily a place of business. At another level, Brady's Bar is a place where men can come to play out exaggerated masculine roles, acting out their fantasies of sexual prowess, and reaffirming their own male identities. Brady's Bar is a men's ceremonial center (1975:130–131).

This level of ethnographic writing contains many of the themes that the ethnographer wants to present to the reader. Thus, the theme of males expressing their identities in many different ways—in the way space is organized, the way drinks are ordered, etc.—is described in statements at this level. Sometimes one can encapsulate general statements at level four in a quotation from an informant; they still remain statements of a very general nature. Making use of an informant quotation helps provide a sense of immediacy and gives the reader a closer acquaintance with the culture, but we must move to even more specific levels.

Level Five: Specific Statements about a Cultural Domain. At this level, the ethnographer begins to make use of folk terms and the specific contrasts elicited from informants. We are now dealing with a class of events, objects, or activities as labeled by informants. The ethnographer should show how the informant uses these terms. For example, here is an ethnographic statement at level five from my own research on the Valley, a company that produces tannery equipment. "One of the most important jobs that the men at the Valley do is to make *drums*. A drum can be small, such as a barrel, or more than thirty feet across. There are many minute stages in making a drum, including *making heads, making pins, making cross pieces, making staves, making doors,* and *making door frames.* The entire process of making a drum can take as long as a week and involve the work of several men."

Descriptive statements at this level can make reference to taxonomies and paradigms that encapsulate a great deal of information. However, these representations in themselves seldom communicate more than a skeleton of the relationships. In order to translate these into a description that will be understood, a great deal of narrative description at this level and the next more specific level is required.

Here is a brief example of a specific statement about the domain *asking for a drink,* which makes up part of the culture of cocktail waitresses.

One frequent way that men ask for a drink is not to ask for a drink at all. In the situation where it is appropriate to ask for a drink, they ask instead for the waitress. This may be done in the form of *teasing, hustling, hassling,* or some other speech act (1975:132).

Level Six: Specific Incident Statements. In one sense, levels one through five all contrast sharply with level six. This level takes the reader immediately to the actual level of behavior and objects, to the level of perceiving these things. Consider an example from Brady's Bar, closely related to all the examples given at the other five levels of abstraction:

Sandy is working the upper section on Friday night. She walks up to the corner table where there is a group of five she has never seen before: four guys and a girl who are loud and boisterous. She steps up to the table and asks, "Are you ready to order now?" One of the males grabs her by the waist and jerks her towards him. "I already know what I want! I'll take you," he says as he smiles innocently up at her (1975:132).

As a reader, you immediately begin to see things happening, perhaps feel things that the actors in this situation feel. Instead of merely being *told* what people know, how they generate behavior from this knowledge, and how they interpret things, you have been *shown* this cultural knowledge in action. *A good ethnographic translation shows; a poor one only tells*.

Perhaps another example of the six levels in ethnographic writing will clarify the effect on the reader. Draw from my research among tramps, the following statements all describe a single aspect of their experience: begging, borrowing, panhandling, lending, and otherwise exchanging things.

LEVEL 1: Reciprocity among human beings is balanced where two people give to each other over time, each giving and each receiving. Such reciprocity occurs in all societies.

LEVEL 2: Tramps, like those who live in tribal villages, depend on one another in time of need. They expect others to reciprocate. A Kwakiutl Indian will give in a potlatch and later receive gifts at someone else's potlatch. A tramp will give to another tramp and also beg from another tramp.

LEVEL 3: Tramps engage in much more reciprocal exchange than do other members of the larger society. This kind of exchange takes many forms.

LEVEL. 4: A tramp in the Seattle City Jail will exchange goods and services with other tramps. If he is a trusty in the jail, he might exchange a service for money with someone in lockup.

LEVEL 5: (Informant's statement) "Yes, a tramp will beg from other tramps. If you're panhandling you can expect another tramp to give you money or a cigarette if he has it. You realize that sometime he will need something and then it will be your turn."

LEVEL 6: It was a dull Tuesday afternoon and a slight mist of rain was blowing gently in from the Puget Sound. Joe had become a kickout an hour earlier; several minutes ago he walked off the elevator on the first floor of the Public Safety Building and found his way to the street. Pulling the collar of his worn tweed jacket up around his neck, he hunched his shoulders slightly and headed downtown, wondering where he would find money for a drink or even a cigarette. He might have to make a flop under the bridge on Washington Street tonight to stay out of the rain. He saw a man approaching him as he headed slowly down James Street, obviously another tramp. Looked like a home guard tramp, but he couldn't tell for sure. "Can you spare a quarter for a jug?" he asked. "I just got a kickout." "No, I'm flat on my ass myself," the other man said, "but how about a smoke, all I got are Bull Durhams." After taking a light too, Joe started on down James Street looking for a tourist or businessman to panhandle.

Ethnographic writing includes statements at all six levels from the general to the particular. Effective writing, which serves to communicate the meanings of a culture to the reader, is achieved by making all these statements, but doing so in a certain *proportion*. Professional journals, in which the author writes primarily to colleagues, tend to consist of statements at levels one and two. That is, the description is made in general terms; the author avoids specific incidents. Those outside a narrow professional group often find these articles dense, dull, antiseptic, and inadequate translations. Some ethnographic writing, whether articles, papers, or books, adopts a formal style using levels three and four. Most dissertations and theses are written at these middle levels of abstractions, although they may also contain a great deal of information at level five. They tend to present the bare bones, the skeleton of knowledge, without the flesh of examples and specific incidents of level six. At the other extreme, some ethnographic novels and personal accounts consist entirely of statements at level six with a few statements from level five thrown in now and then. This kind of writing holds the reader's attention but may fail to communicate the overall structure of a culture or the nature of ethnography.

It should be clear that mixing the various levels in a desirable proportion depends on the goals of the ethnographer. In *You Owe Yourself a Drunk: An Ethnography of Urban Nomads* (1970), I made a great deal of use of levels three through six, ranging back and forth from statements about tramps generally to specific incidents. Many of the incidents were contained in quotations from informants. In *The Cocktail Waitress: Women's Work in a Man's World* (Spradley and Mann 1975), we sought to communicate to a wider audience and included many more statements at level six, the most specific level. We also tried to relate the culture of Brady's Bar to the universal level of writing. In retrospect, we tended to scale down the middle level of generalizations. In *Deaf Like Me* (Spradley and Spradley 1978), an in-depth study of a family coping with a deaf child, we moved almost entirely to the most concrete level. We did this in order to communicate with the widest possible audience. Although much of the data we gathered by ethnographic interviewing and other ethnographic techniques, we recounted specific incidents in order to communicate more effectively to the reader. We sought to *show* the culture of this family, how they coped with a deaf child, what strategies they used, and the consequences for communication. Although statements appear in this study at all the other levels of generalization, they are woven into the particular so thoroughly that they do not stand out. We attempted to communicate more general statements through the use of particular statements.

Each ethnographer will have to determine the intended audience. I believe ethnographic research holds important values for all people and that ethnographers should write for those outside the academic world. I urge students and others to avoid the middle levels of generalizations, to use them, but sparingly. Emphasize the most general and the most specific. In ethnographic writing, the concern with the general is incidental to an understanding of the particular for an important reason. It is because generalities are best communicated through particulars. And the second half of all translation involve *communicating* to outsiders the meanings of a culture.

STEPS IN WRITING AN ETHNOGRAPHY

Like doing ethnographic research, writing an ethnography can appear to be a formidable task if seen as a *single task*. All too often, the beginning ethnographer conceives the writing as simply *writing*. You sit down with blank paper and all your field notes and begin writing the ethnography. When it is completed it will require some revision and editing, but the work is largely one long, arduous task.

Underlying the D.R.S. Method of research is the assumption that breaking a large task into smaller ones and placing these in sequence will simplify the work and improve one's performance. This assumption applies equally to writing. However, because each of us has developed patterns of writing from years of experience, it is far more difficult to create a series of steps that have wide applicability.[4] The following steps must be considered as suggestions only. Each reader will want to create his own series of steps to organize writing in a manner that best fits patterns developed through past experience. However, the underlying premise, that it is valuable to divide up the writing of an ethnography into tasks, does have wide applicability.

Step One: Select an audience. Because the audience will influence every aspect of your ethnography, this is one of the first things to do. All writing is an act of communication between human beings and in that sense it is similar to talking. When speaking to someone, there are innumerable cues that remind us that our audience is present. The writer needs to select an audience, identify it clearly, and then keep in mind throughout the writing who that audience is.

When writing for a specific journal or magazine, the ethnographer must carefully scrutinize past issues of that journal to discover the style of writing. You are, in fact, discovering the audience that such a journal is written for.

If one intends to write a book-length ethnography, then the audience may be scholars in the field, students, the general public, or some other group.

The best advice I have ever received for selecting an audience came from Marshall Townsend, the editor at the University of Arizona Press:

A basic concept we stress at the University of Arizona Press is that of the "target reader." What we urge YOU as an author to do is to pick out a "target reader" and write in book form for only *one reader*. Pick out some real person *whom you know*, then set down your materials so this person will understand what you are saying. When you have a "target reader," you effect a single level of presentation, rather than trying to provide information to everyone from those who have their doctorates to students in high school who want to delve into the subject just a bit. Choose your level of communication and stay with it—by addressing yourself in your writing to only this one person. We believe you will find this concept a highly workable one.

When you as an author write successfully for one, we as a publisher may be able to take your book and sell thousands of copies because each person feels "this was meant for *me*." On the other hand, if you try to write for thousands, and embrace all of their varied interests and viewpoints, we may not be able to sell a single copy. Stick to your one-level approach, and we as publishers will take care of informing readers at all levels of interest and of understanding how the book will fit into their realm.

Step Two: Select a thesis. In order to communicate with your audience, you need to have something to say. All too often, ethnographic descriptions are like conversations meandering, without a destination. Although of interest to the ethnographer and a few colleagues, such writing will not hold the attention of many more. A thesis is the central message, the point you want to make. There are several sources for finding a thesis.

First, the major themes you have discovered in ethnographic research represent possible theses. For example, a major theme in the culture of tramps was that being in jail affected one's identity, even made a man want to go out and get drunk. In jail a man learned to "hustle," and this reinforced his identity as a tramp trying to "make it" on the street. This theme became the thesis of the ethnography: That jailing drunks, rather than being therapeutic, actually played an important role in creating the identity of tramp. This thesis was summed up in the title of the ethnography, which came from one informant who said, "After thirty days in jail, *you owe yourself a drunk!*"

Second, a thesis for your ethnography may come from the overall goals of ethnography. You may for example, state your thesis in the following way: "To most people, a bar is a place to drink. But to a cocktail waitress, it is much more complex. It is a world of varied cultural meanings that she learns in order to carry out her work and cope with difficulties. In this paper I want to show just how complex the cultural knowledge of cocktail waitresses is, in contrast to the casual impressions of the outsider." Your thesis can simply be to show that cultural meaning systems are much more complex than we usually think.

Another way to formulate this type of thesis is in terms of a set of recipes for behavior. Culture can be viewed as a set of instructions for carrying out ordinary activities of life. Your thesis would be to show the reader the recipe for being a tramp, a cocktail waitress, or some other kind of person. Charles Frake, in a series of articles, has made effective use of this kind of thesis. For example, he has written on "How to ask for a drink," and "How to enter a house" among groups in the Philippines (1964c, 1975).

Still another way to formulate this type of thesis is to show the tacit rules for behavior. This thesis argues that much goes on in social life that we do not see; that there are tacit rules of behavior that people have learned but seldom discuss. The point of your paper is to make those tacit rules explicit.

Third, a thesis may come from the literature of social sciences. In one paper on tramps I reviewed the literature on the concept of "reciprocity." Then, I formulated a thesis that linked the patterns of reciprocity among tramps to these more general concepts (1968).

When a thesis has been selected, it is useful to state it briefly, perhaps in a single sentence, and place it before you as a constant reminder as you write. This will help organize your paper and integrate it around a single major idea. It will also help the reader to grasp the meanings of the culture in a way that a simple listing of domains and their meanings will not.

Step Three: Make a list of topics and create an outline. Any ethnography will necessarily deal with only selected aspects of a culture. Furthermore, you will use only part of the material you have collected. Step three involves reviewing your field notes and the cultural inventory you have made and listing topics you think should be included in the final description. Some of these topics will be things like "introduction" and "conclusion." Once listed, you can then make an outline built around your thesis. This will divide up your actual writing into sections, each of which can be done as a separate unit. If you have been writing short descriptive pieces throughout the project (see Appendix B), many or all of these may fit into the outline.

Step Four: Write a rough draft of each section. A rough draft is intended to be rough, unfinished, unpolished. One of the great roadblocks for many writers is the desire to revise each sentence as it goes down on paper. Constant revision not only slows the entire writing process but takes away from the free flow of communication. Constant revision seldom occurs in speaking; we may occasionally restate something, but usually we talk without revising. *Write as you talk* is an excellent rule to follow in composing a rough draft of each section.

Step Five: Revise the outline and create subheads. Almost always the outline from which one writes becomes changed in the process of writing. Once a rough draft is completed for each section, it is a good idea to make a new outline, rearranging sections as appropriate. You may want to use subheads to give your reader a clue to the structure of the paper and also to act as transitions from one part to another. Native folk terms can often be used as subheads in an ethnography, helping to create a view which reflects the cultural knowledge of your informants.

Step Six: Edit the rough draft. At this point in the writing you will have a rough draft of your paper, a fairly clear outline, and a number of subheadings you want to use throughout the paper. Now it is time to go over it with an eye to improving the details of writing. Work through each section and at the same time keep the entire description in mind. Make changes directly on the pages you had previously written. When you want to add a paragraph or sentence, write them on the back of the page or on a separate piece of paper with instructions as to where they will appear. At this stage it is often useful to ask a friend to read over the manuscript and make general comments. An outside perspective is especially useful for making improvements that will enhance the communicative power of the description.

Step Seven: Write the introduction and conclusion. By now the description has taken on substantial form and you can write these two parts of the paper in a more effective manner. Some writers find that they write better if they write a rough introduction at the start of the writing but save the conclusion until the end. In either case, now is the time to review both the introduction and conclusion and revise them to fit the paper.

Step Eight: Reread the manuscript for examples. Examples involve writing at the lowest level of abstraction. Because of their importance in communication, a special reading of the paper to see if you have used enough examples is highly desirable. Look for places where general statements have made your writing too "dense" and see if you can insert a brief or extended example at those places.

Step Nine: Write the final draft. In some cases this will merely involve typing the paper or turning it over to someone else to type. In other cases, you will need to go carefully over the manuscript again, making the final editorial changes. Using steps such as these means you have been over the entire manuscript numerous times during the course of writing. Instead of a single first-draft-as-final-draft, your paper has gone through a series of developmental stages.

In this chapter we have discussed ethnographic writing as a part of the

215

translation process. In the notes for this chapter are several excellent references on writing which you may want to consult. Writing is a skill learned slowly. It is one that shows great variation from one person to another. The suggestions in this chapter are offered only as general guidelines, not as hard and fast rules that every writer should try to follow.

Tasks

12.1 Write a rough draft of an ethnography.
12.2 Conduct additional interviews as needed to fill gaps in your data.
12.3 Write a final draft of an ethnography.

NOTES

CHAPTER ONE: ETHNOGRAPHY AND CULTURE

1. There are many excellent books on the field work experience. See Freilich (1970), Kimball and Watson (1972), and Spindler (1970) for accounts of field work.
2. The term "ethnography" is used to refer to both the work of studying a culture and the end product, "an ethnography." In this book I will use it to refer to books, monographs, and any articles or papers that set forth a cultural description. All ethnographies are incomplete, whether they consist of many volumes or a short paper.
3. See Kroeber and Kluckhohn for an early review of definitions (1952). Also see Spradley (1972a, 1972b) for a discussion of concepts of culture. Kaplan and Manners (1972) and Keesing (1974) review theories and concepts of culture.
4. Many of the more important articles on symbolic interactionism have been collected in Manis and Meltzer (1967). See also Blumer (1969) for an introduction to this theoretical perspective.
5. The focus of this book is on *ethnography*. Ethnographic semantics methodologies form the core of the techniques presented in this book, but this book is not limited to the semantic approach. As we shall see in some of the later steps, ethnography draws from many different approaches in anthropology and sociology.
6. In his presidential address to the American Psychological Association, Donald Campbell (1975) cogently argued that social scientists need to take the folk theories of all the world's societies more seriously.
7. Their book, *The Discovery of Grounded Theory* (Glaser and Strauss 1967), shares many similarities with the present work. However, the approach presented here makes systematic use of a linguistic theory of meaning.
8. See Spradley (1969) and (1971b).
9. This approach is known as ethnopsychology. For two excellent examples see Straus (1977) and Valentine (1963).
10. See my chapter "Trouble in the Tank" (1976b), which appeared in *Ethics and Anthropology: Dilemmas in Field Work* (Rynkiewich and Spradley 1976), for a description of the events that led up to this publishing decision.
11. In addition, Werner and his associates have undertaken systematic ethnographic research on Navaho schools. These are being used by the Navaho in improving the schools for their children.

CHAPTER TWO: LANGUAGE AND FIELD WORK

1. The primary resource for this research is *You Owe Yourself a Drunk: An Ethnography of Urban Nomads*, James P. Spradley (1970). See especially Chapter Three, which deals with *making a flop*, as does "Adaptive strategies of urban nomads the ethnoscience of tramp culture," Spradley (1972c). Other reports on

my research with skid row men appear in the following articles: (1968, 1971a, 1972d, 1972e, 1978, 1975, 1976b). All references to research on tramps (or skid row men) in this book are drawn from my field notes or these published sources.

2. The concept of *cultural scene* is used in this book to refer to the shared knowledge people use in a particular social situation or which has been acquired as a result of membership in a particular group or participation in a particular setting. Each society is made up of diverse subgroups and many different settings, each with its own cultural definitions and rules. The concept of cultural scene is particularly useful in doing ethnography in complex societies.

3. See Bateson (1937).

4. I am indebted to Oswald Werner of Northwestern University for suggesting this concept for a type of ethnography.

CHAPTER THREE: INFORMANTS

1. There is a growing literature in the social sciences which explicitly recognizes the importance of ethics in doing research. J.A. Barnes, in *The Ethics of Inquiry in Social Science* (1977), examines some of the important ethical issues and provides a good source of references. For selected cases dealing with ethical issues in doing ethnography see *Ethics and Anthropology: Dilemmas in Field Work,* Michael Rynkiewich and James P. Spradley, eds. (1976).

2. See Mann (1976).

3. This study is reported in Allen (1974).

STEP ONE: LOCATING AN INFORMANT

1. See Wallace (1965).

2. See Nash (1976, 1977, 1978) for descriptions of the culture of long-distance runners by a participant. In addition, Nash has written on the culture of bus riders based on his own experience (1975).

3. This study of matchbox cars appears in Hansen (1976).

4. This study appears in Sloane (1975).

STEP TWO: INTERVIEWING AN INFORMANT

1. I use the concept of speech event here in the ethnographic sense of an event that is labeled by the kind of speech that occurs with a folk term. This concept has been developed by Dell Hymes in his work on the ethnography of speaking. See his *Foundations in Sociolinguistics: An Ethnographic Approach* (1974). See "How to Ask for a Drink," Chapter Seven in *The Cocktail Waitress: Woman's Work in a Man's World,* Spradley and Mann (1975), for a specific study of speech acts.

STEP THREE: MAKING AN ETHNOGRAPHIC RECORD

1. It is important not to confuse an ethnography with the ethnographic record. My ethnography of selected aspects of tramp culture (1970) makes use of only parts of the ethnographic record built up during the research.

STEP FOUR: ASKING DESCRIPTIVE QUESTIONS

1. See Ehrman (1977).

STEP FIVE: ANALYZING ETHNOGRAPHIC INTERVIEWS

1. This represents an ideal conception of the research sequence. In practice, many social scientists deviate from this pattern or modify it to fit the needs of the project. However, as an ideal, it is one most social scientists strive to achieve. In doing ethnography or qualitative research, the sequence is different. Some researchers attempt to combine ethnography with the more usual type of social science research, wearing two hats as they carry out their research. This is a perfectly acceptable procedure as long as the two types of investigation do not become confused and the procedures mixed.

2. Ethnographers do formulate hypotheses on the basis of previous ethnographic research or on the basis of a general theory of culture. However, these hypotheses concern the meanings which informants have acquired rather than relationships among variables of a noncultural kind.

3. In this sense, ethnography aims to develop hypotheses to test a theory of a specific culture. Ultimately, using the data of ethnography, anthropologists seek to develop a general theory of culture.

4. Although this theory is intended as a set of propositions that will explain how meaning works in human cultural systems, it is presented here primarily as a heuristic theory, that is, one designed to further the investigation of meaning. I am especially indebted to the work of Oswald Werner and Charles Frake and their particular analyses of semantic relations in semantic systems. See especially Frake (1964a), Perchonock and Werner (1968), Werner et al. (1974), and Evens, Litowitz, Markowitz, Smith, and Werner (1977). In addition, my thinking has been greatly influenced by numerous personal communications with Oswald Werner.

5. I use the concept symbol here as one kind of sign (Pierce, 1931). For a fuller discussion of signs and symbols see my article, "Foundations of Cultural Knowledge" (1972b).

6. All categories involve some form of inclusion in a set theory sense. All categories *include* members. Thus, the category "stages in the life cycle" includes things like childhood and middle age. "Ways to drink beer from a bottle" is a category that includes a variety of acts. I will use the term *strict inclusion* to refer to that relationship in which an object is a *kind of* something, i.e., a pine is a kind of tree. Some writers restrict the concept of inclusion to this strict inclusion, but I will use it to refer to any kind of category relationships among symbols.

7. *Domain* is sometimes used in anthropology to refer to the large areas or realms of culture as anthropologists have divided them up—such things as kinship, family, government, technology, etc. I will use domain in the more restricted sense that it is defined in in this chapter. It is a *folk domain,* a category of culture as identified by members of a particular society.
8. Semantic relationships form the central concept of the relational theory of meaning on which ethnographic semantics is based. I will discuss this concept at greater length in Step Six.
9. This figure is adapted from Cavan (1974). Cavan's research on rural hippies discussed in this article makes much use of native terminology for ethnographic purposes, but mixes these with the topic categories generated by anthropologists and others. My own conception of ethnography seeks to maintain a closer adherence to the native categories of thought. Cavan's study is an excellent discussion of how to integrate native categories with the investigator's categories in doing ethnographic research.

STEP SIX: MAKING A DOMAIN ANALYSIS

1. See Evens et al. (1977) for a review of the literature on semantic relations.
2. See Perchonock and Werner (1969), Werner et al. (1974), and Evens et al. (1977), which review the work of scholars in various disciplines who have proposed universal semantic relations.
3. See Werner and Topper (1976).
4. See Walker (1965) for a valuable discussion of generic terms and their function in human communication. As noted earlier, *inclusion* is used to refer to any category relationship. Thus you can create a *set* included in a cover term by using any semantic relationship. Strict inclusion will be used here to refer to a single class of categories: X is a kind of Y.
5. This list is adapted from another longer one prepared by Kruft (1977) in her research on encyclopedia salespeople.

STEP SEVEN: ASKING STRUCTURAL QUESTIONS

1. References to the culture of the deaf are based on my own research in collaboration with Thomas S. Spradley. See our study of a family coping with a child born deaf entitled *Deaf Like Me,* Thomas Spradley and James Spradley (1978). I am indebted to Nina Verin (1978) for identifying the different modes of communication.
2. This example is based on Noren (1974).
3. This example is based on Kruft (1977).
4. This example is drawn from Gores (1972).
5. It is easy to fall into the trap of treating informants as if they only had knowledge about themselves. But all informants are, in a sense, participant observers. They can report on what others do and know; they can offer their understanding of the usual patterns of behavior; they can, in short, give cultural information as well as personal information.

6. See Step Nine: "Asking Contrast Questions" for further discussion of the use of cards in asking ethnographic questions.

STEP EIGHT: MAKING A TAXONOMIC ANALYSIS

1. See Harris (1968), especially Chapter Twenty, and Berreman (1966) for a discussion of some of these issues.
2. See Conklin (1962) for one of the early theoretical discussions in anthropology of folk taxonomies and their significance. In addition, Conklin has provided a comprehensive bibliography of articles on folk classification (1972). Other valuable discussions of folk taxonomies can be found in Frake (1962), Berlin, Breedlove, and Raven (1968), and Kay (1966).
3. See Spradley (1975) for a complete analysis of this domain.

STEP NINE: ASKING CONTRAST QUESTIONS

1. Many of my ideas concerning the principle of contrast are based on the work of psychologist George Kelly (1955).
2. This distinction was initially made by Conklin (1962).
3. A contrast set, when viewed from the perspective of a folk taxonomy, is any set of terms at a single level whch are all included in a single term at the next higher level in the taxonomy.
4. Triadic contrast questions are based on a strategy for the study of personal constructs developed by Kelly (1955).

STEP TEN: MAKING A COMPONENTIAL ANALYSIS

1. See Goodenough (1956), Wallace and Atkins (1960), and Wallace (1962).
2. For a discussion of attributes see "On Attributes and Concepts," Chapter Two in Bruner, Goodnow, and Austin (1956).
3. See Wallace and Atkins (1960) for a discussion of psychological and structural reality.
4. Studies which focus on structural reality often seek to identify the minimum number of attributes or criteria necessary to define or identify a particular concept. Thus, studies of kinship terms often only identify the criteria necessary to distinguish all the terms in a set. In studying the psychological reality of folk terms, we want to go well beyond the minimum bits of information and include as much information as informants are using to organize their worlds. This results in a much larger number of attributes than a structural analysis.
5. I use the concept of paradigm in this book as it was originally used in linguistic analysis, not in the broader sense of "world view" made popular by Thomas Kuhn in his *The Structure of Scientific Revolutions* (1970).
6. This paradigm is based on data presented in Spradley (1970).

STEP ELEVEN: DISCOVERING CULTURAL THEMES

1. For a review and discussion of many of these concepts see "World View and Values," Chapter 14 in *Anthropology: The Cultural Perspective,* James P. Spradley and David W. McCurdy (1975).
2. See Agar (1976) for an excellent discussion of the concept of theme. Agar identifies themes as broad premises that have expressed themselves in many areas of a person's cultural knowledge, premises that make up a part of an individual's communicative competence. In this paper, Agar makes some tentative suggestions for identifying themes.
3. See Meggitt (1974) for a discussion of this theme.
4. See Rohlen (1974).
5. See Spradley and Mann (1975:120-143) for further discussion of this theme.
6. See Davis (1974) for an excellent discussion of ways to discover themes in literature for use in social science.

STEP TWELVE: WRITING AN ETHNOGRAPY

1. This is not to say that studying the writing process is not helpful. Among the books on writing that I have found the most useful are *Writing Without Teachers,* Peter Elbow (1973), *The Practical Stylist,* Sheridan Baker (1969), *Telling Writing,* Ken Macrorie (1970), and *A Writer Teaches Writing,* Donald Murray (1968).
2. For an excellent discussion of translation see Nida (1964).
3. Some of these ideas were originally presented in a paper called "The Art and Style of Ethnographic Writing," presented to a special session on Anthropological Writing and Publishing for Nonprofessional Audiences, as part of the 74th Annual Meeting of the American Anthropological Association, December 2-6, 1975, San Francisco.
4. As with all suggestions on writing, I believe it is best to try them out, then adapt them to one's own peculiar writing style, or discard them entirely.

APPENDIX A. A Taxonomy of Ethnographic Questions

1.0 DESCRIPTIVE QUESTIONS
    1.1 Grand Tour Questions
        1.11 Typical Grand Tour Questions
        1.12 Specific Grand Tour Questions
        1.13 Guided Grand Tour Questions
        1.14 Task-Related Grand Tour Questions
    1.2 Mini-Tour Questions
        1.21 Typical Mini-Tour Questions
        1.22 Specific Mini-Tour Questions
        1.23 Guided Mini-Tour Questions
        1.24 Task-Related Mini-Tour Questions
    1.3 Example Questions
    1.4 Experience Questions
    1.5 Native-Language Questions
        1.51 Direct Language Questions
        1.52 Hypothetical-Interaction Questions
        1.53 Typical-Sentence Questions

2.0 STRUCTURAL QUESTIONS
    2.1 Verification Questions
        2.11 Domain Verification Questions
        2.12 Included Term Verification Questions
        2.13 Semantic Relationship Verification Questions
        2.14 Native-Language Verification Questions
    2.2 Cover Term Questions
    2.3 Included Term Questions
    2.4 Substitution Frame Questions
    2.5 Card Sorting Structural Questions

3.0 CONTRAST QUESTIONS
    3.1 Contrast Verification Questions
    3.2 Directed Contrast Questions
    3.3 Dyadic Contrast Questions
    3.4 Triadic Contrast Questions
    3.5 Contrast Set Sorting Questions
    3.6 Twenty Questions Game
    3.7 Rating Questions

In completing each step in the D.R.S. Method, it is useful to do some writing. Beginning to write early will result in rough draft material that can find its way into the final ethnography. Of course, you will be writing field notes, a journal, and interpretations that suggest themselves. Also, each of the assignments involves some writing. The tasks outlined here are designed specifically with the final written ethnography in mind. Writing two to four pages each week about topics that may fit into the final report will influence your research. These projects will stimulate you to make certain kinds of analyses and continually think about the end product of the research. These topics are *suggestions;* you may want to follow some or all of them, or design specific writing that fits more directly your own research.

1. Locating an Informant

The nature of ethnographic research. One cannot assume that the reader of an ethnographic description will understand the nature of the investigation. Write a brief statement that tells the reader what an ethnography is. Identify and define key concepts such as culture, ethnography, ethnographic interview, and informant. Illustrate these concepts from your own experience. Several pages about the nature of ethnography may serve as an introduction to the final report and will certainly help to clarify the concepts as you begin research.

2. Interviewing an Informant

The role of language in ethnographic research. Discuss briefly the role of language in all phases of ethnographic research. See if you can use examples of translation competence in operation from the practice interview you conducted.

3. Making an Ethnographic Record

Beginning an ethnographic research project. Describe for a reader how you started ethnographic research. Write in the first person to test that style as one option for the final ethnography. Include details on how you made the decision to select the cultural scene, how you located an informant, and what took place when you contacted your informant. Include your own reactions to this early phase of field work.

4. Asking Descriptive Questions

The physical setting. Describe the setting in which your informant carries out routine activities. Base your writing on observations made during interviews, visits to the setting, and the first interview. Begin by making a list of specific locales and objects. This writing task will make use of your first impressions before they fade and also bring to light needed information.

5. Analyzing Ethnographic Interviews

Summary of the cultural scene. Write a preliminary overview of the cultural scene on the basis of the domains you have identified in your preliminary search. Write in broad terms to describe the total scene, or what you know about it. Underline all key folk terms in your writing to highlight their role in the cultural knowledge of your informant.

6. Making a Domain Analysis

Revise the summary of the cultural scene. Rewrite the paper you wrote for Step Five, adding important domains, revising the style into a coherent but brief overview of the cultural scene.

7. Asking Structural Questions

Describe a cultural domain. Select a set of terms that make up one domain or are part of a larger domain and write a description of this segment of your informant's knowledge. Show how informants use the terms in this domain in ordinary speech; give specific examples which will enable the uninformed reader to grasp the meaning of the domain.

8. Making a Taxonomic Analysis

Write a dialogue on a cultural domain. Select a domain you have analyzed and create a meaningful dialogue between two people who know the culture. Describe the situation in which they are communicating. This form of writing will enable you to experiment with a slightly different style.

9. Asking Contrast Questions

Describe a cultural domain. Select a different cultural domain and write a formal description of that domain, making clear the meaning of terms and their relationships. Give specific examples to show some of the attributes that reveal contrasts among the terms.

10. Making a Componential Analysis

Describe the development of your relationship with an informant. Describe your informant, the atmosphere of interviews, how interviews changed, and then characterize your relationship with the informant. Include a discussion of ethical problems that have arisen and how these have been solved.

11. Discovering Cultural Themes

Describe a cultural theme. Select one or more cultural themes and write a brief paper that shows how the theme connects several domains of the culture.

12. Writing an Ethnography

Suggestions for future research. Write a brief paper that identifies several of the most important areas for future research on the cultural scene in light of your discoveries. What would you study if you had more time or recommended that someone else study in this scene?

The Developmental Research Sequence Method (D.R.S. Method) has developed by doing a kind of informal ethnography of ethnography. In addition to searching for the actual steps I followed, I interviewed other ethnographers and students doing ethnography. In identifying the basic principles of the D.R.S. Method, it is helpful to briefly characterize traditional approaches to learning to do ethnography.

Traditionally, anthropologists have learned to do field work toward the end of their professional training. Frequently, as in my own case, it has meant a kind of sink-or-swim experience. After years of listening to lectures, reading journals, and writing library research papers, the ethnographer arrived in some strange community where people spoke an alien language. The goal was clear: to discover the cultural patterns that made life meaningful to these people. The field techniques were also clear: interviewing and participant observation. But we only vaguely understood the way to actually conduct interviews or engage in participant observation. The skills for doing ethnography had to be learned in the field in a hit-or-miss fashion.

And so the ethnographer started hanging around, watching, listening, and writing things down. Those who seemed willing or talkative became key informants. In a few months, the stack of field notes about what people said and did grew quite large. Through trial and error, through persistence and patience, most ethnographers somehow learned to do rather good ethnography. Staying in the field for six months, a year, or eighteen months, they learned a great deal about the culture, worrying now and then whether they had missed some important area of life.

The field work period drew to a close and the ethnographer returned home with notebooks filled with observations and interpretations. Sorting through field notes in the months that followed, the ethnographer discovered questions that should have been asked, important lines of inquiry that should have been followed. But even with many gaps in the field notes, the ethnographer compared, contrasted, analyzed, synthesized, and wrote. And rewrote. The end was in sight: an ethnographic description that translated an alien way of life into terms that others could understand. By the end of the project, one had finally learned to do ethnography—*by doing it*.

The Developmental Research Sequence approach shares a common feature with this traditional way of learning to do field work. Both rest on the assumption that the best way to learn to do ethnography is by doing it. This is reflected in Part Two of this book, which consists of specific tasks arranged in sequential order. Part One, "Ethnographic Research," can be read quickly to review some basic concepts related to doing field work. But Part Two, "The Developmental Research Sequence," requires a different approach. Each step begins with a statement of D.R.S. objectives—what one must learn by doing before proceeding to the next step. After a discussion of concepts and techniques, each step ends with a list of D.R.S. tasks required for doing field work. Many of the later steps in the sequence only make sense *after* one has gained at least minimal experience in conducting ethnographic interviews. Although this book is designed for the person seeking to acquire some skill in ethnographic interviewing, I believe it will also be of value to the experienced ethnographer. In the latter case, the sequence of steps must be adapted to what one has found works best from previous experience in the field.

Five principles underly the D.R.S. Method of learning and doing ethnography. These principles form the basis for the way this book is organized, for the inclusion of some ideas and the omission of others. My goal is not to survey the professional literature on ethnographic interviewing, but rather to provide a workable approach to learning this field technique for doing ethnography.

1. The Single Technique Principle. The D.R.S. Method makes a distinction among ethnographic techniques and selects one for learning purposes. In order to describe another culture, ethnographers use many techniques. They act as participant observers, recording what people do and say in the course of ordinary activities. They observe ceremonies and work activities such as fishing and building houses. They make casual inquiries as they follow people around watching what they do. They record life histories to discover how individuals experience their culture. They record folktales and legends. They conduct ethnographic interviews with key informants, carefully analyzing responses to questions. They record genealogies. They may use projective tests. In the field, the experienced ethnographer may pursue all of these approaches at the same time. However, for purposes of learning to do ethnography, it is best to focus on mastering one technique at a time. This book deals only with the ethnographic interview, not because this is the best source of data, but because it is one indispensable technique for doing ethnography.

2. The Task Identification Principle. The D.R.S. Method identifies the basic tasks and specific objectives required by a particular field technique. In this book I have identified twelve major tasks. When a person carries out these tasks, two things occur. First, one learns the basic skills of informant interviewing and writing a cultural description. Second, one carries out original research on a particular cultural scene.

Take the example of one ethnographer who followed this method in studying the culture of air traffic controllers.[1] She contacted an air traffic controller at a large airport and secured his cooperation to participate in a series of interviews. After one or two interviews she undertook a basic task called "making a domain analysis" (Step Six). Air traffic controllers, like people everywhere, organize their cultural knowledge, and as an ethnographer she wanted to discover that organization. She had come to the research with her own categories like "airplane," and "unidentified flying object," but her informant did not share them. He had a much more elaborate way to organize things that fly. This ethnographer's task was to discover how her informant organized his cultural knowledge, and she began to do this by following the instructions in Step Six.

When she had completed that step, she had accomplished two things. On the one hand, she knew how to carry out a domain analysis from interviews in *any* culture, whether that of air traffic controllers, bail bondsmen, quadriplegics, Bushmen, or United States congressmen. On the other hand, she had taken a significant step into the cultural world of air traffic controllers.

3. The Developmental Sequence Principle. The D.R.S. Method is based on a developmental sequence of specific tasks necessary to complete each of the major steps. The sequenced nature of the assignments helps to *focus* ethnographic research. The ethnographer in the field is confronted with hundreds of things that could be studied. Even in a single interview there are many possible ways to go. The sequenced nature of the steps does two things: (a) it enables a person to improve basic research skills in a systematic manner, and (b) it allows one to study a cultural scene in a way that is efficient and workable. This will lead to a rapid growth in interviewing competence, a sense of control, and reduction in the anxiety of field work.

4. The Original Research Principle. The D.R.S. Method takes one through to the completion of an original ethnographic research project. The steps in Part Two of this book are *not* merely training exercises; they represent steps in carrying out original research. Because of this goal, the Developmental Research Sequence covers, in addition to interviewing skills, techniques for analysis of interview data, suggestions for organizing a cultural description based on interviews, and specific guidelines for writing the final ethnographic description.

I have known a number of graduate and undergraduate students who have published their research which resulted from following the D.R.S. Method. Others have read their papers at professional meetings. Many continue their projects with additional informants or shift from ethnographic interviews to participant observation on the same cultural scene. Throughout this book I have drawn examples from the work of professionals and students alike. I refer to all of them as *ethnographers;* through their use of the D.R.S. Method, they were engaged in doing original research.

5. The Problem-Solving Principle. The D.R.S. Method is based on the problem-solving process. Every ethnographer knows that field work presents an endless series of problems. In one way or another, the successful ethnographer must become a successful problem solver. Part of the excitement of doing field work comes from the challenge of problem solving, a process that involves six steps: (1) define the problem, (2) identify possible causes, (3) consider possible solutions, (4) select the best solution, (5) carry out your plan, and (6) evaluate the results.[2]

The objectives and tasks presented in each of the twelve steps were developed by applying this problem-solving process to informant interviewing and ethnographic writing. From my own experience, from talking with other professional ethnographers, and from the experiences of hundreds of students, certain recurrent problems became apparent. Some were *informant problems:* cancelled appointments, unwillingness to answer questions, suspicion, failure to gain rapport. *Conceptual problems* arose from lack of understanding of fundamental concepts related to doing ethnography. *Analysis problems* came from not knowing what to do with the raw information gathered from an imformant. *Writing problems* included organizing the final report and knowing what to include as well as how to go about the task of writing. The sequence of objectives and tasks throughout the twelve steps anticipates all of these problems as well as others. The concepts, objectives, tasks, and examples in each step arose, in part, from applying the problem-solving process to the most common difficulties in ethnographic interviewing.

However, every field work project is unique and presents new problems. For this reason, the ethnographer must apply the problem-solving process throughout a research project. I encourage beginning ethnographers to make a systematic effort to do this—monitoring their progress, identifying problems, developing lists of possible solutions, selecting the best ones, carrying them out, and evaluating the results.

Working in a group can often facilitate the application of the problem-solving process to ethnographic field work. In both graduate and undergraduate classes I have scheduled a weekly problem-solving laboratory which begins with my asking for difficulties encountered during the previous week of research. The first statement of a problem usually needs to be refined. Once the group has clearly defined the problem, we try to generate as many solutions as possible. From this list, we can discuss the best solutions and how to carry them out. Sometimes students meet in small groups of four or five and use the problem-solving process to work through their current difficulties or evaluate the success of carrying out a solution.

There are as many ways to do ethnography as there are ethnographers. More than in most academic pursuits, ethnographers tend to work alone in isolated situations. As a result, highly individualistic approaches to research have developed with a consequent lack of agreed-upon procedures and techniques. This has been intensified by the vagaries of field work conditions: what works well in one society is sometimes ineffective in another. Individualism in doing ethnography has stimulated many innovations in field work technique, but at the same time it has made both replication of ethnographies and learning to do ethnography much more difficult.

Any book that sets forth a set of strategies for doing ethnography, as this one does, runs into this spirit of individualism. Any book that goes further to suggest that ethnography might be done in a series of steps, as this one does, runs the risk of serious criticism—if not outright rejection. Some readers may misunderstand the present volume because of stereotypes about *ethnoscience*, an approach to ethnography with which this book shares many similarities. Other questions will undoubtedly arise from the fact that I have imposed certain limitations on myself in writing this book for a particular audience: the professional and student alike who have never done ethnographic field work. I want to discuss briefly each of these issues in the following paragraphs.

During the 1950s several anthropologists began to apply a linguistic model to cultural description, and their work came to be known as ethnoscience.[3] As Sturtevant points out in his lengthy review (quoting an unpublished paper by Spaulding): "The term ethnoscience is unfortunate for two reasons— first, because it suggests that other kinds of ethnography are *not* science, and second, because it suggests that folk classifications and folk taxonomies *are* science" (1964:99). The prefix ethno- refers to the system of knowledge typical of a given society or subgroup within a society. The *ethnobotany* of a particular group is that group's classification of botanical phenomena; *ethnoanatomy* refers to how a particular society classifies parts of the human body; *ethnomedicine* is the way a group classifies disease and its treatment. The fundamental assumption in ethnoscience is that native classifications of phenomena must be taken seriously and studied exhaustively.

Ethnoscience has its roots in linguistics and the work of Franz Boas and Edward Sapir. One of the first attempts to use advances in descriptive linguistics to further the study of human behavior generally was made by Kenneth Pike (1967), who distinguished between "emic" and "etic" descriptions on the basis of the phonological analogy. Phon*etics* is the study of all possible sounds useable in speech production. At one time, phonetics set as a goal the accurate description of all sounds. During the early part of this century linguists shifted their attention to phon*emics*, the study of sound categories recognized and used by a particular language group. Emic descriptions of sound depended on discovering the native's categories and perceptions. In the same way, emic descriptions of behavior depended on discovering native categories of action. Etic descriptions, on the other hand, of sound or anything else are based on categories created by the investigator, and are usually employed to compare things cross-culturally. Ethnoscience took the emic–etic distinction seriously; it emphasized that the first goal of ethnography was a thorough emic description based on native categories. Sophisticated methods of elicitation and analysis were developed to achieve this goal. Etic descriptions and cross-cultural comparisons were considered worthy goals, but since they depended on the primary work of emic ethnography, they were largely relegated to the future.[4]

Most ethnographers agreed with the basic goal of ethnoscience—to discover native categories of thought. However, during the 1960s, ethnoscience came to be associated with a narrow scholasticism. Instead of wholistic cultural descriptions, ethnoscience produced a flood of studies that focused almost exclusively on kinship terminology. Instead of discovering the texture of life in another society, it tended to give us increasingly abstract and restricted descriptions. Because ethnoscientists wanted to *thoroughly* investigate native categories of thought, the goal of broad descriptions receded into the future. Ethnoscience became, in the minds of many ethnographers, only the analysis of kinship terms, the study of cognitive processes, and the production of abstract mathematical models for cultural rules.

In 1967 I shared this view; I completed my doctoral research with hardly a passing glance at ethnoscience. Then I began an ethnographic study in Seattle of skid row drunks, with the intention of describing the cultural worlds of these men. It didn't cross my mind that ethnoscience could contribute to my research. Several months after I started field work, a graduate assistant, Per Hage, urged me to investigate the folk categories of my informants. Skeptical, I watched him interview several long-time skid row men. With great care he elicited the folk terms that informants used to label ordinary events in their lives. They said things and talked in ways I had not previously observed. I realized that I had skipped over the first step in ethnographic field work—learning the native language. It had seemed unnecessary because my informants all spoke English; I had overlooked the special usages my informants employed, the street argot of tramps. I set about in earnest to use the techniques of ethnoscience and thereby to learn the language of my informants. In the process the culture of skid row men became clearer than it ever would have through the lens of my language and observations. Ethnoscience showed me how to let skid row "bums" become my teachers. It led me to discover how my informants organized their culture, setting me free from the need to impose an order from the outside. Later I discovered that the ethnoscience approach gave beginning ethnographers the necessary tools to study other cultures.

I see ethnoscience as a set of tools for achieving the larger goals of ethnography—the wholistic, emic description of a way of life. I seek "thick descriptions" that will communicate to outsiders the full context and meaning of a culture in all its human dimensions.[5] It is my conviction that ethnoscience techniques can serve the same goals as traditional ethnography. These techniques represent a systematic approach to doing what every good ethnographer has always done—study the language and categories of informants. At the same time, it should be recognized that this book does represent only one particular approach to doing ethnography. Some may want to adopt all of these strategies; others will find that only certain strategies presented here will be useful in their own research. Still others will want to build on suggestions given in this book to continue the development of more effective ways to discover and describe the cultural meanings people live by in other societies.[6]

In order to make this book most useful to those who wish to learn to do ethnography, I have limited its scope in several important ways. Some have already been mentioned, but I want to briefly summarize what I have *not* attempted to do.

1. *This book does not survey the various methods used in ethnographic research.*[7] I focus exclusively on interviewing, isolating it from other approaches in a manner that will undoubtedly seem artificial to many experienced ethnographers. This, I believe, is necessary in order to deal effectively with the skills of interviewing and analysis. However, I do not assume that one should ever attempt a full scale ethnography using this technique alone. Ethnographic research that aims at an adequate description requires a number of methods. At the same time, it is possible to do a *partial* description of *selected aspects* of a culture by means of ethnographic interviewing. Moreover, some ethnographers will use intensive interviews as their most important means for gathering data.

2. *This book does not systematically examine how to integrate data from multiple informants to produce an ethnographic description.* I focus on working with a single informant in order to show how one can learn ethnographic interviewing and analysis skills. This does not mean that a complete ethnography can ever be done with a single informant. Again, a partial description of selected aspects of a culture can be made from one informant's point of view.[8] In order to make generalizations about a culture, the ethnographer will need additional informants as well as data from other sources.

Culture, as I use the concept (see p. 5), is neither totally shared by a group nor is it something totally unique to every individual. In studying a college bar, for example, I had to recognize at the outset that not everyone who entered the bar shared in its culture. One group of about ten women, the cocktail waitresses, did share most features of a distinct cultural perspective in that bar, and they became informants. But variations did occur even among this group.[9] In my research with skid row men, I concentrated on the culture of a city jail. However, my ethnography was limited to the inmates' perspective of that jail and did not try to integrate that perspective with cultural rules shared by civilians and police officers who worked in the jail. Even among inmates I discovered variations, something I examined by using multiple informants and through a detailed ethnographic questionnaire.[10]

3. *This book does not systematically examine strategies for studying culture change.* It may seem to some readers that I assume culture is a static, unchanging phenomenon. Such is not the case. Every culture is

changing, whether in a primary school classroom or in a Samoan village. Indeed, ethnographic interviews provide an excellent tool for discovering native cultural categories and perceptions of these changes. Ethnohistory (i.e., history from the perspective of informants) will almost always include native ideas about the causes and processes of change. Again, I focus primarily on interviewing informants about their current way of life; this simplifies the task of learning to interview. At the same time, use of this book does not make it impossible to adapt the principles of interviewing to the study of culture change.[11]

4. *This book does not systematically examine theories of ethnography or theories of culture.* It does contain considerable discussion of ethnographic theory *in the context of doing field work.* But because the focus is on strategies for interviewing and analyzing data, many important theoretical issues are intentionally omitted. Theoretical discussions in this book are brought in to serve the purpose of doing field work rather than to review a coherent body of theory.[12]

5. *This book does not examine strategies for participant observation or how to integrate data from observation with data from interviews.* Again, I have imposed this limitation in order to more carefully examine the interview in ethnographic research. However, one may use this book and *at the same time* do participant observation. The two approaches serve as a kind of check and balance in doing ethnography and are seldom used in isolation by experienced ethnographers.[13]

6. *This book does not discuss the range of experiences that usually occur during ethnographic field work.* Doing ethnography by following the steps in this book cannot be equated with doing field work in a non Western community for a year or more. It cannot be equated with an intensive field work experience in a school, a hospital, or on the streets in a large city. For example, the problems of culture shock and loneliness are often intense during field work but are at a minimum in carrying out a series of interviews with a single informant. This book does deal with one of the most important experiences of doing field work anywhere: interviewing key informants and analyzing the interview data.

7. *Finally, this book does not limit ethnographic research to English-speaking informants from cultural scenes within American society.* I do draw most examples from ethnographic studies with such informants. I do this to make clear the principles one must master to do ethnographic interviewing. But most of these techniques were originally developed in non-western contexts and all can be adapted to other languages and other settings.

NOTES

1. Gelb (1978).
2. For a discussion of the problem-solving process as well as a general source to the literature see Koberg and Bagnall (1972).
3. For a review of ethnoscience see Sturtevant (1964), Tyler (1969), and Werner (1977). This field is also referred to as ethnographic semantics. For a brief introduction to ethnographic semantics see Spradley and McCurdy (1972).
4. Etic descriptions of human behavior and broad cross-cultural studies based on ethnoscience have become more frequent in recent years. See Berlin and Kay (1969) and Brown (1976).
5. See Geertz (1973).
6. Ethnographic methods in general, and ethnoscience theory and methodology, are still very much in a state of development. Oswald Werner and his coworkers at Northwestern University are now in the process of compiling a *Handbook of Ethnoscience: Ethnographies and Encyclopaedia* which will contain recent developments. See Werner (1977).
7. For other discussions of ethnographic and related research methods see Pelto (1970), Lofland (1976), and Glazer (1972).
8. Anthony Wallace has described the cultural rules for one aspect of his own culture using himself as sole informant (1965).
9. Because the total population of waitresses was small (less than ten persons) we used informal means for constructing a composite picture of this culture. See Spradley and Mann (1975) for a description of this college bar from the perspective of cocktail waitresses. For a discussion of variability among informants and methods for handling this variability see Sanjek (1977) and Sankoff (1971). Pelto and Pelto (1975) have discussed many of the issues dealing with intracultural variability.
10. A copy of this ethnographic survey questionnaire is included as Appendix A, pp. 281–291, in Spradley (1970). This questionnaire was developed only after I had analyzed the culture in its own terms; the questions arose from out of the culture itself.
11. Both Barnett (1953) and Wallace (1970) have developed theories of culture change based on cognitive models of culture. For a study in culture change based on the methods presented here see Basso (1967).
12. For a review of culture theory see Kaplan and Manners (1972) and Keesing (1974).
13. See Lofland (1976) and Spradley (1979). Filstead (1970) has edited a valuable collection that deals with both approaches.

BIBLIOGRAPHY

AGAR, MICHAEL
  1969 "The simulated situation: a methodological note," *Human Organization* 28:322-329.
  1973 *Ripping and Running: A Formal Ethnography of Urban Heroin Addicts.* New York: Seminar Press.
  1976 "Themes Revisited: Some Problems in Cognitive Anthropology." Unpublished paper, Department of Anthropology, University of Houston.
ALLEN, JANICE
  1974 "Ethnography of the dope dealer on a college campus." B.A. Honors Thesis, Department of Anthropology, Macalester College, St. Paul, Minn.
BAHR, HOWARD M.
  1973 *Skid Row: An Introduction to Disaffiliation.* New York: Oxford University Press.
BAKER, SHERIDAN
  1969 *The Practical Stylist.* New York: Crowell.
BARNES, J. A.
  1977 *The Ethics of Inquiry in Social Science.* Delhi: Oxford University Press.
BARNETT, H. G.
  1953 *Innovation: The Basis of Cultural Change.* New York: McGraw-Hill.
BASSO, KEITH
  1967 "Semantic aspects of linguistic acculturation." *American Anthropologist* 69:471-477.
BATESON, GREGORY
  1937 *Naven.* New York: Macmillan.
BERLIN, BRENT, DENNIS E. BREEDLOVE, AND PETER H. RAVEN
  1968 "Covert categories and folk taxonomies." *American Anthropologist* 70:290-299.
BERLIN, BRENT, AND PAUL KAY
  1969 *Basic Color Terms.* Berkeley: University of California Press.
BERREMAN, GERALD D.
  1966 "Anemic and emetic analyses in social anthropology." *American Anthropologist* 68:346-354.
BLACK, MARY, AND DUANE METZGER
  1965 "Ethnographic description and the study of law." In The Ethnography of Law, Laura Nader, ed. *American Anthropologist* 67(2):141-165.
BLUMER, HERBERT
  1969 *Symbolic Interactionism.* Englewood Cliffs, N.J.: Prentice-Hall.
BOAS, FRANZ
  1943 "Recent anthropology." *Science* 98:311-314, 334-337.
BROWN, CECIL H.
  1976 "General principles of human anatomical partonomy and speculations on the growth of partonomic nomenclature." *American Ethnologist* 3:400-424.
BRUNER, JEROME S., J. J. GOODNOW, AND G. A. AUSTIN
  1956 *A Study of Thinking.* New York: Wiley.

236

CAMPBELL, DONALD T.
1975   "On the conflict between biological and social evolution and between psychology and moral tradition." *American Psychologist* 30:1103-1126.

CARLSON, KATHERINE
1977   "Reciprocity in the marketplace: tipping in an urban nightclub." In *Conformity and Conflict: Readings in Cultural Anthropology*, 3rd ed. James P. Spradley and David W. McCurdy, eds., pp. 337-347. Boston: Little, Brown.

CASAGRANDE, J. B., AND K. L. HALE
1967   "Semantic relations in Papago folk-definitions." In *Studies in Southwestern Ethnolinguistics*. D. Hymes and W. E. Bittle, eds., pp. 165-196. The Hague: Mouton.

CAVAN, SHERRI
1974   "Seeing social structure in a rural setting." *Urban Life and Culture* 3:329-346.

CONKLIN, HAROLD C.
1962   "Lexicographical treatment of folk taxonomies." In *Problems in Lexicography*. F. W. Householder and S. Saporta, eds. *Indiana University Research Center in Anthropology, Folklore, and Linguistics Publication 21*, pp. 119-141.

1954   *The Relation of Hanunoo Culture to the Plant World*. Ph.D. dissertation in anthropology, Yale University, New Haven. Published by University Microfilms, Ann Arbor, Mich., 1967, No. 67-4119.

1972   *Folk Classification: A Topically Arranged Bibliography of Contemporary and Background References through 1971*. New Haven: Department of Anthropology, Yale University.

D'ANDRADE, ROY
1976   "A propositional analysis of U.S. American beliefs about illness." In *Meaning in Anthropology*, Keith Basso and Henry A. Selby, eds., pp. 155-180. Albuquerque: University of New Mexico Press.

DAVIS, FRED
1974   "Stories and sociology." *Urban Life and Culture* 3:310-316.

DENNEY, ROBERT
1974   "The health and social culture of quadriplegics," B.A. Honors Thesis, Department of Anthropology, Macalester College, St. Paul, Minn.

EHRMAN, SUZI
1977   "The lord of the rings: Ethnography of a directory assistance telephone operator." Unpublished seminar paper, Department of Anthropology, Macalester College, St. Paul, Minn.

ELBOW, PETER
1973   *Writing without Teachers*. New York: Oxford University Press.

EVENS, MARTHA, BONNIE LITOWITZ, JUDITH MARKOWITZ, RAOUL SMITH, AND OSWALD WERNER
1977   "Lexical/semantic relations: A comparative survey." Unpublished manuscript. Department of Anthropology. Northwestern University.

FRAKE, CHARLES O.
1962   "The ethnographic study of cognitive systems." In *Anthropology and Human Behavior*, T. Gladwin and W. C. Sturtevant, eds., pp. 72-85. Washington: Anthropological Society of Washington.

1964a "Notes on queries in ethnography." *American Anthropologist* 66(3), Part 2:132-145.

1964b "A structural description of Subanun religious behavior." In *Explorations in Cultural Anthropology,* Ward Goodenough, ed, pp. 111-130. New York: McGraw-Hill.

1964c "How to ask for a drink in Subanun." *American Anthropologist* 66(2):127-132.

1975 "How to enter a Yakan house." In *Sociocultural Dimensions of Language Use,* Mary Sanchez and Ben Blount, eds., pp. 25-40. New York: Academic Press.

1977 "Plying frames can be dangerous: some reflections on methodology in cognitive anthropology." *Quarterly Newsletter of the Institute For Comparative Human Development,* Vol. 1, No. 3, pp. 1-7. New York: Rockerfeller University.

FREILICH, MORRIS, ED.

1970 *Marginal Natives: Anthropologists at Work.* New York: Harper and Row.

FILSTEAD, WILLIAM J., ED.

1970 *Qualitative Methodology.* Chicago: Markham.

GEERTZ, CLIFFORD

1973 "Thick description: Toward an interpretive theory of culture." In *The Interpretation of Cultures,* Clifford Geertz, pp. 3-32. New York: Basic Books.

GELB, MOLLY

1973 "Two zero yankee hold short of one eight: an ethnography of air traffic controllers." Unpublished seminar paper, Department of Anthropology, Macalester College, St. Paul, Minn.

GLASER, BARNEY G., AND ANSELM L. STRAUSS

1967 *The Discovery of Grounded Theory: Strategies for Qualitative Research.* Chicago: Aldine.

GLAZER, MYRON

1972 *The Research Adventure: Promise and Problems of Field Work.* New York: Random House.

GODWIN, DONALD W., ET AL.

1974 "Drinking problems in adopted and nonadopted sons of alcoholics." *Archives of General Psychiatry* 31:164-169.

GOODENOUGH, WARD H.

1956 "Componential analysis and the study of meaning." *Language* 32:195-216.

GORES, NANCY

1972 "Everybody wants to be a gorilla: ethnography of a costume shop." Unpublished B.A. Honors Thesis, Department of Anthropology, Macalester College, St. Paul, Minn.

GREGORY KATHLEEN L.

1976 " 'Stop throwing books out of my window!' An ethnography of junior high teachers," B.A. Honors Thesis, Macalester College, St. Paul, Minn.

HANSEN, JENNIFER

1976 "Ethnography of second-grade boys playing matchbox cars." Unpublished seminar paper, Department of Anthropology, Macalester College, St. Paul, Minn.

HARRIS, MARVIN

1968   *The Rise of Anthropological Theory.* New York: Crowell.

1976   "History and significance of the emic/etic distinction." *Annual Review of Anthropology* 5:329-350.

HYMES, DELL

1974   *Foundations in Sociolinguistics: An Ethnographic Approach.* Philadelphia: University of Pennsylvania Press.

KAPLAN, DAVID, AND ROBERT A. MANNERS

1972   *Culture Theory.* Englewood Cliffs, N.J.: Prentice-Hall.

KAY, PAUL

1966   "Comment." *Current Anthropology* 7:20-23.

KEESING, ROGER

1974   "Theories of culture." *Annual Review of Anthropology* 3:73-98.

KELLY, GEORGE A.

1955   *The Psychology of Personal Constructs.* New York: Norton.

KIEFER, THOMAS M.

1968   "Institutionalized friendship and warfare among the Tausaug of Jolo." *Ethnology* 7:225-244.

KIMBALL, SOLON T., AND JAMES B. WATSON

1972   *Crossing Cultural Boundaries: The Anthropological Experience.* San Francisco: Chandler.

KOBERG, DON, AND JIM BAGNALL

1972   *The Universal Traveler: A Soft-Systems Guide to Creativity, Problem-Solving, and the Process of Reaching Goals.* Los Altos, Calif.: William Kaufmann.

KROEBER, A. L., AND CLYDE KLUCKHOHN

1952   *Culture: A Critical Review of Concepts and Definitions.* Vol. XLVII, No. 1, Papers of the Peabody Museum of American Archaeology and Ethnology. Cambridge: Harvard University.

KRUFT, JEAN

1977   "No soliciting on Sunday." Unpublished seminar paper, Department of Anthropology, Macalester College, St. Paul, Minn.

KUHN, THOMAS

1970   *The Structure of Scientific Revolutions,* 2nd ed. Chicago: University of Chicago Press.

LIEBOW, ELLIOT

1967   *Tally's Corner.* Boston: Little, Brown.

LOFLAND, JOHN

1976   *Doing Social Life: The Qualitative Study of Human Interaction in Natural Settings.* New York: Wiley.

LOFLAND, LYN H.

1973   *A World of Strangers: Order and Action in Urban Public Space.* New York: Basic Books.

LYND, ROBERT S.

1939   *Knowledge for What?* Princeton, N.J.: Princeton University Press.

MACRORIE, KEN

1970   *Telling Writing.* Roselle Park, N.J.: Hayden.

MALINOWSKI, BRONISLAW
1922 *Argonauts of the Western Pacific*. London: Routledge.
1950 *Argonauts of the Western Pacific*. New York: Dutton.
MANIS, JEROME, AND BERNARD MELTZER, EDS.
1967 *Symbolic Interaction: A Reader in Social Psychology*. Boston: Allyn and Bacon.
MANN, BRENDA
1976 "The ethics of field work in an urban bar." In Rynkiewich and Spradley, 1976, pp. 95-109.
MEGGITT, MERVYN
1974 "Pigs are our hearts!" *Oceania* 44:165-203.
MURRAY, DONALD
1968 *A Writer Teaches Writing*. Boston: Houghton Mifflin.
NASH, JEFFREY E.
1975 "Bus riding: community on wheels." *Urban Life and Culture* 4:99-124.
1976 "The short and the long of it: legitimizing motives for running." In *Sociology: A Descriptive Approach*, J. Nash and J. Spradley, eds., pp. 161-181. Chicago: Rand McNally.
1977 "Decoding the runner's wardrobe." In *Conformity and Conflict: Readings in Cultural Anthropology*, 3rd ed. James P. Spradley and David W. McCurdy, eds., pp. 172-186. Boston: Little, Brown.
1978 "Weekend racing as an eventful experience: understanding the accomplishment of well being." *Urban Life and Culture*, 6.
NIDA, EUGENE A.
1964 *Toward a Science of Translating*. Leiden: Brill.
NOREN, JULIE
1974 "Classical ballet: an ethnographic study of an art form in western society." Unpublished B.A. Honors Thesis, Department of Anthropology, Macalester College, St. Paul, Minn.
OPLER, MORRIS E.
1945 "Themes as dynamic forces in culture," *American Journal of Sociology* 53:198-206.
ORBACH, MICHAEL K.
1977 *Hunters, Seamen, and Entrepreneurs*. Berkeley: University of California Press.
PELTO, PERTTI J.
1970 *Anthropological Research: The Structure of Inquiry*. New York: Harper & Row.
PELTO, PERTTI J., AND GRETEL H. PELTO
1975 "Intra-cultural diversity: some theoretical issues." *American Ethnologist* 2:1-18.
PERCHONOCK, NORMA, AND OSWALD WERNER
1968 "Navajo systems of classification: the domains of food." *Ethnology* 8:229-242.
PIERCE, CHARLES SANDERS
1931 *Collected Papers*. Cambridge: Harvard University Press.

PIKE, KENNETH L.
1967   *Language in Relation to a Unified Theory of the Structures of Human Behavior*, 2nd ed. The Hague: Mouton.
READ, KENNETH E.
1965   *The High Valley*. New York: Scribner's.
REED, RICHARD
1973   "Thrills and skills: ethnography of sky diving." Unpublished seminar paper, Department of Anthropology, Macalester College, St. Paul, Minn.
ROHLEN, THOMAS P.
1974   *For Harmony and Strength*. Berkeley: University of California Press.
RYNKIEWICH, MICHAEL A., AND JAMES P. SPRADLEY, EDS.
1976   *Ethics and Anthropology: Dilemmas in Fieldwork*. New York: Wiley.
SANJEK ROGER
1977   "Cognitive maps of the ethnic domain in urban Ghana: reflections on variability and change." *American Ethnologist* 4:603-622.
SANKOFF, GILLIAN
1971   "Quantitative analysis of sharing and variability of cognitive models." *Ethnology* 10:389-408.
SLOANE, NATHANIEL
1975   "Language and Culture." Unpublished B.A. Honors Thesis, Department of Anthropology, Macalester College, St. Paul, Minn.
SOLOMON, PHILIP
1966   "Psychiatric treatment of the alcoholic patient." In *Alcoholism*, J. H. Mendelson, ed., pp. 159-188. Boston: Little, Brown.
SPINDLER, GEORGE, ED.
1970   *Being an Anthropologist*. New York: Holt, Rinehart and Winston.
SPRADLEY, JAMES P.
1968   "A cognitive analysis of tramp behavior." *Proceedings of the 8th International Congress of Anthropological and Ethnological Sciences*. Tokyo: Japan Science Council.
1969   *Guests Never Leave Hungry: The Autobiography of James Sewid, a Kwakiutl Indian*. New Haven: Yale University Press.
1970   *You Owe Yourself a Drunk: An Ethnography of Urban Nomads*. Boston: Little, Brown.
1971a   "Beating the drunk charge." In Spradley and McCurdy, 1971:351-358.
1971b   "Cultural deprivation or cultural innundation." *Western Canadian Journal of Anthropology* 2:65-82.
1972a   *Culture and Cognition: Rules, Maps and Plans*, ed. San Francisco: Chandler.
1972b   "Foundations of cultural knowledge." In Spradley, 1972a:3-38.
1972c   "Adaptive strategies of urban nomads: the ethnoscience of tramp culture." In *The Anthropology of Urban Environments*. Thomas Weaver and Douglas White, eds., pp. 21-38. *The Society for Applied Anthropology Monograph Series, Monograph Number 11*.
1972d   "Down and out on skid row." In *Life Styles: Diversity in American Society*, Saul Feldman and Gerald W. Thielbar, eds., pp. 340-350. Boston: Little, Brown.

1972e "An ethnographic approach to the study of organizations: the city jail." In *Complex Organizations and their Environments*. Merlin Brinkerhoff and Phillip Kunz, eds., pp. 94-105. Dubuque: W. C. Brown.

1973 "The ethnography of crime in American society." In *Cultural Illness and Health*, Laura Nader and Thomas Maretzki, eds. Anthropological Studies, No. 9. Washington, D.C.: American Anthropological Association.

1975 "Public health services and the culture of skid row bums." *Proceedings of Conference on Public Inebriates*, pp. 1-19. National Institute on Alcohol and Alcohol Abuse. Washington, D.C.: U.S. Government Printing Office.

1976a "The revitalization of American culture: an anthropological perspective." In *Qualities of Life: Critical Choices for Americans, Vol. III*, pp. 99-122. Lexington, Mass.: Heath.

1976b "Trouble in the tank." In Rynkiewich and Spradley, 1976:17-31.

1979 *Participant Observation*. New York: Holt, Rinehart and Winston.

SPRADLEY, JAMES P., AND BRENDA MANN

1975 *The Cocktail Waitress: Woman's Work in a Man's World*. New York: Wiley.

SPRADLEY, JAMES P., AND DAVID W. MC CURDY

1971 *Conformity and Conflict: Readings in Cultural Anthropology*. Boston: Little, Brown (2nd ed., 1974; 3rd ed., 1977).

1972 *The Cultural Experience*. Chicago: Science Research Associates.

1975 *Anthropology: The Cultural Perspective:* New York: Wiley.

SPRADLEY, THOMAS S., AND JAMES P. SPRADLEY

1978 *Deaf Like Me*. New York: Random House.

STARR, PAUL D.

1978 "Ethnic categories and identification in Lebanon." *Urban Life and Culture* 7:111-142.

STRAUS, ANNE S.

1977 "Northern Cheyenne Ethnopsychology." *Ethos* 5:326-357.

STURTEVANT, WILLIAM C.

1964 "Studies in ethnoscience." *American Anthropologist* 66(2), No. 1:99-131.

THOMAS, ELIZABETH MARSHALL

1958 *The Harmless People*. New York: Random House.

TURNBULL, COLIN

1962 *The Forest People*. New York: Simon & Schuster.

TYLER, STEVEN A., ED.

1969 *Cognitive Anthropology: Readings*. New York: Holt, Rinehart and Winston.

VALENTINE, CHARLES

1963 "Men of anger and men of shame: Lakalai ethnopsychology and its implications for sociopsychological theory." *Ethnology* 2:441-478.

VERIN, NINA

1978 "An ethnography of an interpreter for the deaf." Unpublished seminar paper, Department of Anthropology, Macalester College, St. Paul, Minn.

WALKER, WILLARD

1965 "Taxonomic structure and the pursuit of meaning." *Southwestern Journal of Anthropology* 21:265-275.

WALLACE, ANTHONY F. C.
1962 "Culture and cognition." *Science* 135:351-357.
1965 "Driving to work." In *Context and Meaning in Cultural Anthropology,* Melford E. Spiro, ed., pp. 277-294. New York: The Free Press.
1970 *Culture and Personality,* 2nd ed. New York: Random House.
WALLACE, ANTHONY F. C., AND JOHN ATKINS
1960 "The meaning of kinship terms." *American Anthropologist* 62:58-80.
WARD, BARBARA
1966 *Spaceship Earth.* New York: Columbia University Press.
WERNER, OSWALD
1977 "A Theory of Ethnoscience." Unpublished manuscript, Department of Anthropology, Northwestern University.
WERNER, OSWALD, AND GLADYS LEVIS
1975 "Context and memory: toward a theory of context in ethnoscience." In press.
WERNER, OSWALD, AND MARTIN TOPPER
1976 "On the theoretical unity of ethnoscience lexicography and ethnoscience ethnographies. *Proceedings of the Georgetown University Roundtable on Languages and Linguistics.*
WERNER, OSWALD, JUDITH REMINGTON, AND FRANK PASQUALE
1976 "Prologomena toward a theory of values in ethnoscience." Unpublished manuscript, Department of Anthropology, Northwestern University.
WERNER, OSWALD, W. HAGEDORN, GEORGE ROTH, E. SCHEPERS, AND L. URIARTE
1974 "Some new developments in ethnosemantics and the theory and practice of lexical/semantic fields." In *Current Trends in Linguistics, Volume 12,* Thomas A. Sebeok, ed., pp. 1477-1543. The Hague: Mouton.

INDEX